Advance Praise for
First Things First

"With *The 7 Habits of Highly Effective People*, Stephen Covey helped to focus our steering committee and, in fact, our company on the principles and values of our organization. He now has accomplished our focus on the integrity of life itself and we are grateful."

—Horst Schulze, President and Chief Operating Officer,
The Ritz-Carlton Hotel Company

"Time is gone forever, once spent, and is the ultimate equal opportunity employer. The Covey team gives a priceless compass and brilliant, timely directions, based upon timeless truth, as we navigate a world reeling in fast-forward. *First Things First* will last a lifetime!"

—Dr. Denis Waitley, author of
The Psychology of Winning and *Time to Win*

"Covey is the hottest self-improvement consultant to hit U.S. business since Dale Carnegie."

—*USA Today*

"Profound and powerful, *First Things First* shines a brilliant light into the semidarkness of time management techniques. Instead of seeing fragments of our lives, we can now see the whole picture. This book can be the lever with which you can *truly* change your life."

—Scott DeGarmo, Editor-in-Chief, *Success* magazine

"Any leader who wants to move from time management to personal leadership should read this book, embrace its principles, and use the excellent tools provided."

—The Honorable Hazel O'Leary,
former President of Northern States Power and former
Assistant Attorney General for the State of New Jersey

"Covey has reached the apex with this publication. This is an important work. I can't think of anyone who wouldn't be helped by reading it."

—Larry King

"If *The 7 Habits of Highly Effective People* was the best personal development book of the 80s, and I believe it was, *First Things First* is my front-runner for the 90s. My graduate students are studying *The 7 Habits*. *First Things First* takes up the hard and practical questions they are now asking. It will be a great resource."

    —David Davenport, President,
    Pepperdine University and Immediate Past President
    of the American Association of Presidents of
    Independent Colleges and Universities

"Time management gives us the tools but *First Things First* delivers us to a place where we can each make the right choices; fueled by a powerful vision of a life lived as a legacy—a life of enduring meaning. This book is the ultimate legacy! Covey and the Merrills lovingly show us the way to create lives enriched by goals and personal vision so that we may each become living tapestries of fulfillment."

    —Melody Mackenzie, coauthor of *Managing Your Goals*
    and President, Alec Mackenzie's Time Tactics

"Finally—a book on time management that goes beyond the simple quick fixes of behavioral engineering. A book that connects the investment of time to our deeper priorities in life. Both inspirational and practical, *First Things First* is a priority reading."

    —Charles A. Garfield, Ph.D., author of *Peak Performers:*
    New Heroes of American Business and *Second to*
    None: How Our Smartest Companies Put People First

"A universal characteristic of our aging population is the wish to leave a legacy of a better world for future generations. This book, with its emphasis on personal vision and mission, will ensure old and young alike who apply these principles as their foundations of life the opportunity to leave a rich legacy for the future."

    —Kirk L. Stromberg, Director of Strategic Planning
    and Development, American Association of
    Retired Persons (AARP)

"If you liked reading *The 7 Habits of Highly Effective People*, you'll love reading *First Things First*. Steve Covey's principle-centered approach to time management does indeed provide the reader a 'compass' for what is truly important in life."

    —Nolan D. Archibald, Chairman, President and CEO,
    The Black & Decker Corporation

"Practical, insightful wisdom at its best is Stephen Covey's newest book, *First Things First*. A must for the survival of your family!"
—Dr. Robert H. Schuller
Reverend of Crystal Cathedral and Hour of Power

"Stephen Covey offers a roadmap toward making a thumbprint of distinction in your own life, thereby allowing those around you to see an excellent model for living a quality life."
—Dr. Sonya Friedman, Ph.D., host of "Sonya Live," CNN

"The best book yet on managing one's time. *First Things First* will truly unleash the 'fire within' whereby living, loving, learning, and leaving a legacy are more than mere platitudes—they're valued and pursued."
—Loren J. Hulber, President and CEO, Day-Timers, Inc.

"The great successes I've had in my life can be attributed to the life-changing principles Covey teaches in *First Things First*."
—Steve Young, Quarterback, San Francisco Forty-Niners,
and 1992 NFL Most Valuable Player

"I hate time management systems. Do lists, day planners, and breathing-by-objective systems give me the hives. But I love *First Things First*—Covey and the Merrills' approach to making your life meaningful and successful on purpose. The subtitle tells it all, 'To Live, to Love, to Learn, to Leave a Legacy.' That's making your life work instead of making work of your life. Super!"
—Ron Zemke, Senior Editor, *Training* magazine,
and coauthor of *Service America* and
Sustaining Knock Your Socks Off Service

"Harder, smarter, and faster has always worked for us. The principle-centered concepts in *First Things First* provide a better way. We are studying, highlighting, and applying these concepts already."
—Mick Shannon, President and CEO
Joseph E. Lake, Executive Vice-President and COO,
Cofounders of Children's Miracle Network

"Quality as defined by W. Edwards Deming is first and foremost a new way of thinking, a new way of life, that begins with each and every person. *First Things First* is a practical and effective way to begin the process of personal reflection and change. It is *the* next level of thinking in time and life management."
—Barbara B. Lawton
W. Edwards Deming Professor of Management,
University of Colorado, Boulder

"Trilogy: *The 7 Habits of Highly Effective People, Principle-Centered Leadership, First Things First* . . .
To 'read' the Trilogy is 'to add value to your life';
To 'understand' the Trilogy is 'to develop insights for a better life';
To 'live' the Trilogy is 'to be the "Best Individual You" and the "Best Interdependent You (Teammate)", you can be!' "

> —Victor N. Goulet, Chairman of the Board and CEO,
> Electronic Realty Associates, L.P., and Bob, Mac, Tom,
> and Team ERA Worldwide

"In my reading, *First Things First* is another first for Stephen Covey and the Merrills. It is not only a culmination of a trilogy (*The 7 Habits of Highly Effective People, Principle-Centered Leadership, First Things First*), but it also takes to a higher plane of regard, the dilemma of how to prioritize the many demands on one's time. I was particularly struck by Stephen, Roger, and Rebecca's ability to combine substance, form, and human values within highly readable prose."

> —John R. Seffrin, Ph.D., Executive Vice President,
> American Cancer Society

"What we stand for shapes our lives! *First Things First* breaks the mold in showing us how our heart guides us and how our conscience is the compass pointing us toward true success. Read this book and reignite the fire of meaning in your life!"

> —Anthony Robbins, author *Unlimited Power*
> and *Awaken the Giant Within*

"*First Things First* lays to rest the myths of rugged individualism and self-sufficiency by showing compelling evidence that peace of mind and spirit are achieved only by aligning our lives with governing principles. The reader is given a map into a world of principle-centered living that gives the term liberation a whole new meaning. This isn't *new age* philosophy. It's timeless wisdom packaged in an understandable, recognizable, and usable fashion."

> —Bruce L. Christensen, Former President,
> Public Broadcasting Service (PBS)

"The principles found in *First Things First* create a new paradigm for school leaders that will challenge them to become and remain focused on those truths that will transform education."

> —Judy Nash, Director, NASE Programming,
> American Association of School Administrators

"Highly recommended. I found this an immensely thought-provoking book. For many people, Time—or being over-busy—is a dragon that they cannot figure out how to slay. Here, Stephen Covey, author of *The 7 Habits of Highly Effective People*, gives them *the map* of the dragon's lair, and *the sword*, forged on the anvil of principles and priorities—just the things they need, to slay the beast."
> —Richard Bolles, author of
> *What Color Is Your Parachute?*

"Quadrant II is the Quadrant of Quality and executives who become proficient at this technique can significantly improve their personal and organizational leadership."
> —N. E. Rickard, President of Xerox Business Services,
> and Cofounder of Quality at Xerox

"The authors are right! In this ever-changing world, the only things we really control are the choices we make. *First Things First* guides us in that effort with understandable tools and useful metaphors. It encourages each of us to lead lives of integrity, courage, and contribution."
> —Kathleen D. Ryan, coauthor,
> *Driving Fear Out of the Workplace*

"Steve Covey has done it again. Together with the Merrills he has written a thought-provoking book that makes us look at ourselves in life, and more importantly, *First Things First* gently guides us to basic principles."
> —Ken Blanchard, Ph.D.,
> coauthor of *The One Minute Manager*

"Becoming aware of what we really want—and then finding a way to accomplish it, is not just good time management; it is freedom. *First Things First* is about fulfillment and freedom—not through "quick fix time manipulation," but through real lasting change."
> —Dave Checketts, President, New York Knicks

"This book portrays the deep sense of mooring in lives and organizations based on principles and character."
> —J. McDonald Williams, President and CEO,
> Trammell Crow Company

Also by Stephen R. Covey

The 7 Habits of Highly Effective People
Principle-Centered Leadership

Also by A. Roger Merrill and Rebecca R. Merrill

Connections: Quadrant II Time Management

FIRST THINGS FIRST

To Live, to Love, to Learn, to Leave a Legacy

STEPHEN R. COVEY
A. ROGER MERRILL
REBECCA R. MERRILL

SIMON & SCHUSTER

New York   London   Toronto   Sydney   Tokyo   Singapore

First published in Great Britain by Simon & Schuster Ltd, 1994
A Paramount Communications Company

Simon & Schuster Ltd
West Garden Place
Kendal Street
London W2 2AQ

Simon & Schuster of Australia Pty Ltd
Sydney

A CIP catalogue record for this book is available from the British Library.

ISBN 0–671–71283–7

Chapter opening illustrations are by Randall Royter, Royter Snow Design

Covey Leadership Center, Principle-Centered Leadership, The Seven Habits of Highly Effective
People, Principle-Centered Living, Quadrant II Time Management and *Executive Excellence* are
registered trademarks of Covey Leadership Center

Printed and bound in Great Britain by
Butler & Tanner Ltd, Frome and London

ACKNOWLEDGMENTS

We gratefully acknowledge and express deep appreciation to the many wonderful people who have made this project possible:

—to those through whose lives and writings has come the wisdom of the ages. We have tried to learn from your legacy.

—to our colleagues, clients, and seminar participants whose deep sharing and synergy have moved us many levels beyond our own thinking.

—to our associates at the Covey Leadership Center for their synergy and extra-mile support.

—to Bob Asahina of Simon & Schuster, for his patience, insight, and guidance.

—to the members of the *First Things First* team—Boyd Craig, Greg Link, Toni Harris, Adam Merrill, and Ken Shelton—for their significant contributions. In very challenging situations, they have demonstrated the character and competency we've tried to write about.

—most of all, to our families and the families of the team, whose loving support has made all the difference. Thank you for helping to teach us what "first things" are and why they're first.

To our grandchildren,
born and unborn,
who constantly inspire us
to keep first things first.

CONTENTS

Section Four

THE POWER AND PEACE OF PRINCIPLE-CENTERED LIVING   267

Appendices

Introduction

If working harder, smarter, and faster won't solve it, what will?

IF you were to pause and think seriously about the "first things" in your life—the three or four things that matter most—what would they be?

Are these things receiving the care, emphasis, and time you really want to give them?

Through our work at the Covey Leadership Center, we've come in contact with many people from around the world, and we're constantly impressed with what they represent. They're active, hardworking, competent, caring people dedicated to making a difference. Yet, these people consistently tell us of the tremendous struggles they face daily while trying to put first things first in their lives. The fact that you picked up this book indicates that you can probably identify with what they're feeling.

Why is it that so often our first things aren't first? For years we've been given methods, techniques, tools, and information on how to manage and control our time. We've been told that if we keep working harder, learn to do things better and faster, use some new device or tool, or file or organize in a particular way, then we'll be able to do it all. So we buy the new planner, go to the new class, read the new book. We learn it, apply it, try harder, and what happens? For most of the people we meet, the result is increased frustration and guilt.

- I need more time!
- I want to enjoy my life more. I'm always running around. I never have time for myself.
- My friends and family want more of me—but how do I give it to them?

- I'm always in crisis because I procrastinate, but I procrastinate because I'm always in crisis.
- I have no balance between my personal life and work. It seems like when I take time from one for the other, it just makes matters worse.
- There's too much stress!
- There's too much to do—and it's all good. How do I choose?

Traditional time management suggests that by doing things more efficiently you'll eventually gain control of your life, and that increased control will bring the peace and fulfillment you're looking for.

We disagree.

Basing our happiness on our ability to control everything is futile. While we do control our choice of action, we cannot control the consequences of our choices. Universal laws or principles do. Thus, *we* are not in control of our lives; *principles* are. We suggest that this idea provides key insight into the frustration people have had with the traditional "time management" approach to life.

In this book, we present a dramatically different approach to time management. This is a principle-centered approach. It transcends the traditional prescriptions of faster, harder, smarter, and more. Rather than offering you another clock, this approach provides you with a compass—because more important than how fast you're going, is where you're headed.

In one sense, this approach is new; in another, it's very old. It's deeply rooted in classic, timeless principles that represent a distinct contrast to the quick-fix, wealth-without-work approach to life promoted by so much of the current time management and "success" literature. We live in a modern society that loves shortcut techniques. Yet quality of life cannot be achieved by taking the right shortcut.

There is no shortcut. But there is a path. The path is based on principles revered throughout history. If there is one message to glean from this wisdom, it is that a meaningful life is not a matter of speed or efficiency. It's much more a matter of what you do and why you do it, than how fast you get it done.

We'd like to let you know what you can expect from *First Things First:*

- In Section One, "The Clock and the Compass," we'll look at the gap many of us feel between the way we spend our time and what's deeply important to us. We'll describe the three "generations" of traditional time management that comprise the current paradigm of efficiency and control, and discuss why this traditional "clock only" approach essentially increases the gap instead of closing it. We'll look at the need for a new level of thinking—for a fourth generation that's different in kind. We'll encourage you to examine the way you spend your time now to determine if you're doing what's merely "urgent" or what's really "important" in your life, and we'll look at the consequences of "urgency addiction." Finally, we'll take a look at "first things"—our basic human needs and capacities to live, to love, to learn, and to leave a legacy—and how to put them first by using our inner compass to align our lives with the "true north" realities that govern quality of life.

• In Section Two, "The Main Thing Is to Keep the Main Thing the Main Thing," we'll introduce the Quadrant II organizing process—a thirty-minute weekly process that subordinates the clock to the compass and empowers you to shift the focus from "urgency" to "importance." We'll go through the process once to give you a sense of the immediate benefits; then we'll go through each part of the process in depth to show you the richness of what it can do in your life over time. We'll look at:

- how to detect your mission and create an empowering future vision that gives meaning and purpose and, in effect, becomes the DNA of your life.
- how to create balance and synergy among the various roles in your life.
- how to set and achieve principle-based goals that create quality-of-life results.
- how to maintain a perspective that empowers you to keep first things first.
- how to act with integrity in the moment of choice—to have the wisdom and judgment to know whether "putting first things first" means sticking to your plan or changing . . . and to be able to do whichever you decide with confidence and peace.
- how to turn your weeks into an upward spiral of learning and living.

• In Section Three, "The Synergy of Interdependence," we'll address the problems and the potential of the interdependent reality in which we spend 80 percent of our time—an area essentially ignored or inadequately dealt with by traditional time management. We'll look at the difference between transactional and transformational interactions with others. Instead of seeing other people merely as resources through which we can get more done through delegation, we'll see how to create powerful synergy through shared vision and synergistic agreements. We'll look at empowerment— the ultimate "moving the fulcrum over"—and offer insight into things you can do to nurture personal and organizational empowerment and become a change catalyst for your family, work group, or other organization.

• In Section Four, "The Power and Peace of Principle-Centered Living," we'll look at some real-life examples, and show how the fourth-generation approach will literally transform the quality of your day and the nature of what you do. We'll conclude the book by focusing on the principles of peace and how to avoid the main obstacles to a life of fulfillment, meaning, and joy.

To get the most out of this material requires that you become involved with it in a deep way—to be willing to examine your life, your scripts, your motives, your "first things," and what you represent. This is a highly introspective process. As you work with the material, we encourage you to pause frequently and listen to your own mind and heart. It's impossible to get deeply absorbed in this kind of profound self-knowledge and not emerge unchanged. You'll see the world differently. You'll see relationships differently. You'll see time differently. You'll see yourself differently. We are convinced that this material can empower you to close the gap between what's deeply important to you and the way you spend your time.

We thank you for being willing to consider what we believe to be a better way. We're convinced from our own experience that principles produce both personal peace and dramatic results.

The power is in the principles.

It's our belief that the material in this book can help you escape the tyranny of the clock and rediscover your compass. This compass will empower you to live, love, learn, and leave a great and enduring legacy . . . with joy.

Section One

THE CLOCK AND THE COMPASS

Stephen: My daughter Maria, who recently had her third child, was talking with me one evening. She said, "I'm so frustrated, Dad! You know how much I love this baby, but she is literally taking all my time. I'm just not getting anything else done, including many things that only I can do."

I could understand how this was frustrating to her. Maria is bright and capable, and she's always been involved in many good things. She was feeling pulled by good things—projects she wanted to accomplish, contributions she wanted to make, things around the house that weren't getting done.

As we talked, we came to the realization that her frustration was essentially a result of her expectations. And for now, only one thing was needful—enjoying that baby.

"Just relax," I said. "Relax and enjoy the nature of this new experience. Let this infant feel your joy in the role of mother. No one else can love and nurture that child the way you can. All other interests pale in comparison for now."

Maria realized that, in the short run, her life was going to be imbalanced . . . and that it should be. "There is a time and a season for everything under the sun." She also realized that as the baby grew and entered a different phase in life, she would be able to reach her goals and contribute in other powerful ways.

Finally, I said, "Don't even keep a schedule. Forget your calendar. Stop using your planning tools if they only induce guilt. This baby is the first thing in your life right now. Just enjoy the baby and don't worry. Be governed by your internal compass, not by some clock on the wall."

For many of us, there's a gap between the compass and the clock—between what's deeply important to us and the way we spend our time. And this gap is not closed by the traditional "time management" approach of doing more things faster. In fact, many of us find that increasing our speed only makes things worse.

Consider this question: If someone were to wave a magic wand and suddenly grant you the 15 or 20 percent increase in efficiency promised by traditional time management, would it solve your time management concerns? While you may feel initially excited about the prospect of increasing your efficiency, if you're like most of the people we work with, you'll probably conclude that the challenges you face cannot be solved simply by increasing your ability to get more things done in less time.

In this section, we'll take an in-depth look at the three generations of traditional time management and explore the reasons why they fail to close that gap. We'll ask you to consider whether you look at life through a basic paradigm of "urgency" or "importance," and we'll discuss the effects of urgency addiction. We'll look at the need for a fourth generation that's different in kind. More than "time management," it's a generation of personal leadership. More than doing things right, it's focused on doing the right things.

In Chapter 3, we'll address the hard questions about what "first things" are in our lives and our capacity to put them first. This chapter deals with the three core ideas at the very heart of the fourth generation. It will probably challenge the way you think about time and life. This chapter requires an emotional willingness to do some deep interior work. We suggest you go through it in sequence, but if you feel it would be more useful for you, go on to Section Two, get into the Quadrant II organizing process, see the benefits of what we're talking about, and then come back to Chapter 3. We guarantee that understanding and applying the three fundamental ideas in this chapter will have a dramatic impact on your time and the quality of your life.

1: *How Many People on Their Deathbed Wish They'd Spent More Time at the Office?*

The enemy of the "best" is the "good."

WE'RE constantly making choices about the way we spend our time, from the major seasons to the individual moments in our lives. We're also living with the consequences of those choices. And many of us don't like those consequences—especially when we feel there's a gap between how we're spending our time and what we feel is deeply important in our lives.

My life is hectic! I'm running all day—meetings, phone calls, paperwork, appointments. I push myself to the limit, fall into bed exhausted, and get up early the next morning to do it all again. My output is tremendous; I'm getting a lot done. But I get this feeling inside sometimes, "So what? What are you doing that really counts?" I have to admit, I don't know.

I feel like I'm being torn apart. My family is important to me; so is my work. I live with constant conflict, trying to juggle the demands of both. Is it possible to be really successful—and happy—at the office and at home?

There is simply too little of me to go around. The board and shareholders are on me like a swarm of bees for our declining share prices. I'm constantly playing referee in turf wars between members of my executive team. I feel tremendous pressure to be leading our organization's quality improvement initiative. The morale among our employees is low and I feel guilty for not getting out with them and listening more. On top of all this, despite our family vacations, my family has all but written me off because they never see me.

I don't feel in control of my life. I try to figure out what's important and set goals to do it, but other people—my boss, my work associates, my spouse—continually throw wrenches into the works. What I set out to do is blocked by what other people want me to do for them. What's important to me is getting swept away in the current of what's important to everybody else.

Everyone tells me I'm highly successful. I've worked and scraped and sacrificed, and I've made it to the top. But I'm not happy. Way down inside I have this empty feeling. It's like the song says, "Is that all there is?"

Most of the time, I just don't enjoy life. For every one thing I do, I can think of ten things I don't do, and it makes me feel guilty. The constant stress of trying to decide what I should do in the middle of all I could do creates a constant tension. How can I know what's most important? How can I do it? How can I enjoy it?

I feel like I have some sense of what I should do with my life. I've written down what I feel is really important and I set goals to make it happen. But somewhere between my vision and my daily action, I lose it. How can I translate what really counts into my daily life?

Putting first things first is an issue at the very heart of life. Almost all of us feel torn by the things we want to do, by the demands placed on us, by the many responsibilities we have. We all feel challenged by the day-to-day and moment-by-moment decisions we must make regarding the best use of our time.

Decisions are easier when it's a question of "good" or "bad." We can easily see how some ways we could spend our time are wasteful, mind-numbing, even destructive. But for most of us, the issue is not between the "good" and the "bad," but between the "good" and the "best." So often, the enemy of the best is the good.

Stephen: I knew a man who was asked to be the new dean of the College of Business of a large university. When he first arrived, he studied the situation the college faced and felt that what it needed most was money. He recognized that he had a unique capacity to raise money, and he developed a real sense of vision about fund-raising as his primary function.

This created a problem in the college because past deans had focused mainly on meeting day-to-day faculty needs. This new dean was never there. He was running around the country trying to raise money for research, scholarships, and other endowments. But he was not attending to the day-to-day things as the previous dean had. The faculty had to work through his administrative assistant, which was demeaning to many of them who were used to working with the person at the top.

The faculty became so upset with his absence that they sent a delegation to the president of the university to demand a new dean or a fundamental change in his leadership style. The president, who knew what the dean was doing, said, "Relax. He has a good administrative assistant. Give him some more time."

Within a short time, the money started pouring in and the faculty began to recognize the vision. It wasn't long until every time they saw the dean, they would say, "Get out of here! We don't want to see you. Go out and bring in more funds. Your administrative assistant runs this office better than anyone else."

This man admitted to me later that the mistake he made was in not doing enough team building, enough explaining, enough educating about what he was trying to accomplish. I'm sure he could have done better, but I learned a powerful lesson from him. We need to constantly be asking ourselves, "What is needed out there, and what is my unique strength, my gift?"

It would have been easy for this man to meet the urgent expectations of others. He could have had a career at the university filled with many good things. But had he not discerned both the real needs and his own unique capacities, and carried out the vision he developed, he would never have achieved the *best* for him, the faculty, or the college.

What is "best" for you? What keeps you from giving those "best" things the time and energy you want to give them? Are too many "good" things getting in the way? For many people, they are. And the result is the unsettling feeling that they're not putting first things first in their lives.

THE CLOCK AND THE COMPASS

Our struggle to put first things first can be characterized by the contrast between two powerful tools that direct us: the clock and the compass. The clock represents our commitments, appointments, schedules, goals, activities—what we do with, and how we *manage* our time. The compass represents our vision, values, principles, mission, conscience, direction—what we feel is important and how we *lead* our lives.

The struggle comes when we sense a gap between the clock and the compass—when what we do doesn't contribute to what is most important in our lives.

For some of us, the pain of the gap is intense. We can't seem to walk our talk. We feel trapped, controlled by other people or situations. We're always responding to crises. We're constantly caught up in "the thick of thin things"[1]—putting out fires and never making time to do what we know would make a difference. We feel as though our lives are being lived for us.

For others of us, the pain is a vague discomfort. We just can't get what we feel we *should* do, what we *want* to do, and what we actually *do* all together. We're caught in dilemmas. We feel so guilty over what we're not doing, we can't enjoy what we do.

Some of us feel empty. We've defined happiness solely in terms of professional or financial achievement, and we find that our "success" did not bring us the satisfaction we thought it would. We've painstakingly climbed the "ladder of success" rung by rung—the diploma, the late nights, the promotions—only to discover as we reached the top rung that the ladder is leaning against the wrong wall. Absorbed in the ascent, we've left a trail of shattered relationships or missed moments of deep, rich living in the wake of the intense, overfocused effort. In our race up the rungs, we simply did not take the time to do what really mattered most.

Others of us feel disoriented or confused. We have no real sense of what "first things" are. We move from one activity to another on automatic. Life is mechanical. Once in a while, we wonder if there's any meaning in our doing.

Some of us know we're out of balance, but we don't have confidence in other alternatives. Or we feel the cost of change is too high. Or we're afraid to try. It's easier to just live with the imbalance.

WAKE UP CALLS

We may be brought to an awareness of this gap in a dramatic way. A loved one dies. Suddenly she's gone and we see the stark reality of what could have been, but wasn't, because we were too busy climbing the "ladder of success" to cherish and nurture a deeply satisfying relationship.

We may find out our teenage son is on drugs. Pictures flood our minds—times we could have spent through the years doing things together, sharing, building the relationship . . . but didn't because we were too busy earning a living, making the right connections, or simply reading the newspaper.

The company's downsizing and our job's on the line. Or our doctor tells us we have just a few months to live. Or our marriage is threatened by divorce. Some crisis brings us to an awareness that what we're doing with our time and what we feel is deeply important don't match.

Rebecca: Years ago, I was visiting with a young woman in the hospital who was only twenty-three years old and had two small children at home. She had just been told she had incurable cancer. As I held her hand and tried to think of something to say that might comfort her, she cried, "I would give anything just to go home and change a messy diaper!"

As I thought about her words and my experience with my own small children, I wondered how many times both of us had changed diapers out of a sense of duty, hurriedly, even frustrated by the seeming inconvenience in our busy lives, rather than cherishing precious moments of life and love we had no way of knowing would ever come again.

In the absence of such "wake-up calls," many of us never really confront the critical issues of life. Instead of looking for deep chronic causes, we look for quick-fix Band-Aids and aspirin to treat the acute pain. Fortified by temporary relief, we get busier and busier doing "good" things and never even stop to ask ourselves if what we're doing really matters most.

THE THREE GENERATIONS OF TIME MANAGEMENT

In our effort to close the gap between the clock and the compass in our lives, many of us turn to the field of "time management." While just three decades ago there were fewer than a dozen significant books on the subject, our most recent survey led us through well over a hundred books, hundreds of articles, and a wide variety of calendars, planners, software, and other time management tools. It reflects something of a "popcorn phenomenon," with the increasing heat and pressure of the culture creating a rapidly exploding body of literature and tools.

In making this survey, we read, digested, and boiled down the information to eight basic approaches to time management. These range from the more traditional "efficiency"-oriented approaches such as the *"Get Organized" Approach*, the *Warrior Approach*, and the *ABC* or *Prioritization Approach*, to some of the newer approaches that are pushing traditional paradigms. These include the more Far Eastern *"Go with the Flow" Approach*, which encourages us to get in touch with the natural rhythms of life—to connect with those "timeless" moments in time when the tick of the clock simply fades away in the joy of the moment. They also include the *Recovery Approach*, which shows how such time wasters as procrastination and ineffective delegation are often the result of deep psychological scripting, and how environmentally scripted "people pleasers" often overcommit and overwork out of fear of rejection and shame.

We've provided both a brief explanation of each of these approaches and a bibliography in Appendix B for those who are interested. But we generally find that most people relate more to what could be called the three "generations" of time management. Each generation builds on the one before it and moves toward greater efficiency and control.

First Generation. The first generation is based on "reminders." It's "go with the flow," but try to keep track of things you want to do with your time—write the report, attend the meeting, fix the car, clean out the garage. This generation is characterized by simple notes and checklists. If you're in this generation, you carry these lists with you and refer to them so you don't forget to do things. Hopefully, at the end of the day, you've accomplished many of the things that you set out to do and you can check them off your list. If those tasks are not accomplished, you put them on your list for tomorrow.

Second Generation. The second generation is one of "planning and preparation." It's characterized by calendars and appointment books. It's efficiency, personal responsibility, and achievement in goal setting, planning ahead, and scheduling future activities and events. If you're in this generation, you make appointments, write down commitments, identify deadlines, note where meetings will be held. You may even keep this in some kind of computer or network.

Third Generation. The third generation approach is "planning, prioritizing, and controlling." If you're in this generation, you've probably spent some time clarifying your values and priorities. You've asked yourself, "What do I want?" You've set long-, medium-, and short-range goals to obtain these values. You prioritize your activities on a daily basis. This generation is characterized by a wide variety of planners and organizers—electronic as well as paper-based—with detailed forms for daily planning.

In some ways, these three generations of time management have brought us a long way toward increased effectiveness in our lives. Such things as efficiency, planning, prioritization, values clarification, and goal setting have made a significant positive difference.

But, bottom-line, for most people—even with the tremendous increase in interest and material—the gap remains between what's deeply important to them and the way they spend their time. In many cases, it's exacerbated. "We're getting more done in less time," people are saying, "but where are the rich relationships, the inner peace, the balance, the confidence that we're doing what matters most and doing it well?"

Roger: These three generations describe a chronicle of my history in time management. I was raised in the Carmel, Pebble Beach area in California. The artistic, free-thinking, philosophical environment was certainly in generation one. I would jot down, from time to time, things I didn't want to forget—particularly golf tournaments, which were a big part of my life. Because I was also involved in ranches and quarter horses, there were certain seasons and other important things not to forget.

As I moved on, the need to get more done in less time, the demands of the many things I wanted to do, and the rich opportunities that were around drove me deeply into the second generation. I read everything I could get my hands on in the area of time management. In fact, my business, for a period of time, was as a time management consultant. I would work with individuals to help them become more efficient, organize things better, learn how to handle the telephone and so forth. Typically, after observing and analyzing their activities for a day, I would make specific suggestions on things they could do to get more done in less time.

As time went on, I found to my dismay that I wasn't really sure that I was helping. In fact, I began to wonder if I was just helping people fail faster. The problem wasn't how much they were getting done. It was where they were trying to go, and what they were trying to accomplish. People wanted to know how they were doing, but I realized I couldn't tell them unless I knew what it was they were trying to do. This drove me into generation three. In fact, both Stephen and I were quite involved in some of the work that began this third generation and worked with some of the people who have been very influential in that field. Our interest was in tying values to goals to help people do more that was congruent and in priority. At the time, it seemed like a clear path that needed to be pursued.

But over time, it became evident that there was a real difference between what people wanted and what they apparently needed in their lives. Many were achieving more and more goals . . . and feeling less and less happy and fulfilled.

As a result, I began to question some of the fundamental paradigms and the ways I had been thinking. I began to realize the answers weren't in these three generations of time management. They were at the fundamental paradigm level. They were in the very assumptions by which we determine and approach what we're trying to do.

THE STRENGTHS AND WEAKNESSES OF EACH GENERATION

Let's take a closer look at the strengths and weaknesses of each of these generations and see specifically how they help . . . but why they fail to meet the deeper need.

People in the *first generation* tend to be flexible. They're able to respond to people and changing needs. They're good at adapting and working things out. They work on their own timetable and do whatever they feel they need to do or seems pressing at the time.

But things often fall through the cracks. Appointments are forgotten; commitments are not kept. Without an empowering sense of lifetime vision and goal setting, meaningful accomplishment is less than it could be. "First things" for people in this generation are essentially whatever happens to be in front of them.

People in the *second generation* plan and prepare. They generally feel a higher level of personal responsibility to results and commitments. Calendars and schedules not only serve as reminders, but encourage better preparation for meetings and presentations—professionally and with family, friends, and associates. Preparation increases efficiency and effectiveness. Goal setting and planning increase performance and results.

But the focus on schedule, goals, and efficiency enthrones the schedule. Although many in the second generation sincerely value other people and relationships, this schedule focus often leads them to act as though others are "the enemy." Other people become interruptions or distractions that keep them from sticking to their schedule and carrying out their plans. They insulate or isolate themselves from others, or they delegate to them, seeing people primarily as a resource through which they can increase their personal leverage. In addition, those in the second generation may be getting more of what they want, but what they're getting does not necessarily fulfill deep needs or create peace of mind. "First things" for people in the second generation are a function of calendar and goals.

The *third generation* makes a major contribution by tying goals and plans to values. People in this generation achieve sizable gains in personal productivity through focused daily planning and prioritization. "First things" become a function of values and goals.

The results of this generation seem very promising. In fact, for many people, the zenith of "time management" is this third generation. They feel that if they were deeply into this generation, they'd be on top of everything. But this third generation has some serious flaws—not in intent, but in unintended results created by incomplete paradigms and vital missing elements. We want to look at these flaws in depth because this generation represents the "ideal" for many and the goal toward which many in the first and second generations aspire.

Let's consider some of the underlying *paradigms*, or mind-sets. These paradigms are like maps. They're not the territory; they describe the territory. And if the map is wrong—if we're trying to get to some place in Detroit and all we have is a map of Chicago—it's going to be very difficult for us to get where we want to go. We can work on our behavior—we can travel more efficiently, get a different car with better gas mileage, increase our speed—but we're only going to wind up in the wrong place faster. We can work on our attitude—we can get so "psyched up" about trying to get there we don't even care that we're in the wrong place. But the problem really has nothing to do with attitude or behavior. The problem is that we have the wrong map.

While these paradigms underlie the entire traditional time management approach, they're emphasized by the third generation.

• **Control.** The primary paradigm of the third generation is one of control—plan it, schedule it, manage it. Take it a step at a time. Don't let anything fall through the cracks. Most of us feel it would be great to be in "control" of our lives. But the fact is, *we're* not in control; *principles* are. We can control our choices, but we can't control the consequences of those choices. When we pick up one end of the stick, we pick up the other. To think we're in control is an illusion. It puts us in the position of trying to manage consequences. In addition, we can't control other people. And because the basic paradigm is one of control, time management essentially ignores the reality that most of our time is spent living and working with other people who cannot be controlled.

• **Efficiency.** Efficiency is "getting more done in less time." It makes good sense. We get more done. We reduce or even eliminate waste. We're streamlined. We're faster. We're leveraged. The increase in productivity is incredible. But the underlying assumption is that "more" and "faster" are better. Is that necessarily true? There's a vital difference between efficiency and effectiveness. You may be driving down the highway, enjoying great traveling weather, and getting terrific mileage. You may be very efficient. But if you're headed south down the California coast on Highway 101 and your destination is New York City—some three thousand miles to the east—you're not being very effective.

In addition, how can you be "efficient" with people? Have you ever tried to be efficient with your spouse or your teenager or an employee on an emotional jugular issue? How did it go?

"Sorry, but you can't express your deepest feelings. I only have ten minutes scheduled for this interview."

"Don't bother me now, son. Just take your emotionally broken and bleeding self somewhere else for a few minutes while I finish this 'to do' item I have here on my schedule."

While you can be efficient with things, you can't be efficient—effectively—with people.

• **Values.** To value something is to esteem it to be of worth. And values are critically important. Our values drive our choices and actions. But we can value many different things—love, security, a big house, money in the bank, status, recognition, fame. Just because we value something does not necessarily mean it will create quality-of-life results. When what we value is in opposition to the natural laws that govern peace of mind and quality of life, we base our lives on illusion and set ourselves up for failure. We cannot be a law unto ourselves.

• **Independent achievement.** The traditional time management focus is on achieving, accomplishing, getting what you want, and not letting anything get in the way. Other people are essentially seen as resources through which you can get more done faster—or as obstacles or interruptions. Relationships are essentially transactional. But the reality is that most of the greatest achievements and the greatest joys in life come through relationships that are *transformational*. In the very nature of the interaction, people are altered. They are transformed. Something new is created and neither person is controlling it. Neither could have anticipated it. It isn't a function of efficiency. It's a function of the exchange of understanding, insights, new learnings, and excitement around those new learnings. To access the transformational power of interdependent synergy is the ultimate "moving of the fulcrum" in terms of time and quality-of-life results.

• **Chronos.** Time management deals with *chronos*, the Greek word for chronological time. Chronos time is seen as linear and sequential. No second is worth any more than any other second. The clock essentially dictates the rhythm of our lives. But there are entire cultures in the world that approach life from a *kairos*— an "appropriate time" or "quality time"—paradigm. Time is something to be *experienced*. It's exponential, existential. The essence of kairos time is how much value you get out of it rather than how much chronos time you put into it. Our language reflects recognition of kairos time when we ask, "Did you have a good time?" We're not asking about the amount of chronos time spent in a particular way, but about the value, the quality, of that time.

• **Competence**. Time management is essentially a set of competencies. The idea is that if you can develop certain competencies, you'll be able to create quality-of-life results. But personal effectiveness is a function of competence *and character*. In one way or another, almost all of the literature says, "Time is life," but like most of the "success" literature of the past seventy years, the time management literature essentially truncates what we *do* from what we *are*.[2] The wisdom literature of centuries, on the other hand, validates the supreme importance of developing character as well as competence in creating quality-of-life results.

• **Management**. Time management itself is a *management*—not *leadership*—perspective. Management works within the paradigm. Leadership creates new paradigms. Management works within the system. Leadership works on the system. You manage "things"; but you lead people. Fundamental to putting first things first in our lives is leadership *before* management: "Am I doing the right things?" *before* "Am I doing things right?"

The strengths and weakness of the three generations of time management are summarized in the chart on the next page.

WHAT YOU SEE IS WHAT YOU GET

What are the underlying paradigms that produce these kinds of results—efficiency, control, management, competence, chronos? Are these accurate maps of the territory? Do they fulfill the expectations they create around quality of life? The very fact that we invest increasing effort in techniques and tools based on these paradigms—and that the fundamental problem remains (in many cases, in fact, it's exacerbated)—is a good indication that the basic paradigms are flawed.

Think back to some of the concerns we identified earlier.

My life is hectic! I'm running all day—meetings, phone calls, paperwork, appointments. I push myself to the limit, fall into bed exhausted, and get up early the next morning to do it all again. My output is tremendous; I'm getting a lot done. But I get this feeling inside sometimes, "So what? What are you doing that really counts?" I have to admit, "I don't know."

"The within is ceaselessly becoming the without," said James Allen, author of the classic *As a Man Thinketh*. "From the state of a man's heart proceed the conditions of his life; his thoughts blossom into deeds, and his deeds bear the fruitage of character and destiny."[3]

Understanding these underlying paradigms of time management is vitally important because our paradigms are the maps of our minds and hearts out of which our attitudes and behaviors and the results in our lives grow. It creates something of a "see/do/get" cycle.

The way we see (our paradigm) leads to what we do (our attitudes and behaviors); and what we do leads to the results we get in our lives. So if we want to create significant change in the results, we can't just change attitudes and behaviors, methods or techniques; we have to change the basic paradigms out of which they grow. When we try to change the behavior or the method without changing the paradigm, the paradigm eventually overpowers the change. That's why attempts to "install" total quality or empowerment in organizations are unsuc-

	Strengths	**Weaknesses**
First Generation	• Ability to adapt when something more important arises—Go-with-the-flow flexibility • More responsive to people • Not overscheduled and overstructured • Less stress • Tracks "to-do's"	• No real structure • Things fall through the cracks • Commitments to others ignored or forgotten, relationships suffer • Relatively little accomplished • Move from crisis to crisis as consequence of ignoring schedules and structure • "First things"—those things right in front of you
Second Generation	• Tracks commitments and appointments • Much more accomplished through goals and planning • More effective meetings and presentations through preparation	• Leads to putting schedule over people • More of what you *want*—not necessarily what you *need* or what is fulfilling • Independent thinking and action—sees people as means or barriers to goals • "First things"—those things on the schedule
Third Generation	• Assumes responsibility for results • Connects with values • Taps into the power of long-, medium-, and short-term goals • Translates values into goals and actions • Increases personal productivity through daily planning and prioritization • Increases efficiency • Gives structure/order to life • Strengthens skill of managing time and self	• Can lead you to believe *you* are in control, rather than natural laws or principles—"Law unto oneself" pride • Values clarification not necessarily aligned with principles that govern • Power of vision untapped • Daily planning rarely gets past prioritizing the urgent, the pressing, and crises management • Can lead to guilt, overprogramming, and imbalance between roles • May put schedule over people and see people as things • Less flexibility/spontaneity • Skills alone don't produce effectiveness and leadership—need character • "First things" set by urgency and values

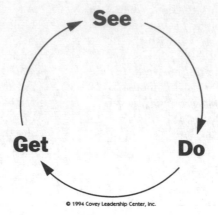

© 1994 Covey Leadership Center, Inc.

cessful. They can't be installed; they have to be grown. They emerge naturally out of the paradigms that create them.

Changing a planning tool or a method won't create significant change in the results we're getting in our lives—although the implied promise is that it will. It's not a matter of controlling things more, better, or faster; it's questioning the whole assumption of control.

As Albert Einstein said:

The significant problems we face cannot be solved by the same level of thinking that created them.[4]

More essential than working on attitudes and behaviors is examining the paradigms out of which those attitudes and behaviors flow. "The unexamined life is not worth living," observed Plato.[5] But the number of people who come out of our leadership development programs saying "I haven't thought that deeply in years!" is astonishing. As human beings, we're trying—sometimes with disastrous results— to run our businesses, raise our children, teach our students, be involved in relationships without giving serious and careful consideration to the roots out of which the fruits in our lives are growing. And somehow time management is something of a mechanical skill, segmented from these vital things we spend our time trying to do.

THE NEED FOR THE FOURTH GENERATION

One thing's for sure: if we keep doing what we're doing, we're going to keep getting what we're getting. One definition of insanity is "to keep doing the same things and expect different results." If time management were the answer, surely the sheer abundance of good ideas would have made a big difference by now. But we find that concerns about quality of life are *just as likely* to come from someone with a high level of time management training as from someone without it.

Time management—especially the third generation—sounds good. It gives the promise of achievement, a sense of hope. But it doesn't deliver. And for many people, the pinnacle third generation approach feels rigid, structured, and unnatural. The intensity is hard to maintain. The first thing many do when they get ready to go on vacation is to leave their planners—the symbols of the third generation—at home!

There's clearly a need for a fourth generation—one that embraces all the strengths of generations 1, 2, and 3, but eliminates the weaknesses . . . and moves beyond. This requires a paradigm and an approach that is not different by degree, but in kind—a fundamental break with less effective ways of thinking and doing.

More than an evolution, we need a revolution. We need to move beyond time management to life leadership—to a fourth generation based on paradigms that will create quality-of-life results.

2: *The Urgency Addiction*

*Anything less than
a conscious commitment to the important
is an unconscious commitment
to the unimportant.*

AS we begin this chapter, take a moment to consider your answer to the following questions:

*What is the one activity that you **know** if you did superbly well and consistently would have significant positive results in your personal life?*

*What is the one activity that you **know** if you did superbly well and consistently would have significant positive results in your professional or work life?*

*If you **know** these things would make such a significant difference, why are you not doing them now?*

As you consider your response, let's look at the two primary factors that drive our choices concerning how we use our time: *urgency* and *importance*. Although we deal with both factors, one of them is the basic paradigm through which we view our time and our lives.

The fourth generation is based on the "importance" paradigm. Knowing and doing what's important rather than simply responding to what's urgent is foundational to putting first things first.

As you go through this chapter, we'll ask you to examine your own paradigms carefully. Whether you're operating from a paradigm of urgency or one of importance has a profound effect on the results you're getting in your life.

URGENCY

Few of us realize how powerfully urgency affects our choices. The phone rings. The baby cries. Someone knocks at the door. A deadline approaches.

"I need this *now.*"

"I'm in a jam, can you come right over?"

"You're late for your appointment."

How much does urgency control your life? We'd like to suggest that you take a few moments and look at some of the attitudes and behaviors that grow out of it as reflected in the Urgency Index on the following page. The degree to which you relate to the statements in the Index will give you some idea of the extent to which you may be looking at life through a paradigm of urgency. As you read each statement, mark the number on the continuum that best describes your response.

After going through the Index, add up your total score and measure yourself with the following key:

0–25   Low urgency mind-set
26–45   Strong urgency mind-set
46+   Urgency addiction

If most of your responses are on the low end, the urgency paradigm is probably not a significant factor in your life. If they're in the middle or toward the higher end, there's a good chance urgency is your fundamental operational paradigm. If your responses are consistently high, urgency may be more than just the way you see. It may actually be an addiction.

THE URGENCY ADDICTION

Some of us get so used to the adrenaline rush of handling crises that we become dependent on it for a sense of excitement and energy. How does urgency feel? Stressful? Pressured? Tense? Exhausting? Sure. But let's be honest. It's also sometimes exhilarating. We feel useful. We feel successful. We feel validated. And we get good at it. Whenever there's trouble, we ride into town, pull out our six shooter, do the varmit in, blow the smoke off the gun barrel, and ride into the sunset like a hero. It brings instant results and instant gratification.

We get a temporary high from solving urgent and important crises. Then when the importance isn't there, the urgency fix is so powerful

The Urgency Index©

Circle the number along the matrix that most closely represents your normal behaviors or attitudes regarding the statements at the left (0=Never, 2=Sometimes, 4=Always).

	N	S	A

1. I seem to do my best work when I'm under pressure.
   0 1 2 3 4

2. I often blame the rush and press of external things for my failure to spend deep, introspective time with myself.
   0 1 2 3 4

3. I'm often frustrated by the slowness of people and things around me. I hate to wait or stand in line.
   0 1 2 3 4

4. I feel guilty when I take time off work.
   0 1 2 3 4

5. I always seem to be rushing between places and events.
   0 1 2 3 4

6. I frequently find myself pushing people away so that I can finish a project.
   0 1 2 3 4

7. I feel anxious when I'm out of touch with the office for more than a few minutes.
   0 1 2 3 4

8. I'm often preoccupied with one thing when I'm doing something else.
   0 1 2 3 4

9. I'm at my best when I'm handling a crisis situation.
   0 1 2 3 4

10. The adrenaline rush from a new crisis seems more satisfying to me than the steady accomplishment of long-term results.
    0 1 2 3 4

11. I often give up quality time with important people in my life to handle a crisis.
    0 1 2 3 4

12. I assume people will naturally understand if I have to disappoint them or let things go in order to handle a crisis.
    0 1 2 3 4

13. I rely on solving some crisis to give my day a sense of meaning and purpose.
    0 1 2 3 4

14. I often eat lunch or other meals while I work.
    0 1 2 3 4

15. I keep thinking that someday I'll be able to do what I really want to do.
    0 1 2 3 4

16. A huge stack in my "out" basket at the end of the day makes me feel like I've really been productive.
    0 1 2 3 4

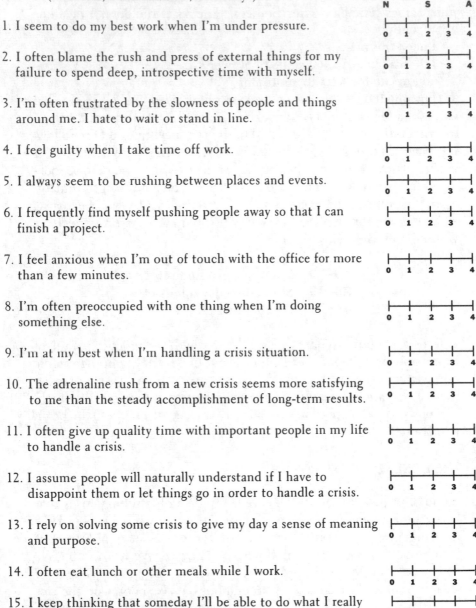

we are drawn to do anything urgent, just to stay in motion. People expect us to be busy, overworked. It's become a status symbol in our society—if we're busy, we're important; if we're not busy, we're almost embarrassed to admit it. Busyness is where we get our security. It's validating, popular, and pleasing. It's also a good excuse for not dealing with the first things in our lives.

"I'd love to spend quality time with you, but I have to work. There's this deadline. It's urgent. Of course you understand."

"I just don't have time to exercise. I know it's important, but there are so many pressing things right now. Maybe when things slow down a little."

Urgency addiction is a self-destructive behavior that temporarily fills the void created by unmet needs. And instead of meeting these needs, the tools and approaches of time management often feed the addiction. They keep us focused on daily prioritization of the urgent.

Addiction to urgency is every bit as dangerous as other commonly recognized dependencies. The following list of characteristics comes out of recovery literature not even connected with time management. It deals primarily with addiction to such things as chemical substances, gambling, and overeating. But look at the similarities! [1]

The Addictive Experience

1. Creates predictable, reliable sensations
2. Becomes the primary focus and absorbs attention
3. Temporarily eradicates pain and other negative sensations
4. Provides artificial sense of self-worth, power, control, security, intimacy, accomplishment
5. Exacerbates the problems and feelings it is sought to remedy
6. Worsens functioning, creates loss of relationships

How well these characteristics describe urgency addiction! And our society is literally inundated with it. Everywhere we turn, urgency addiction is reinforced in our lives and in our culture.

Roger: At one of our programs, I'd just gone through the Urgency Index with a group of senior executives from a multinational firm. At the break, the senior manager from Australia came up to me with a wry smile on his face. "I can't believe it!" he exclaimed. "I am absolutely addicted! It's the whole culture of our business. We live from crisis to crisis. Nothing ever gets done until somebody says it's urgent."

As he was speaking, the number two man in his operation came up beside him and nodded his head in agreement. They joked about their situation for a minute, but their joking had a serious undertone. Then the senior manager turned to me and said, "You know, when this man joined our company, he wasn't that way. But now he is too."

His eyes opened wide with sudden realization. "You know what?" he asked. "I'm not only an addict—I'm a pusher!"

It's important to realize that urgency itself is not the problem. The problem is that when urgency is the *dominant factor* in our lives, importance isn't. What we regard as "first things" are urgent things. We're so caught up in doing, we don't even stop to ask if what we're doing really needs to be done. As a result, we exacerbate the gap between the compass and the clock. As Charles Hummel observes in his booklet, *Tyranny of the Urgent:*

The Important task rarely must be done today, or even this week. . . . The urgent task calls for instant action. . . . The momentary appeal of these tasks seems irresistible and important, and they devour our energy. But in the light of time's perspective, their deceptive prominence fades; with a sense of loss we recall the vital task we pushed aside. We realize we've become slaves to the tyranny of the urgent.[2]

Many of the traditional time management tools actually feed the addiction. Daily planning and "to do" lists essentially keep us focused on prioritizing and doing the urgent. And the more urgency we have in our lives, the less importance we have.

IMPORTANCE

Many important things that contribute to our overall objectives and give richness and meaning to life don't tend to act upon us or press us. Because they're not "urgent," they are the things that we must act upon.

In order to focus on the issues of urgency and importance more effectively, let's look at the Time Management Matrix below. As you can see it categorizes our activities into four quadrants. We spend time in one of these four ways:

	Urgent	**Not Urgent**
Important	**I** • Crises • Pressing problems • Deadline-driven projects, meetings, preparations	**II** • Preparation • Prevention • Values clarification • Planning • Relationship building • True re-creation • Empowerment
Not Important	**III** • Interruptions, some phone calls • Some mail, some reports • Some meetings • Many proximate, pressing matters • Many popular activities	**IV** • Trivia, busywork • Junk mail • Some phone calls • Time wasters • "Escape" activities

Quadrant I represents things that are both "urgent" and "important." Here's where we handle an irate client, meet a deadline, repair a broken-down machine, undergo heart surgery, or help a crying child who has been hurt. We need to spend time in Quadrant I. This is where we manage, where we produce, where we bring our experience and judgment to bear in responding to many needs and challenges. If we ignore it, we become buried alive. But we also need to realize that many important activities become urgent through procrastination, or because we don't do enough prevention and planning.

Quadrant II includes activities that are "important, but not urgent." This is the Quadrant of Quality. Here's where we do our long-range planning, anticipate and prevent problems, empower others, broaden our minds and increase our skills through reading and continuous professional development, envision how we're going to help a struggling son or daughter, prepare for important meetings and presentations, or invest in relationships through deep, honest listening. Increasing time spent in this quadrant *increases our ability to do.* Ignoring this quadrant feeds and enlarges Quadrant I, creating stress, burnout, and deeper crises for the person consumed by it. On the other hand, investing in this quadrant shrinks Quadrant I. Planning, preparation, and prevention keep many things from becoming urgent. Quadrant II does not act on us; we must act on it. This is the Quadrant of personal leadership.

Quadrant III is almost the phantom of Quadrant I. It includes things that are "urgent, but not important." This is the Quadrant of Deception. The noise of urgency creates the illusion of importance. But the actual activities, if they're important at all, are only important to someone else. Many phone calls, meetings, and drop-in visitors fall into this category. We spend a lot of time in Quadrant III meeting other people's priorities and expectations, thinking we're really in Quadrant I.

Quadrant IV is reserved for those activities that are "not urgent and not important." This is the Quadrant of Waste. Of course, we really shouldn't be there at all. But we get so battle-scarred from being tossed around in Quadrants I and III that we often "escape" to Quadrant IV for survival. What kinds of things are in Quadrant IV? Not necessarily recreational things, because recreation in the true sense of re-creation is a valuable Quadrant II activity. But reading addictive light novels, habitually watching "mindless" television shows, or gossiping around the water fountain at the office would qualify as Quadrant IV time wasters. Quadrant IV is not survival; it's deterioration. It may have an initial cotton candy feel, but we quickly find there's nothing there.

We'd like to suggest now that you look at the Time Management Matrix and think back over the past week of your life. If you were to place each of your last week's activities in one of these quadrants, where would you say you spent the majority of your time?

Think carefully as you consider Quadrants I and III. It's easy to think because something is urgent, it's important. A quick way to differentiate between these two quadrants is to ask yourself if the urgent activity contributed to an important objective. If not, it probably belongs in Quadrant III.

If you're like most of the people we work with, there's a good chance you spent the majority of your time in Quadrants I and III. And what's the cost? If urgency is driving you, what important things—maybe even "first things"—are not receiving your time and attention?

Think again about the questions you answered at the first of the chapter:

*What is the one activity that you **know** if you did superbly well and consistently would have significant positive results in your personal life?*

*What is the one activity that you **know** if you did superbly well and consistently would have significant positive results in your professional or work life?*

Analyze what quadrant your answers are in. Our guess is that they're probably in Quadrant II. As we've asked these questions of thousands of people, we find that a great majority of them fall under seven key activities:

1. Improving communication with people
2. Better preparation
3. Better planning and organizing
4. Taking better care of self
5. Seizing new opportunities
6. Personal development
7. Empowerment

All of these are in Quadrant II. They're important.

So why aren't people doing them? Why aren't you doing the things you identified from the questions above?

Probably because they're not urgent. They aren't pressing. They don't act on you. You have to act on them.

THE IMPORTANCE PARADIGM

Clearly, we deal with both factors—urgency and importance—in our lives. But in our day-to-day decision making, one of these factors tends to dominate. The problem comes when we operate primarily from a paradigm of urgency rather than a paradigm of importance.

When we operate out of the importance paradigm, we live in Quadrants I and II. We're out of Quadrants III and IV, and as we spend more time in preparation, prevention, planning, and empowerment, we decrease the amount of time we spend putting out fires in Quadrant I. Even the nature of Quadrant I changes. Most of the time, we're there by choice rather than default. We may even choose to make something urgent or timely because it's important.

An associate shared this experience:

Recently one of my friends was going through a crisis in her relationship. I was extremely busy with home and work, but was managing to keep on top of things and maintain my personal renewal time. One day in particular, I was scheduled for three meetings, some car service, shopping, and an important lunch date when she called. I knew immediately that she was having a really rough day and quickly decided to shelve my other activities and make the hour drive to her home. I knew that my next day would be heavy in Quadrant I activities because there were things I wasn't going to be able to do today in preparation. But this was important, very important. I chose to place myself in a position where I would live with urgency, but it was a decision I could feel good about.

In our seminars, we often ask people to identify the feelings they associate with the different paradigms. When they talk about urgency, they typically use words such as "stressed out," "used up," "unfulfilled," and "worn out." But when they talk about importance they use words like "confident," "fulfilled," "on track," "meaningful," and "peaceful." You might try this exercise yourself. How do you feel when operating from one paradigm or the other? These feelings can tell you a lot about the source of the results you're getting in your life.

QUESTIONS PEOPLE ASK ABOUT THE MATRIX

Now we know that real life is not as neat and tight and logical as the four quadrants would suggest. There's a continuum within and between each quadrant. There's some overlapping. The categories are a matter of degree as well as kind.

Below are some common questions people ask about the matrix:

• **Among all the urgent and important things that face us, how do we know what to do?** This is the dilemma that fills our lives. It's what leads us to feel we need to hunker down and do more, faster. But almost always, there *is* one thing among all the others that should be done first. In a sense there is a Quadrant I of

Quadrant I, or a Quadrant II of Quadrant II. How we decide what's *most* important at any given time is one of the primary issues we'll address in the following chapters of this book.

• *Is it bad to be in Quadrant I?* No, it's not. In fact, many people will spend a significant amount of their time in Quadrant I. The key issue is why you're there. Are you in Quadrant I based on urgency or importance? If urgency dominates, when importance fades, you'll slip into Quadrant III—it's the urgency addiction. But if you're in Quadrant I because of importance, when urgency fades you'll move to Quadrant II. Both Quadrant I and Quadrant II describe what's important; it's only the time factor that changes. The real problem is when you're spending time in Quadrants III and IV.

• *Where do I get the time to spend in Quadrant II?* If you're looking for time to spend in Quadrant II, Quadrant III is the primary place to get it. Time spent in Quadrant I is both urgent and important—we already know we need to be there. And we know we shouldn't be in Quadrant IV. But Quadrant III can fool us. The key is learning to see all of our activities in terms of their importance. Then we're able to reclaim time lost to the deception of urgency, and spend it in Quadrant II.

• *What if I'm in a Quadrant I environment?* Some professions are, by nature, almost completely in Quadrant I. For example, it's the job of firefighters, many doctors and nurses, police officers, news reporters, and editors to respond to the urgent and important. For these people it's even more critical to capture Quadrant II time for the simple reason that it builds their capacity to handle Quadrant I. Time spent in Quadrant II increases our capacity to do.

• *Is there anything in Quadrant I that doesn't act on us and demand our attention "right now"?* Some things are crises or problems in the making if we don't attend to them. We can *choose* to make these things urgent. In addition, what may be a Quadrant II activity to an organization, such as long-term visioning, planning, and relationship building, may be Quadrant I to its top executive. This is his or her unique charge, the need for these things is great, and the consequences of either doing these things or not doing them are significant. The need for that executive is "now," it's urgent, and it must be acted on.

The value of the matrix is that it helps us to see how importance and urgency affect the choices we make about how to spend our time. It allows us to see where we spend most of our time and why we spend it there. We can also see that *the degree to which urgency is dominant is the degree to which importance is not.*

ON THE FAR SIDE OF COMPLEXITY

Like chemical abuse, urgency addiction is a temporary painkiller used in excess. It relieves some of the acute pain caused by the gap between the compass and the clock. And the relief may feel good at the time. But it's cotton-candy satisfaction. It quickly evaporates. And the pain remains. Simply doing more faster fails to get at the chronic causes, the underlying issues, the *reason* for the pain. It's doing second (or third or fourth) things faster . . . but doing nothing to really solve the chronic pain that comes from not putting first things first.

To get at the chronic issues requires a different kind of thinking. It's like the difference between "prevention" and "treatment" thinking in medicine. Treatment deals with the acute or the painful level of illness; prevention deals with lifestyle issues and the maintenance of health. These are two different paradigms, and even though a doctor may operate out of both paradigms, one paradigm usually predominates.

Stephen: I've had physicals from doctors who operate out of both paradigms, and they are altogether different. They're looking for different things. For example, I've had doctors who operate primarily out of the treatment paradigm look at my blood chemistry and report that because the total cholesterol was less than 200, I was okay. I've had doctors with a prevention paradigm look at the blood chemistry—particularly the LDL/HDL/total cholesterol ratio—and say that I was not okay, that I was in a moderate risk area, and prescribe a regimen of exercise, diet, and medication.

Most of us realize that a good percentage of the health problems we have are lifestyle-related. Without an extreme "wake-up call," such as a heart attack, many of us live in a rescue fantasy. We live the way we want to live—little or no exercise, poor nutrition, burning the candle at both ends—and when we have a problem, we expect the medical profession to pick up the pieces. While we may be able to diminish the pain with prescriptions and Band-Aids, if we're really going to make a difference, we need to go to the underlying root cause of the pain. We need to attend to prevention in a profound way.

The same is true in all areas of our lives. As Oliver Wendell Holmes said, "I wouldn't give a fig for the simplicity on this side of complexity; I would give my right arm for the simplicity on the far side of complexity." [3] The simplistic answers on this side of complexity do not address the full reality we're in. They may give a sense of being quick and easy, but their promise is empty. And most people know it. It's our experience that people are tired of the Band-Aids and aspirin offered by quick-fix solutions and personality ethic techniques. They want to address and resolve the chronic issues that keep them from putting first things first in their lives.

In the following chapter, we'd like to go beyond the acute pain of the problems we've talked about in Chapters 1 and 2 and into the chronic, underlying causes. We'd like to move through the heart of complexity, through the full reality that impacts our time and the quality of our lives. The three ideas in Chapter 3 may challenge your thinking, but we encourage you to pay the price and interact with these ideas on a deep personal level. We believe they will affirm a deeper knowing that transcends your paradigms and will empower you to create maps that accurately describe the territory.

Out of these ideas—on the far side of complexity—come the simple and powerful paradigms and processes in Section Two that will empower you to more effectively put first things first in your life.

3: *To Live, to Love, to Learn, to Leave a Legacy*

Doing more things faster is no substitute for doing the right things.

AS we move from urgency to importance, we encounter the fundamental question at hand: What are "first things" and how do we put them first in our lives?

At the heart of the fourth generation are three fundamental ideas that empower us to answer that question:

1. the fulfillment of the four human needs and capacities
2. the reality of "true north" principles
3. the potentiality of the four human endowments

1. THE FULFILLMENT OF THE FOUR HUMAN NEEDS AND CAPACITIES

There are certain things that are fundamental to human fulfillment. If these basic needs aren't met, we feel empty, incomplete. We may try to fill the void through urgency addiction. Or we may become complacent, temporarily satisfied with partial fulfillment.

But whether or not we fully acknowledge or address these needs on a conscious level, deep inside we know they're there. And they're important. We can validate them through our own experience. We can validate them through the experience of other people. We can validate them through our combined experience that stretches around the globe and throughout time. These needs have been recognized in the wisdom literature* throughout time as vital areas of human fulfillment.

---

* "Wisdom literature" is that portion of the classic, philosophical, and religious literature of a society that deals specifically with the art of living (see Appendix C for further explanation and suggested readings).

The essence of these needs is captured in the phrase "to live, to love, to learn, to leave a legacy." The need to live is our *physical* need for such things as food, clothing, shelter, economic well-being, health. The need to love is our *social* need to relate to other people, to belong, to love, to be loved. The need to learn is our *mental* need to develop and to grow. And the need to leave a legacy is our *spiritual* need to have a sense of meaning, purpose, personal congruence, and contribution.

How powerfully do these needs affect our time and the quality of our lives? You may find it helpful to think about the questions below:

- Do you have sustained energy and physical capacity throughout the day—or are there things you'd like to do that you can't do because you feel tired, ill, or out of shape?
- Are you in a position of financial security? Are you able to meet your own needs and have resources set aside for the future—or are you in debt, working long hours, and barely scraping by?
- Do you have rich, satisfying relationships with others? Are you able to work with others effectively to accomplish common purposes—or do you feel alienated and alone, unable to spend quality time with the people you love, or challenged in trying to work with others because of misunderstanding, miscommunication, politicking, backbiting, or blaming and accusing?
- Are you constantly learning, growing, gaining new perspectives, acquiring new skills—or do you feel stagnant? Are you being held back from career advancement or other things you'd like to do because you don't have the education or skills?
- Do you have a clear sense of direction and purpose that inspires and energizes you—or do you feel vague about what's important to you and unclear about what you really want to do with your life?

Each of these needs is vitally important. *Any one of these needs, unmet, reduces quality of life.* If you're in debt or poor health, if you don't have adequate food, clothing, and shelter, if you feel alienated and alone, if you're mentally stagnant, if you don't have a sense of purpose and integrity, your quality of life suffers. Vibrant health, economic security, rich, satisfying relationships, ongoing personal and professional development, and a deep sense of purpose, contribution, and personal congruence create quality of life.

Any one of these needs, unmet, can become a black hole that devours your energy and attention. If you have a financial problem, or you're going through a deep social trauma such as divorce, or you lose your health, that unmet need can become the urgent, dominating, pressing factor that consumes you. Other needs tend to be ignored, and quality of life suffers in every dimension.

Any one of these needs, unmet, can drive you to urgency addiction. As you respond time and again to urgent, unmet needs, you tend to become an excellent crisis manager. You may begin to prioritize the crises and do the urgent more efficiently, thinking, "If I'm busy, I must be effective." And you may get reinforcement from the adrenaline highs that come with putting out fires and responding to other people's urgent demands. But these activities don't bring quality-of-life results. They don't meet the underlying needs. The more urgent things we try to do, the more we feed the addiction. We keep substituting the artificial "high" of the urgency fix for the deep satisfaction of effectively meeting our four fundamental needs.

BALANCE AND SYNERGY AMONG THE FOUR NEEDS

These needs are real and deep and highly interrelated. Some of us recognize that we have these needs, but we tend to see them as separate "compartments" of life. We think of "balance" as running from one area to another fast enough to spend time in each one on a regular basis.

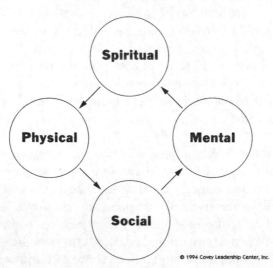

© 1994 Covey Leadership Center, Inc.

But the "touching bases" paradigm ignores the reality of their powerful synergy. It's where these four needs overlap that we find true inner balance, deep fulfillment, and joy.

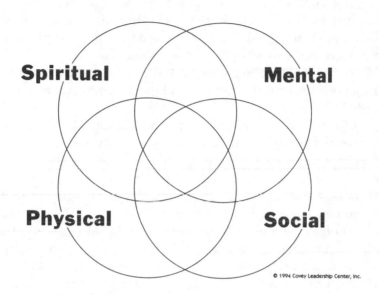

© 1994 Covey Leadership Center, Inc.

Just look at the difference. If we operate from the "touching bases" paradigm, we may see the physical need of earning a living as separate from our spiritual need to contribute to society. The work we choose to do may be monotonous, dull, and unfulfilling. It may even be counterproductive to society's welfare.

If we see our psychological need to learn and develop as separate from our social need to love and be loved, we may not seek to learn how to really, deeply love other human beings. While we increase our academic knowledge, we may shrink in our ability to relate meaningfully to others.

If we see our physical need as separate from all others, we may not fully realize how the quality of our health affects the quality of each of the other areas. When we aren't feeling well, it's much harder to think clearly, to relate in positive ways to others, to focus on contribution instead of survival.

If we see our spiritual need as separate from all other needs, we may not realize that what we believe about ourselves and our purpose has a powerful impact on how we live, how we love, and what we learn. To compartmentalize or even ignore the spiritual dimension of life powerfully affects each of the other dimensions. It is meaning and purpose that give context to fulfillment in all other dimensions.

Only as we see the interrelatedness and the powerful synergy of these four needs do we become empowered to fulfill them in a way that creates true inner balance, deep human fulfillment, and joy. Work has meaning, relationships have depth and growth, health becomes a resource to accomplish worthwhile purposes.

By seeing the interrelatedness of these needs, we realize that the key to meeting an unmet need is in addressing, not ignoring the other needs.

This is one of the strengths of personal leadership. While management is problem-oriented, leadership is opportunity-oriented. Instead of seeing a problem as segmented and mechanical—a broken part that needs to be fixed—it's seeing it as part of a living, synergistic whole. It's looking at what's around a problem, what's connected to it, what can influence it, as well as the problem itself.

If you have a problem in the physical area, for example—you're in debt or you have a financial crisis—instead of ignoring your social, mental, and spiritual needs, you can seek help and counsel from other people, increase your knowledge of money management and your awareness of problem-solving options, and define a reason for wanting to get out of debt that will give meaning, context, and purpose to whatever path you choose to take. By addressing these areas in your life as they relate to the physical need, you become empowered to meet the need in the most effective way.

If you have a problem in the social area—maybe you're going through a divorce—attention to the physical, mental, and spiritual areas of your life increases your ability to handle it. By exercising and taking care of your health, studying and learning more about the nature of relationships, and strengthening your sense of purpose and meaning in life, you nurture the conditions that empower you to face the social problem in the best possible way.

THE FIRE WITHIN

Fulfilling the four needs in an integrated way is like combining elements in chemistry. When we reach a "critical mass" of integration, we experience spontaneous combustion—an explosion of inner synergy that ignites the fire within and gives vision, passion, and a spirit of adventure to life.

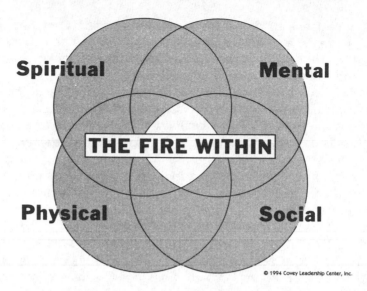

Spiritual   Mental

THE FIRE WITHIN

Physical   Social

© 1994 Covey Leadership Center, Inc.

The key to the fire within is our spiritual need to leave a legacy. *It transforms other needs into capacities for contribution.* Food, money, health, education, and love become resources to reach out and help fill the unmet needs of others.

Think of the impact on the way we spend our time and the quality of our lives when we're able to effectively meet our needs and turn them into capacities for contribution. Abraham Maslow, one of the fathers of modern psychology, developed a "needs hierarchy" in which he identified "self-actualization" as the highest human experience. But in his last years, he revised his earlier theory and acknowledged that this peak experience was not "self-actualization" but "self-transcendence," or living for a purpose higher than self.[1]

In the words of George Bernard Shaw:

This is the true joy in life . . . being used for a purpose recognized by yourself as a mighty one . . . being a force of Nature instead of a feverish selfish little clod of ailments and grievances complaining that the world will not devote itself to making you happy. . . . I am of the opinion that my life belongs to the whole community and as long as I live it is my privilege to do for it whatever I can. I want to be thoroughly used up when I die. For the harder I work the more I live. I rejoice in life for its own sake. Life is no brief candle to me. It's a sort of splendid torch which I've got to hold up for the moment and I want to make it burn as brightly as possible before handing it on to future generations.[2]

Roger: At one of our recent week-long Principle-Centered Leadership programs, a man approached me and asked if he could share a concern. We located a spot on the veranda overlooking a beautiful lake and golf course, and sat down to talk.

As I looked at the man, I had difficulty trying to imagine the nature of the problem he wanted to discuss. He was impressive—in his fifties, vice-president of a multinational corporation, with a nice family. He was an active participant in the program and seemed to grasp the material readily.

"I've felt increasingly uncomfortable as this week has progressed," he admitted. "It started with that exercise on Monday night . . . "

He proceeded to tell me something of his history. He'd been raised in a small town in the Midwest where he was active in sports, a good student, a choirboy. He went on to college where he was also active in a number of clubs and programs. Then came his first big job, marriage, a child, traveling abroad, promotions, a new home, another child, promotion to vice-president. As I listened, I kept waiting for the problem—some life-shattering disaster that must have brought his picturebook world crashing down around him.

"The problem," he finally said, "is that my life is full of good things—a nice house, a nice car, a good job, a busy life. But when you asked us to think deeply about our lives, to come to grips with what matters most, it really brought me up short.

"For most of my life—as a teenager, a college student, a young man—I was involved in some kind of cause. I wanted to make a real difference in the world, to contribute in a meaningful way.

"As I began to think about what really matters most to me, I suddenly realized that over these past years, that feeling, that sense of purpose, has somehow gotten lost. I've been lulled by a sense of security. I haven't made a difference. I haven't taught my children to make a difference. I've basically been watching life go by through the hedges of my country club."

I watched with interest as his entire demeanor changed. "But I've made a decision," he said. "I've determined to reestablish connections with a charitable organization I used to work with. They do incredible work helping people in Third World countries. I want to be a part of it."

There was a light in his eyes, a sense of purpose in his words. He was energized. It was easy to see that the quality of his last few years before retirement and of his life afterward—as well as the quality of life for many other people in the world—would be powerfully impacted by the legacy he would leave.

Whatever else we may value, the reality is that each of these areas of human fulfillment is essential to quality of life. Can you think of any exception—any person who doesn't have these physical, social, mental, and spiritual needs and capacities? Can you think of any time management problem that isn't connected at the root to fulfilling one of these basic needs?

2. THE REALITY OF "TRUE NORTH" PRINCIPLES

As "important" as the needs are to fulfill, is the way we seek to fulfill them. Our ability to create quality of life is a function of the degree to which our lives are aligned with extrinsic realities as we seek to fulfill the basic human needs.

Could you close your eyes right now and point north? When we ask people to do this in seminars, they're surprised when they open their eyes to see people pointing in every direction. If you're home, you may be able to point north easily because you're well oriented and have your bearings. But if you're away from home, without familiar landmarks, you may not find the task so simple.

Is it important for us to know where "true north" is? Most people would say yes. If we're one degree off in air travel from San Francisco, we could wind up in Moscow instead of Jerusalem.

What is "north"? Is it a matter of opinion? Is it something we should vote on? Is it subject to the democratic process? No, because "north" is a reality that is independent of us.

The reality of "true north" gives context and meaning to where we are, where we want to go, and how to get there. Without a compass or stars or a correct understanding of our location, we may have trouble locating it, but it's always there.

Just as real as "true north" in the physical world are the timeless laws of cause and effect that operate in the world of personal effectiveness and human interaction. The collective wisdom of the ages reveals these principles as recurring themes, foundational to every truly great person or society. With that in mind, we'd like to explore "true north" in the human dimension and look at how we can create an inner compass that empowers us to align our lives with it. In using "true north" as a metaphor for principles or external realities, we're not differentiating between technical differences such as "true north," "magnetic north," and "grid north."

WHAT PRINCIPLES ARE *NOT*

When we talk about principles, it's important to know what we aren't talking about as well as what we are.

We're Not Talking about Values.   Many of us think that just because we value something, achieving it will enhance our quality of life. We think, "I'll be happy and fulfilled when I make more money . . . when I get recognition for my talent . . . when I acquire an expensive home or a new car . . . when I finish my college degree."

But the focus on values is one of the major illusions of the traditional time management approach. It's content without context. It has us envisioning success, setting goals, climbing ladders without understanding the true north realities these efforts must be based on to be effective. It essentially says, " 'First things' are your priorities. You decide what you value and go after it in an efficient way." This can lead to arrogance—to thinking we're a law unto ourselves, and to looking at other people as "things" or as resources to help us accomplish what we want to do.

Values will *not* bring quality of life results . . . *unless we value principles*. A vital part of the fourth generation is the humility to realize that there are "first things" that are independent of our values. Quality of life is a function of the extent to which we make these "first things" *our* "first things" and become empowered to actually put them first in our lives. It's also the humility to recognize that quality of life is not "me," it's "us"—that we live in an interdependent reality of abundance and potential that can only be realized when we interact with others in fully authentic, synergistic ways.

All the wishing and even all the work in the world, if it's not based on valid principles, will not produce quality-of-life results. It's not enough to dream. It's not enough to try. It's not enough to set goals or climb ladders. It's not enough to value. The effort has to be based on practical realities that produce the result. Only then can we dream, set goals, and work to achieve them with confidence.

We're Not Talking about Practices.   In the midst of complexity, we tend to seek security in practices—specific, prescribed ways of doing things. We focus on methods instead of results. "Just tell me what to do. Give me the steps." We may get positive results with a particular practice in one situation, but if we try to use the same practice in other situations, we often find it doesn't work. As we encounter situations for which a practice has not been prescribed, we often feel lost and incompetent.

Arnold Toynbee, the great historian, said that all of history can be written in a simple little formula—challenge, response. The challenge is created by the environment, and then the individual, the institution, the society comes up with a response. Then there's another challenge, another response. The formula is constantly being repeated.

The problem is that these responses become codified. They get set in cement. They become a part of the very way we think and the way we perform. They may be good procedures, good practices. But when we're faced with a new challenge the old practices no longer apply. They become obsolete. We're out in the wilderness trying to navigate with a road map.

Our segmented, mechanistic society keeps us in a constantly changing kaleidoscope, so we cling to practices and structures and systems for some sense of predictability in our lives. And, little by little, challenge rubs them out. That's the demise of people and of institutions—even of families where parents can't accommodate the reality of their own children facing different kinds of challenges than they faced when they were growing up.

The power of principles is that they're universal, timeless truths. If we understand and live our lives based on principles, we can quickly adapt; we can apply them anywhere. By teaching our children principles instead of practices, or teaching them the principles behind the practices, we better prepare them to handle the unknown challenges of the future. To understand the application may be to meet the challenge of the moment, but to understand the principle is to meet the challenge of the moment more effectively and to be empowered to meet a thousand challenges of the future as well.

We're Not Talking about "Religion." Because principles deal with meaning and truth, some people tend to associate what we're saying about principles with their own positive or negative experience with religious organization or theology. As we teach in different parts of the world, we've had people express appreciation for our "renewal of the Christian ethic" or for "reminding us of the teachings of Buddha" or for giving them messages that are "so very close to Indian philosophy." On the other hand, a few do a double take when they hear what we teach because they feel it "smacks of religion," and to them, the term "religion" has institutional overtones that are not necessarily positive. At the other end of the spectrum, there are some who wonder if what we teach about principle-centeredness is humanistic and appears to leave out God altogether.

What we're talking about is not religion. We're not dealing with issues such as salvation, life after death, or even the source of these principles. *We do believe these are important issues for each individual to address.* But these issues are beyond the scope of this book. We're not dealing with why "true north" exists, where it came from, or how it came to be. We're simply dealing with the fact that it's there and that it governs the quality of our lives. And while we do find evidence of these principles in the sacred writings of every major religion, facets of them have come from the minds, pens, and spoken words of philosophers, scientists, kings, peasants, and saints throughout the world and throughout history.

These principles are sometimes called by different names as they get translated through different value systems. As Emerson said of the principle of benevolence, "For all things proceed out of this same spirit, which is differently named love, justice, temperance, in its different applications, just as the ocean receives different names on the several shores which it washes."[3] The fundamental principles are there, and recognized—though sometimes by different names—in all major civilizations throughout time.

So we're not talking about values, practices, or religion. What we *are* talking about are the true north realities upon which quality of life is based. These principles deal with things that, in the long run, will create happiness and quality-of-life results. They include principles such as service and reciprocity. They deal with the processes of growth and change. They include the laws that govern effective fulfillment of basic human needs and capacities.

In the chapters that follow we will present many principles that are essential to cultivating a quality life. But our overall objective is not to be comprehensive. It is rather to affirm the effectiveness of an approach to life that is based on the continual search for and effort to live congruently with these timeless, empowering truths.

WHAT PRINCIPLES *ARE*: THE LAW OF THE FARM

One of the best ways to understand how these extrinsic realities govern is to consider the Law of the Farm. In agriculture, we can easily see and agree that natural laws and principles govern the work and determine the harvest. But in social and corporate cultures, we somehow think we can dismiss natural processes, cheat the system, and still win the day. And there's a great deal of evidence that seems to support that belief.

For example, did you ever "cram" in school—goof off during the semester, then spend all night before the big test trying to cram a semester's worth of learning into your head?

Stephen: I'm ashamed to admit it, but I crammed my way through undergraduate school, thinking I was really clever. I learned to psych out the system, to figure out what the teacher wanted. "How does she grade? Mostly on lectures? Great! I don't have to worry about reading the textbook. What about this other class? We have to read the book? Okay, where are the Cliff Notes so I can get a quick summary instead?" I wanted the grade, but I didn't want it to crimp my lifestyle.

Then I got into graduate work, a different league altogether. I spent my first three months trying to cram to make up for four years of undergraduate cramming, and I wound up in the hospital with ulcerated colitis. I was trying to force the natural processes, and I found out that, long term, you simply can't do it. I spent years trying to compensate for the foolishness of getting myself into a value system that was not tied to principles at all.

Can you imagine "cramming" on the farm? Can you imagine forgetting to plant in the spring, flaking out all summer, and hitting it hard in the fall—ripping the soil up, throwing in the seeds, watering, cultivating—and expecting to get a bountiful harvest overnight?

Cramming doesn't work in a natural system, like a farm. That's the fundamental difference between a social and a natural system. A social system is based on values; a natural system is based on principles. In the short term, cramming may appear to work in a social system. You can go for the "quick fixes" and techniques with apparent success.

But in the long run, the Law of the Farm governs in all arenas of life. How many of us wish now we hadn't crammed in school? We got the degree, but we didn't get the education. We eventually find out there's a difference between succeeding in the social system of school and succeeding in the development of the mind—the ability to think analytically, creatively, at deep levels of abstraction, the ability to communicate orally and in writing, to cross borders, to rise above outmoded practices and solve problems in newer, better ways.

What about character? Can you "cram" and suddenly become a person of integrity, courage, or compassion? Or physical health? Can you overcome years of a potato-chip, chocolate-cake, no-exercise lifestyle by spending the night before the marathon working out at the health spa?

What about a marriage? Whether it's governed by the Law of the School or the Law of the Farm depends on how long you want it to last. Many people who marry don't want to change their lifestyle at all. They're married singles. They don't take the time to nurture seeds of shared vision, selflessness, caring, tenderness, and consideration, yet they're surprised at the harvest of weeds. The social system quick fixes and personality ethic techniques they try to install to solve the problem simply don't work. These "solutions" can't take the place of seasons of planting, cultivating, and caring.

What about relationships with children? We can take the short-cuts—we're bigger, smarter, we have the authority. We can talk down, threaten, impose our will. We can try to shift the responsibility for training them to schools, churches, or day-care centers. But over time, will these shortcuts develop responsible, caring, and wise adults empowered to make effective decisions and live happy lives? Will they result in rich, rewarding relationships for us with those who have the potential to be our closest friends?

In the short run, we may be able to go for the "quick fix" with apparent success. We can make impressions, we can put on the charm. We can learn manipulative techniques—what lever to pull, what button to push to get the desired reaction. But long-term, the Law of the Farm governs in all areas of life. And there's no way to fake the harvest. As Dr. Sidney Bremer observed in his book, *Spirit of Apollo:*

> Nature is evenly balanced. We cannot disturb her equilibrium, for we know that the law of Cause and Effect is the unerring and inexorable law of nature; but we do fail to find our own equilibrium as nations and as individuals, because we have not yet learned that the same law works as inexorably in human life and in society as in nature—that what we sow, we must inevitably reap.[4]

ILLUSION VERSUS REALITY

The problems in life come when we're sowing one thing and expecting to reap something entirely different.

Many of our fundamental paradigms and the processes and habits that grow out of them will never produce the results we've been led to expect they will. These paradigms—created by people looking for shortcuts, advertising, program-of-the month training, and seventy years of personality ethic success literature—are fundamentally based on the quick-fix illusion. This not only affects our awareness of our fundamental needs but also the way we attempt to fulfill them.

Physical Needs

Vibrant health is based on natural principles. It grows over time out of regular exercise, proper nutrition, adequate rest, a healthy mind-set, avoiding substances that are harmful to the body. But instead of paying the price, we're caught up in the illusion of appearance—the fantasy that the right clothes, the right makeup, the quick-fix weight-loss programs (actually proven to contribute to the long-term problem instead of solving it) will fulfill our physical need. It's an empty promise. It brings short-term satisfaction, but it's cotton candy. There's no substance to it. It doesn't last.

Economic well-being is based on principles of thrift, industry, saving for future needs, earning interest instead of paying it. But we live with the illusion that having "things" will fulfill the need—regardless of the fact that they're bought on credit and we spend months or even years paying twice what they're worth for the cotton-candy satisfaction of instant gratification. Or we live with the rescue fantasy of winning the lottery or some magazine publisher's sweepstakes—the illusion that somebody or something "out there" is going to magically solve all our problems and absolve us of the need to develop competence in financial affairs.

Social Needs

The reality is that quality relationships are built on principles—especially the principle of trust. And trust grows out of trustworthiness, out of the character to make and keep commitments, to share resources, to be caring and responsible, to belong, to love unconditionally.

But when we're lonely and in the pain of the unmet need, we don't want to be told to go out and earn it, to be trust-worthy—worthy of someone's trust and affection. It's so much easier to believe in the cotton-candy illusion of sexual gratification, or the idea that appearance and personality will win affection, or that we can call the 900 number on late-night TV and have someone talk to us in an affectionate way. It's easier to get a fix of love than to work on being a loving person. And our culture—music, books, advertising, movies, TV programming—is filled with the illusion.

Mental Needs

We often go for the illusion of "cramming" instead of the reality of long-term development and growth. We're into "get the degree . . . so you can get the job . . . so you can get the money . . . so you can buy the things . . . so you'll be successful." But what does that kind of "success" bring? The same character and competence that come from deep, continuous investment in learning and growth?

Spiritual Needs

We settle for the illusion society sells us that meaning is in self-focus—self-esteem, self-development, self-improvement—it's "what *I* want," "let me do my own thing," "I did it *my* way." But the wisdom literature of thousands of years of history repeatedly validates the reality that the greatest fulfillment in improving ourselves comes in our empowerment to more effectively reach out and help others. Quality of life is inside-out. Meaning is in contribution, in living for something higher than self. And the results of the illusion and the reality are as different as the Dead Sea—a stagnant end in itself where there's no outlet and no life—and the Red Sea, where the waters flow on and nurture abundant life along the way.

In the area of time management, many of the techniques and practices masquerade as practical, hard-hitting, bottom-line solutions that address immediate concerns. But their implied promise is quick-fix illusion. The chronic, underlying needs are not addressed. Solutions are truncated from the principles that grow long-term quality-of-life results. We're back to cotton-candy satisfaction, and the results we're getting in our lives validate it.

There is no way quality of life can grow out of illusion. The quick fixes, platitudes, and personality ethic techniques that violate basic principles will never bring quality-of-life results.

So how do we discover and align our lives with true north realities that govern quality of life?

3. THE POTENTIALITY OF THE FOUR HUMAN ENDOWMENTS

As human beings, we have unique endowments that distinguish us from the animal world. These endowments reside in that space between stimulus and response, between those things that happen to us and our response to them.

Stephen: Years ago, as I was wandering between the stacks of books at a university library, I chanced to open a book in which I encountered one of the most powerful, significant ideas I've ever come across. The essence of it was this:
"Between stimulus and response, there is a space.
In that space is our power to choose our response.
In our response lies our growth and our freedom."
That idea hit me with incredible force. In the following days, I reflected on it again and again. It had a powerful effect on my paradigm of life. I began to discover in that space my own ability to make a consciously chosen response.

The endowments that reside in this space—self-awareness, conscience, creative imagination, and independent will—create our ultimate human freedom: the power to choose, to respond, to change. They create the compass that empowers us to align our lives with true north.

© 1994 Covey Leadership Center, Inc.

• **Self-awareness** is our capacity to stand apart from ourselves and examine our thinking, our motives, our history, our scripts, our actions, and our habits and tendencies. It enables us to take off our "glasses" and look at them as well as through them. It makes it possible for us to become aware of the social and psychic history of the programs that are in us and to enlarge the separation between stimulus and response.

   • **Conscience** connects us with the wisdom of the ages and the wisdom of the heart. It's our internal guidance system, which allows us to sense when we act or even contemplate acting in a way that's contrary to principle. It also gives us a sense of our unique gifts and mission.

   • **Independent will** is our capacity to act. It gives us the power to transcend our paradigms, to swim upstream, to rewrite our scripts, to act based on principle rather than reacting based on emotion or circumstance. While environmental or genetic influences may be very powerful, they do not control us. We're not victims. We're not the product of our past. We are the product of our choices. We are "response-able"—able to respond, to choose beyond our moods and tendencies. We have will power to act on self-awareness, conscience, and vision.

   • **Creative imagination** is the power to envision a future state, to create something in our mind, and to solve problems synergistically. It's the endowment that enables us to see ourselves and others differently and better than we are now. It enables us to write a personal mission statement, set a goal, or plan a meeting. It also empowers us to visualize ourselves living our mission statement even in the most challenging circumstances, and to apply principles in effective ways in new situations.

Self-improvement "movements" often recognize these endowments, but tend to segment them and to address them in isolation.

   • **Self-awareness** is the focus of the recovery movement, as well as psychoanalysis and most psychotherapy.
   • **Conscience** is the focus of religion—the world of morality, ethical thought, questions of meaning and right and wrong.
   • **Independent will** is the will power, the "man on the street" approach—white-knuckle your way through life to get what you want. "No pain, no gain."
   • **Creative imagination** is the focus of visualization and mind power movements such as Positive Thinking, Psychocyber-

netics, the Magic of Believing, and Neurolinguistic Programming.

While each approach develops one or more of the human endowments, each fails to recognize all of the endowments as an interrelated, synergistic whole. But each of these endowments—and the synergy among them—is necessary to create quality of life. It's not enough to be self-aware—to recognize we've been scripted in ways that are not in harmony with our deep inner conscience—if we don't have the creative imagination to envision a better way and the independent will to create change. It's not enough to have the independent will to "white-knuckle" our way through life if we don't develop the conscience to discover true north and cut through the rationalizing and justifying that keep us on dead-end paths. Imagination without independent will can create an idealistic dreamer; imagination without conscience can create a Hitler.

The development of each of the four endowments and the synergy between them is the core of personal leadership. This is what empowers us to say, "I can examine my paradigms. I can examine the results they're producing. I can use my conscience to determine new paths that are in harmony with principles and with my own unique ability to contribute. I can use my independent will to make choices to create change. I can use my creative imagination to create beyond my present reality, to find new alternatives."

HOW TO DEVELOP YOUR ENDOWMENTS

We all have each of these endowments. We've all had moments of self-awareness. We've had times when we've listened to and acted in harmony with some inner imperative. We've had experiences where we acted based on what we felt was important instead of reacting to emotion or circumstances. We've had moments of vision, moments of inspired creativity.

But whether we consciously recognize it or not, we've undoubtedly also had times of incredible blindness, times when we've ignored or resisted the urging of that inner guidance system, moments of highly reactive behavior, moments without vision or imagination.

The question is: How fully have we developed our unique endowments and how powerful is the synergy in our lives?

We'd like to suggest that you take a moment and give serious consideration to the questions below. Your answers will give you some idea of the degree to which you've developed and are currently using these endowments in your life.

After going through these questions, add up your score for each of the four endowments. Measure your score in each of the sections by the following key:

0–7   Inactive endowment
8–12   Active endowment
13–16 Highly developed endowment

Circle the number along the matrix that most closely represents your normal behaviors or attitudes regarding the statements at the left. (0=Never, 2=Sometimes, 4=Always)

Self-awareness

1. Am I able to stand apart from my thoughts or feelings and examine and change them?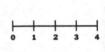

2. Am I aware of my fundamental paradigms and the impact they have on my attitudes and behaviors and the results I'm getting in my life?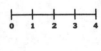

3. Am I aware of a difference between my biological, genealogical, psychological, and sociological scripting— and my own deep inner thoughts?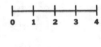

4. When the response of other people to me—or something I do—challenges the way I see myself, am I able to evaluate that feedback against deep personal self-knowledge and learn from it?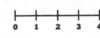

Conscience

1. Do I sometimes feel an inner prompting that I should do something or that I shouldn't do something I'm about to do?

2. Do I sense the difference between "social conscience"—what society has conditioned me to value—and my own inner directives?

3. Do I inwardly sense the reality of true north principles such as integrity and trustworthiness?

4. Do I see a pattern in human experience—bigger than the society in which I live—that validates the reality of principles?

		N	S	A

Independent Will

1. Am I able to make and keep promises to myself as well as to others?

$$\vdash\!\!+\!\!\!+\!\!\!+\!\!\dashv$$
0 1 2 3 4

2. Do I have the capacity to act on my own inner imperatives even when it means swimming upstream?

$$\vdash\!\!+\!\!\!+\!\!\!+\!\!\dashv$$
0 1 2 3 4

3. Have I developed the ability to set and achieve meaningful goals in my life?

$$\vdash\!\!+\!\!\!+\!\!\!+\!\!\dashv$$
0 1 2 3 4

4. Can I subordinate my moods to my commitments?

$$\vdash\!\!+\!\!\!+\!\!\!+\!\!\dashv$$
0 1 2 3 4

Creative Imagination

1. Do I think ahead?

$$\vdash\!\!+\!\!\!+\!\!\!+\!\!\dashv$$
0 1 2 3 4

2. Do I visualize my life beyond its present reality?

$$\vdash\!\!+\!\!\!+\!\!\!+\!\!\dashv$$
0 1 2 3 4

3. Do I use visualization to help reaffirm and realize my goals?

$$\vdash\!\!+\!\!\!+\!\!\!+\!\!\dashv$$
0 1 2 3 4

4. Do I look for new, creative ways to solve problems in a variety of situations and value the different views of others?

$$\vdash\!\!+\!\!\!+\!\!\!+\!\!\dashv$$
0 1 2 3 4

Building these endowments is a process of nurturing and exercising them on a continuing basis. Although there are many ways to nurture these endowments, in this chapter we'd like to suggest one powerful way to develop each and cultivate the synergy among them.

Nurture Self-awareness by Keeping a Personal Journal

Keeping a personal journal is a high-leverage Quadrant II activity that significantly increases self-awareness and enhances all the endowments and the synergy among them.

What things would you write about in a personal journal? If you don't like a result you're getting in your life, write about it. Get it out on paper. Notice how the law of the harvest operates in your life. See how consequences flow from root causes. See how results can be traced to paradigms, processes, and habits.

If you're not sure why you still do some things that you know are harmful or self-defeating, analyze it, process it, write it down. If your parents did something that drove you nuts, and you said to yourself, "When I'm a parent, I'm never going to do that!" —and then you find yourself doing it—write it down. It builds awareness of your scripting. It helps you to make wise choices.

If you gain an insight or learn a principle or observe a situation where a principle produced certain results, write about it. If you feel some inner prompting and you either follow it or ignore it, write about it and what happens as a result. The process helps you pay more attention to that inner guidance system. It strengthens and educates your conscience.

If you make a commitment to yourself or to someone else, write about the way you use your independent will to carry it out. If you commit to exercise four times a week, evaluate the factors that empowered you to do it—or explore the reasons why you didn't. Was your commitment halfhearted, hasty, or unrealistic? Was "mind over mattress" too great a challenge for your current level of independent will? Did the commitment you made to yourself receive the same priority as the commitments you make to others? Increased awareness of your independent will helps you develop it.

Envision possibilities and write them down. Dreaming builds creative imagination. Then test your dreams. Are they based on principles? Are you willing to pay the price to achieve them?

As you develop your imagination, you can use it to create in your mind what you hope to create in your life. It's the blueprint before the finished house, the director's vision before the stage performance. It's creating the long-term, mid-range, and short-term goals that help translate vision into reality.

You may find you're living with unfulfilled dreams. You may be resigned, feeling you're settling for second best, and thinking "if only things were different" you could fulfill those dreams. But if you pay the price and hammer it out, you may find your dreams are delusions—you're wishing and waiting and wanting something that will never bring quality of life.

Stand apart from your dreams. Look at them. Write about them. Wrestle with them until you're convinced they're based on principles that will bring results. Then use your creative imagination to explore new applications, new ways of doing things that have the principle-based power to translate dreaming to doing.

Keeping a personal journal empowers you to see and improve, on a day-by-day basis, the way you're developing and using your endowments. Because writing truly imprints the brain, it also helps you remember and apply the things you're trying to do. In addition, it gives you a powerful contextual tool. As you take occasion—perhaps on a mission statement renewal retreat—to read over your experiences of past weeks, months, or years, you gain invaluable insight into repeating patterns and themes in your life.

Educate the Conscience by Learning, Listening, and Responding

The existence of conscience is one of the most widely validated concepts in psychological, sociological, religious, and philosophical literature throughout time. From the wisdom literature's "inner voice" to psychology's "collective unconscious"—even to Walt Disney's "Jiminy Cricket"—this endowment has been recognized and addressed as a major part of human being. Sigmund Freud said that the conscience is primarily a product of our early life and culture. Carl Jung acknowledged the social conscience, but he also spoke of the "collective unconscious" that taps into the universal spirit of all men and women.[5]

As we work with companies in developing mission statements, we see repeated validation of the "collective unconscious." When most people get into their deep inner lives, regardless of their culture, upbringing, religion, or race, they seem to have a sense of the basic Laws of Life.

Nevertheless, most of us work and live in environments that don't nurture the development of the conscience. To hear conscience clearly often requires us to be "still" or "reflective" or "meditative"—a condition we rarely choose or find. We're inundated by activity, noise, social and cultural conditioning, media messages, and flawed paradigms that dull our sensitivity to that quiet inner voice that would teach us of true north principles and our own degree of congruency with them.

But if we stop and search deeply with an honest heart, we can tap into that inner wellspring of wisdom.

Stephen: Some years ago I was invited to a university to participate in a week-long forum that dealt with many problems and issues of current interest. I was one of a number of people invited, each of whom represented different viewpoints and backgrounds.

On the second night, I was invited to speak at a sorority-fraternity exchange at a sorority house on the subject of "the new morality." The house was packed with about one hundred and fifty young people. They were sitting in the front room, in the dining room, in the hallway, and up the stairs. I had a terrific sense of being overwhelmed and surrounded, and I felt very alone. I put forth my point of view that there are a set of principles that are universal and that operate inde-

pendent of any individual. I sensed throughout my entire presentation considerable resistance and disbelief.

When it came to the question-and-answer period, two articulate students began to express themselves strongly in favor of the situational ethic of the "new morality." The new morality was based on the idea that there are no absolute truths and standards but that each situation must be looked at in terms of the people involved as well as other factors that might be present. One student was particularly effective and persuasive in giving an example of an issue that he believed had no foundation in absolute right or wrong or principle, but was right depending on the situation.

Though I sensed considerable support for this point of view, I continued to make my case for universal principles such as the Law of the Farm, integrity, moderation, self-discipline, fidelity, and responsibility. I knew I wasn't getting through and that the students thought I was pretty much "out of it." I tried to reason that terrible consequences resulted from violating the principle involved in his issue. The persuasive student in the front row didn't buy it. I asked him directly what would happen if a person were to take poison unknowingly. Would it not bring on terrible consequences? He answered that it was a poor analogy, that I wasn't giving enough value to the freedom that individuals have.

At this point, I knew that we weren't getting anywhere. So I looked up at everyone and said, "Each of us knows in our heart the truth of this matter. We all have a conscience. We all know. And if you will take a few moments and just reflect and listen carefully to what your heart tells you, you will know the answer." Many sneered and jeered at this idea.

I responded to this ridicule by renewing the challenge: I asked each person to try it individually, and if each person did not feel their conscience answer the question within one minute, the group could immediately dismiss me and I wouldn't waste any more of their time. This sobered them, and most appeared willing to experiment. I asked them to be very quiet and to do no talking, but to listen internally and ask themselves, "Is the subject, as it has been explained this evening, a true principle or not?"

The first few seconds some looked around to see who was going to take this business seriously, but within about twenty seconds almost every person was sitting quietly and appeared to be very intent in thinking and listening. Many bowed their heads. After a full minute of this silence, which probably seemed like an eternity to some, I looked at the individual at my left who had been so persuasive and vocal and said to him, "In all honesty, my friend, what did you hear?"

He responded quietly but directly, "What I heard is not what I have been saying."

I turned to another who had been disagreeing, and I asked him what he had heard.

He answered, "I don't know—I just don't know. I'm not certain anymore."

There was a totally different spirit among the group. They became subdued and quiet from then on. They became less intellectual and defensive and more open and teachable.

This is the kind of humility we experience when we come to the realization that principles govern—that there is an independent universal reality outside ourselves that conscience affirms.

So how do we develop the endowment of conscience?

Let's compare the development of conscience to the development of physical competence symbolized by five sets of hands. One set belongs to a great concert pianist, who can enthrall audiences with her renditions. Another pair are the hands of a skilled surgeon, who can perform delicate operations on the eye or the brain that can save lives and sight and thinking processes. Another set of hands belongs to a great golfer, who wins tournaments by making great shots under pressure. Another set of hands belongs to a blind man, who can read at incredible speeds by touching the raised markings on a page. And the fifth set of hands belongs to a great sculptor, who can make beautiful art out of solid blocks of marble or granite.

A highly educated conscience is much like any of these sets of hands. A great price has been paid to educate it. Sacrifices have been made and obstacles overcome. In fact, it actually takes even more discipline, sacrifice, and wisdom to develop an educated conscience than it does to become a great sculptor, golfer, surgeon, Braille reader, or concert pianist. But the rewards are far greater—an educated conscience impacts every aspect of our lives.

We can educate our conscience by:

- reading and pondering over the wisdom literature of the ages to broaden our awareness of the true north principles that run as common themes throughout time
- standing apart from and learning from our own experience
- carefully observing the experience of others
- taking time to be still and listen to that deep inner voice
- responding to that voice

It's not enough just to listen to conscience; we must also respond. When we fail to act in harmony with our inner voice, we begin to build a wall around the conscience that blocks its sensitivity and receptivity. As C. S. Lewis observed, "disobedience to conscience makes conscience blind."[6]

As we connect with the wisdom of the ages and the wisdom of the heart, we become less a function of the social mirror and more a person of character and conscience. Our security doesn't come from the way people treat us or in comparing ourselves to others. It comes from our basic integrity.

Nurture Independent Will by Making and Keeping Promises

One of the best ways to strengthen our independent will is to make and keep promises. Each time we do, we make deposits in our Personal Integrity Account. This is a metaphor that describes the amount of trust we have in ourselves, in our ability to walk our talk.

It's important to start small. Make and keep a promise—even if it means you're going to get up in the morning a little earlier and exercise. Even if it means you aren't going to watch television tonight. Even if it means you're going to subordinate taste to nutrition for a week.

Be sure you don't violate that commitment and be sure you don't overpromise and underdeliver. Don't risk making a withdrawal from the Personal Integrity Account. Build slowly until your sense of honor becomes greater than your moods. Think carefully about the full reality you're in, and based on that careful thought, move into it and say, "I will do this." And then, no matter what, do it.

Little by little, your faith in yourself will increase. And if the thing you've committed to do is principle-centered, you gradually become a little more principle-centered. You keep the promise to yourself and your own integrity account goes up.

Stephen: At one time, I counseled with a man whose life was totally broken. It was filled with sloppiness and flakiness. He would put in appearances from time to time like a flying fish that would shimmer into the sunlight, then plow back down into a life of procrastination and selfishness, buffeted by all the urgent things that were afflicting him.

I began to encourage this man to tap into his unique human endowments and to start in very small ways. I said, "Will you get up in the morning when you say you're planning to get up? Will you just get up in the morning?"

He said, "How is that going to affect everything else?"

I said, "Your body is the only instrument through which you operate in life. If you don't get control of your body, how can you control the expressions that come through your body and your mind?"

So he resolved each night to get up, but then a whole new mentality seemed to overcome him in the morning. He was an absolute slave—he worshipped the mattress.

I tried again. "Will you just get up at a certain time for one month?"

He said, "I really don't know if I can."

"Then don't commit to do it. Your integrity is at stake. As you've acknowledged, your life is totally fragmented. You have no internal peace of mind at all. So don't make a promise and break it. Start smaller. Do you think you could do it for a week?"

"Yes, I think I can do it for a week."

*"**Will** you get up at the time you say you're going to get up for one week?"*

"I will."

I saw him a week later. "Did you do it?"

"I did."

"Congratulations! Already your life is getting integrated at a very small level. Now, what's the next thing you're going to commit to do?"

Little by little, this man began to make and keep commitments. No one else knew of his plan but a friend and myself who were encouraging him. But we began to see remarkable change. Before, his emotional life had been a roller coaster. His decisions were a function of circumstances and mood. He would make a promise and it felt great, but when the mood and the circumstance were discouraging, he would get low and break it. And something inside him would break— his integrity.

But as he began the process of making and keeping small promises, his emotional life evened out. He found that making and keeping promises to himself increased his ability to make and keep promises to others as well. He discovered that his lack of integrity had been a great impediment in his relationships with other people. Out of his private victories, public victories began to come.

As one wise man observed, "The greatest battles we fight are in the silent chambers of our own souls." We need to ask ourselves: "Am I willing to be a person of total integrity? Am I willing to apologize when I make mistakes, to love unconditionally, to value someone else's happiness as much as I do my own?"

Part of our scripting and history may say, "No, I'm not. That's not the way I was raised. That's not the environment." But then our independent will says, "Wait a minute! You're capable of this. You don't have to be a function of your scripting or the social mirror and the expedient path others take. You have the opportunity now to decide your response to all that has ever happened to you. Whether others do it or not is irrelevant. You have the power to look at your own involvement, to observe your response, to change it."

To those who say, "Come on! Do you know what it's like out there?" we say, "Come on! Do you know the power you have within you?" We don't want to offend; we say it in love. Our lives are the results of our choices. To blame and accuse other people, the environment, or other extrinsic factors is to choose to empower those things to control us.

We choose—either to live our lives or to let others live them for us. By making and keeping promises to ourselves and to others, little by little we increase our strength until our ability to act is more powerful than any of the forces that act upon us.

Develop Creative Imagination through Visualization

Imagine the following scenario:

Beads of perspiration begin to trickle down your face. The intense heat of the hostile, war-torn tropical Latin American country makes it almost impossible to breathe. The panic-stricken woman you just rescued from the roach-ridden guerrilla prison clings to your arm, just on the edge of hysteria. Your mission: to return her safely to her father, the ambassador. You have no weapons, no food, no transportation, and no way to communicate with the outside world. Surrounded by hostile enemy troops, you realize your barely adequate place of concealment will soon be discovered.

What do you do?

Frankly, we don't know what we would do. We don't know what you would do. But we do know what MacGyver would do.

Star of the television adventure series by that name, MacGyver is the master of ingenuity. There doesn't seem to be any situation this miracle man can't handle. He's the enigma of modern crime drama, the man without weapons, the man with the *mind*. With his vast knowledge and creativity, he makes a reflective parabolic mirror from the remains of a blown-up jeep in the bushes where he's hiding. Focusing the sun's rays on some enemy ammunition, he creates an explosion and diversion to occupy the troops while he and the woman make their way to an abandoned farmer's shed. Finding bits and pieces of old materials and common household chemicals in the shed, he is able to create explosive devices for future protection. He gathers enough parts from a broken radio to create a homing device that signals the rescue helicopter to pick them up.

Fantastic? Yes. Obviously fictional. But how would you like to have a marketing manager like MacGyver?

The "MacGyver Factor," as we like to call it, is the embodiment of the power of creative imagination. It's understanding and being able to apply principles in a wide variety of situations. With the MacGyver Factor, you can still get four by adding two plus two—but you could also consider one plus three, ninety-two minus eighty-eight, two hundred twenty-eight divided by fifty-seven, an infinite variety of fractional combinations, or the square root of sixteen.

The MacGyver Factor illustrates the empowering nature of principles. Had he been thinking in terms of practices instead of principles, MacGyver and the ambassador's daughter might even now be sitting in that roach-ridden Latin American prison, berating the fact that they couldn't find a hand grenade.

Understanding the MacGyver Factor is one of the most exciting and empowering aspects of principle-centered living. Principles are the simplicity on the far side of complexity. In the words of Alfred North Whitehead:

> In a sense, knowledge shrinks as wisdom grows: for details are swallowed up in principles. The details of knowledge which are important will be picked up ad hoc in each avocation of life, but the habit of the active utilisation of well-understood principles is the final possession of wisdom."[7]

With a solid understanding of principles, we can easily see that the Law of the Farm applies as well to personal development as it does to growing tomatoes—or that the same principle of synergy that makes it possible for two boards to hold more weight together than the combined weight held by each separately also empowers two people to come up with a solution better than either could have alone.

The process we suggest to help develop creative imagination is visualization—a high-leverage mental exercise used by world-class athletes and performers. But instead of using it to improve your tennis game or your concert performance, we suggest you try using it to improve your quality of life.

Set aside some time to be alone, away from interruptions. Close your eyes and visualize yourself in some circumstance that would normally create discomfort or pain. Something pushes your button. Your boss yells at you. Your teenage daughter complains that you never buy her any clothes. Your co-worker starts a vicious rumor about you.

Use your self-awareness to separate yourself from your normal thoughts and feelings the situation would create. In your mind's eye, instead of seeing yourself react as you might normally do, see yourself act based on the principles you are convinced will create quality-of-life results. See yourself interacting with others in a way that combines courage and consideration. Use the MacGyver Factor to see how you might apply principles in different situations. The value of this exercise multiplies when you use it to internalize the principles and values in a powerful mission statement.

The best way to predict your future is to create it. You can use the same power of creative imagination that enables you to see a goal before you accomplish it or plan a meeting to create much of the quality of your own reality before you live it.

THE HUMILITY OF PRINCIPLES

Out of the paradigm that principles exist—and that we're only effective to the degree to which we discover and live in harmony with them—comes a sense of humility. We're not in control of our lives; principles are. We cease trying to be a law unto ourselves. We cultivate attitudes of teachability, habits of continual learning. We become involved in an ongoing quest to understand and live in harmony with the Laws of Life. We don't get caught up in the arrogance of values that blinds us to self-awareness and conscience. Our security is not based on the illusion of comparative thinking—I'm better looking, I have more money, I have a better job, or I work harder than somebody else. Nor do we feel any less secure if we're not as good-looking or have less money or prestige than somebody else. It's irrelevant. Our security comes from our own integrity to true north.

When we fail or make a mistake or hit a principle head-on, we say, "What can I learn from this?" We come to the principle to be taught by it. And as we learn where we went wrong in accordance with that principle, we can turn weaknesses into strengths. We confront behavior with truth in a way that represents confidence in the truth and recognition of our own ability to learn and change.

Humility truly is the mother of all virtues. It makes us a vessel, a vehicle, an agent instead of "the source" or the principal. It unleashes all other learning, all growth and process. With the humility that comes from being principle-centered, we're empowered to learn from the past, have hope for the future, and act with confidence in the present. This confidence is an assurance, based on Law of the Farm evidence—across the globe, throughout history, and in our own lives—that if we act based on principles, it will produce quality-of-life results.

MOVING INTO THE FOURTH GENERATION

It's our experience that most people who think deeply about their own experience and the experience of others know that we all have basic needs and capacities that are fundamental to human fulfillment. They have an awareness of some of the true north principles that govern quality of life. They've had some experience with the endowments that make it possible for them to align their lives with true north. In some respects, this chapter is a reminder of things that, deep inside, most of us already know. *The fact that we know it—and that it doesn't get translated into the fabric of our daily lives—is the frustration of the gap between the compass and the clock.* Our problem, as one put it, "is to get at the wisdom we already have."

It's also our experience that most people really want to be in the fourth generation. They want to put people ahead of schedules, compasses ahead of clocks. They want to lead lives of meaning and contribution. They want to live, love, learn, and leave a legacy with balance and joy.

But more often than not, traditional time management gets in the way. Calendars and schedules and third-generation planners keep us focused on the urgent instead of the important. They create guilt when we don't stick to the schedule or check off all the "to do's" on the list. They stifle flexibility and spontaneity. They often create misalignment between what really matters most and the way we live our daily lives. In fact, many people using these tools do not use them in the way they were intended to be used for those very reasons.

Certainly we want the tremendous benefits of the first three generations—efficiency, prioritization, productivity, accomplishment of goals—but we need more. *Doing more things faster is no substitute for doing the right things.* We need a generation of theory and tools that will empower us to use our endowments to fulfill our basic needs and capacities in a balanced, principle-centered way.

Bottom-line, the power to create quality life is not in any planner. It's not in any technique or tool. And it's not limited to our ability to plan a day. None of us is omniscient. We don't know what opportunities, challenges, surprises, sorrows, or unexpected joys the next moment in our lives will bring.

The power to create quality of life is within us—in our ability to develop and use our own inner compass so that we can act with integrity in the moment of choice—whether that moment is spent planning the week, handling a crisis, responding to our conscience, building a relationship, working with an irate client, or taking a walk. To be effective, a tool must be aligned with that reality and enhance the development and use of that inner compass.

*S*ection Two

THE MAIN THING IS TO KEEP THE MAIN THING THE MAIN THING

In this section we'll introduce the Quadrant II organizing process—a thirty-minute weekly process and tool that will empower you to create quality of life based on needs, principles, and endowments. As we move through the parts of the process, we'll address questions such as these:

- Suppose you're planning a day. How do you know what's really most important for you to do? What determines your "first things"—urgency, values . . . or an empowering vision and mission based on the principles that create quality of life?
- What do you do when you feel torn between different roles in your life, such as work and family or contribution and personal development? Is "balance" a matter of running between bases fast enough to touch them all?
- Suppose you have the day planned and someone comes to you with an "urgent" need. How do you know whether it's "best" to change your priorities? Can you change with the confidence and peace that you're putting first things first?
- Suppose you're going through your day and an unexpected opportunity comes up. How do you know whether it's "best" to respond to the opportunity or stick to your plan?

The first time you go through this process, you'll see immediate benefits. You'll be able to start shifting your focus from "urgency" to "importance" and learn how to create a flexible framework for effective decision making instead of a schedule made of cement.

But you'll experience the process on a much more powerful level as we go through each step in depth in Chapters 5 to 10. In these chapters, we'll talk about:

- the transforming power of a principle-based vision and mission
- how to create balance and synergy among the various roles in your life
- how to set and achieve principle-based goals
- why the perspective of the week makes such a vital difference in putting first things first
- how to act with integrity in the moment of choice—where the rubber meets the road in daily living
- how to create an upward spiral of learning and living

At the end of each of these chapters, you'll find specific suggestions for goals you can set during weekly organizing to integrate these things into your life. Some ideas may be more helpful to you than others. We hope you'll come up with many ideas on your own. After going through these chapters, you'll come back to the process with new eyes. You'll be able to see how, over time, Quadrant II organizing can empower you to live, to love, to learn, and to leave a great and enduring legacy.

The key to quality of life is in the compass—it's in the choices we make every day. As we learn to pause in the space between stimulus and response and consult our internal compass, we can face change squarely, confident that we're being true to principle and purpose, and that we're putting first things first in our lives.

4: *Quadrant II Organizing:*
The Process of Putting
First Things First

Where there's no gardener, there's no garden.

*Roger: Some time ago, a friend of mine—a business consultant—
was moving into his new home. He decided to hire a friend of his to
landscape the grounds. She had a doctorate in horticulture and was
extremely bright and knowledgeable.*

*He had a great vision for the grounds, and because he was very
busy and traveled a lot, he kept emphasizing to her the need to create his garden in a way that would require little or no maintenance on
his part. He pointed out the absolute necessity of automatic sprin-
klers and other labor-saving devices. He was always looking for ways
to cut the amount of time he'd have to spend taking care of things.*

*Finally, she stopped and said, "Fred, I can see what you're saying.
But there's one thing you need to deal with before we go any further.*

"If there's no gardener, there's no garden!"

Most of us think it would be great if we could just put our gardens—or our lives—on automatic and somehow get the quality-of-life
results that come from careful, consistent nurturing of the things that
create it.

But life doesn't work that way. We can't just toss out a few seeds, go
ahead and do whatever we want to do and then expect to come back
to find a beautiful, well-groomed garden ready to drop a bountiful
harvest of beans, corn, potatoes, carrots, and peas in our basket. We
have to water, cultivate, and weed on a regular basis if we're going to
enjoy the harvest.

Our lives will bring forth anyway. Things will grow. But the difference between our own active involvement as gardeners and neglect is
the difference between a beautiful garden and a weed patch.

This chapter describes the gardening process. It's identifying what's important and focusing our effort to help it grow. It's planting, cultivating, watering, and weeding. It's applying the importance paradigm to nurture quality of life. It's a "high-leverage" activity you can do in about thirty minutes each week. And whatever your current quality of life, the Quadrant II process will produce significant results.

On one level, this process is a first-aid measure to treat the problem of urgency addiction. If you haven't had a chance to think deeply about needs and principles in your own life and you're basically operating from the urgency paradigm, it will immediately help you begin to shift from urgency to importance thinking. Just going through the process will help you act on the important instead of reacting based on emotion or circumstance.

On another level, it creates the framework in which you can organize your time to focus on needs and principles and begin to work on them in your life. Through the organizing process, you can create Quadrant II time to connect with your deep inner life, create a personal principle-based mission statement that deals with all four needs, and develop your personal capacity to understand and align your life with the principles that govern quality of life.

On yet another level, this process enables you to translate your personal mission statement into the fabric of your daily life. From the mission to the moment, it empowers you to live with integrity and put first things first in a balanced, principle-centered way.

As we present the steps in the process, we suggest that you consider them carefully. Write things down. The more involved you are, the more significant your learning will be. We suggest that you look over the following worksheet and then use it to organize the next week of your life according to the six-step process that follows.

The forms we're using in this chapter are part of an organizing system we've developed based on Quadrant II.* We want to emphasize the fact that the system is not a "magic tool." The system is designed to enhance the process of Quadrant II organizing. But the same process can be done in a modified daily planner, on a computer, in a spiral notebook, or even on a paper napkin. It's important to make sure that whatever system you use is aligned with what you're trying to do. A system that's focused on prioritizing urgent Quadrant I/III activities will get in the way of your effort to transition into Quadrant II.

* Feel free to make one copy of the worksheet for practice. For a complimentary four-week sample of the Seven Habits Organizer, call 1-800-680-6839.

THE WEEKLY WORKSHEET®

As you look at the weekly worksheet on the following page, you'll notice that it's different from most planning tools in that it is a weekly and not a daily page.

The week creates context. You may have seen the wonderful two- or three-minute video clip where the camera pans over what appear to be great hills and valleys, sweeping up and down, giving various perspectives of the apparent contours of a vast geographical area. At each sweep of the camera, we wonder what it is we're seeing. Are those raised areas the undulating hills of some barren wasteland? Are they the huge dunes of a remote desert? After a few moments, the camera slowly backs up so that the whole becomes visible. The "mountains" and "valleys" are the recognizable texture of an orange!

Daily planning provides us with a limited view. It's so "close up" that we're often kept focused on what's right in front of us. Urgency and efficiency take the place of importance and effectiveness. Weekly organizing, on the other hand, provides a broader context to what we do. It takes a bigger picture and lets us see the "mountains" for what they really are. The activities of the day begin to take on more appropriate dimensions when viewed in the context of the week.

STEP ONE: CONNECT WITH YOUR VISION AND MISSION

As you begin to organize for the coming week, the first step is to connect with what's most important in your life as a whole. Context gives meaning. Consider the big picture—what you care about, what makes the moments in your life meaningful. The key to this connection lies in the clarity of your vision around such questions as:

* *What's most important?*
* *What gives your life meaning?*
* *What do you want to be and to do in your life?*

Many people capture their answers to such questions in a written personal creed or mission statement. Such statements capture what you want to be and what you want to do in your life and the principles upon which being and doing are based. Clarity on these issues is critical because it affects everything else—the goals you set, the decisions you make, the paradigms you have, the way you spend your time. Returning to the ladder metaphor, a personal mission statement provides

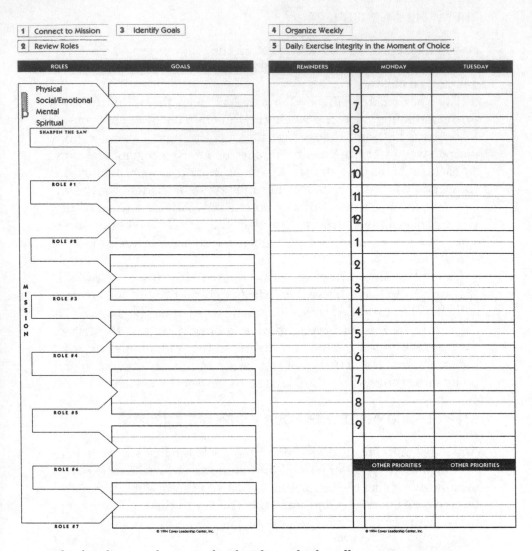

1	Connect to Mission
2	Review Roles
3	Identify Goals
4	Organize Weekly
5	Daily: Exercise Integrity in the Moment of Choice

the fundamental criteria for deciding which wall you want to put your ladder against.

Because it's so foundational, it's the natural first step in the Quadrant II process. Why schedule activities and appointments that aren't aligned with your purpose? Connecting with your personal mission is foundational to operating out of the importance paradigm. It dramatically affects the way you carry out the rest of the Quadrant II process. If your mission includes such things as personal growth, family involvement, qualities of being, or areas of contribution, reviewing it will reinforce these "first things" in your mind. It will create a powerful framework for decision making in the steps that follow.

In Chapter 5, we'll get into the area of personal vision and mission in depth. We'll look at how you can create an empowering mission statement that will produce quality-of-life results and generate a passion for life.

If you don't have a personal mission statement now, you may get some feeling for what's important to you by doing one of the following:

- List the three or four things you would consider "first things" in your life.
- Consider any long-range goals you might have set.

- Think about the most important relationships in your life.
- Think about any contributions you'd like to make.
- Reaffirm the feelings you want to have in your life—peace, confidence, happiness, contribution, meaning.
- Think about how you might spend this week if you knew you only had six months to live.

Consider the impact a personal mission statement could have for you by asking yourself the following questions:

- *What difference would a clear vision of my principles, values, and ultimate objectives make in the way I spend my time?*
- *How would I feel about my life if I knew what was ultimately important for me?*
- *Would a written statement of my life's purpose be valuable to me? Would it affect the way I spend my time and energy?*
- *How would a weekly reconnection to such a statement affect the things I choose to do during the week?*

> If you do have a mission statement, review it now—before you decide how to spend the next seven days of your life. Reconnect with the things that are deeply important to you. If you don't have a mission statement, spend a few moments connecting with your inner compass and thinking about what really matters most in your life.

STEP TWO: IDENTIFY YOUR ROLES

We live our lives in terms of roles—not in the sense of role playing, but in the sense of authentic parts we've chosen to fill. We may have important roles at work, in the family, in the community, or in other areas of life. Roles represent responsibilities, relationships, and areas of contribution.

Much of our pain in life comes from the sense that we're succeeding in one role at the expense of other, possibly even more important roles. We may be doing great as vice-president of the company, but not doing well at all as a parent or spouse. We may be succeeding in meeting the needs of our clients, but failing to meet our own need for personal development and growth.

A clear set of roles provides a natural framework to create order and balance. If you have a mission statement, your roles will grow out of it. Balance among roles does not simply mean that you're spending time in each role, but that these roles work together for the accomplishment of your mission.

We'll take an in-depth look at roles and the balance among them in Chapter 6. For now, just list the roles that come to your mind in whatever way feels comfortable to you. Don't be overly concerned about getting them "right" the first time. It may take several weeks before you feel they capture the various facets of your life in a way that works for you. There's no set way to do it—another person doing almost the same things you do might define the roles differently. In addition, your roles will probably change through the years. You may change jobs, join a club, marry, or become a parent or grandparent.

You may define your family role as simply "family member." Or, you may choose to divide it into two roles, "husband" and "father," "wife" and "mother," "daughter" and "sister." Some areas of your life, such as your job, may involve several roles: one in administration, one in marketing, one in personnel, and one in long-range planning. You may also want to have one role that reflects personal development.

A product-development executive might define his roles like this:

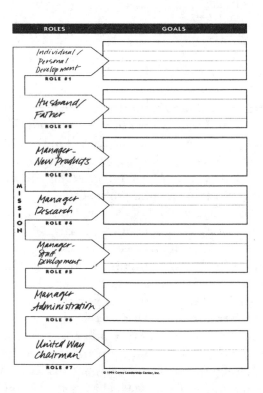

A part-time real estate salesperson might list the following roles:

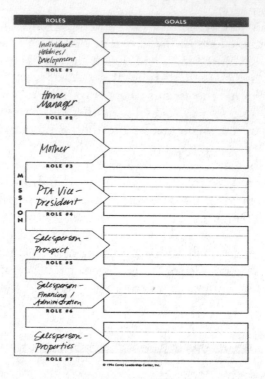

Since studies show that it's less effective to attempt to mentally manage more than seven categories, we recommend that you try to combine functions, such as administration/finance or personnel/team building to keep your total number of roles to seven. This will support mental organization around these role areas. On the other hand, don't feel that you have to come up with seven roles. If you only identify five or six roles, that's fine. The number seven simply represents an upper limit to comfortable mental processing.

Identifying roles gives a sense of the wholeness of quality life—that life is more than just a job, or a family, or a particular relationship. It's all of these together. Identifying roles may also highlight "important, but not urgent" areas that are currently being neglected.

In addition to the roles you've identified, we'd like to suggest a separate and foundational role called "sharpen the saw." We treat this as a separate role for two reasons: 1) it's a role that everyone has, and 2) it's foundational for success in every other role. You'll find this role represented in the upper-left-hand corner of the weekly worksheet.

The term "sharpen the saw" is a metaphor that describes the energy we invest in increasing our personal capacity in the four fundamental

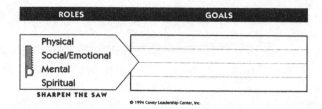

areas—physical, social, mental, and spiritual. We often get so busy "sawing" (producing results) that we forget to "sharpen our saw" (maintain or increase our capacity to produce results in the future). We may neglect to exercise (physical area), or fail to develop key relationships (social/emotional area). We may not keep current in our field (mental area). We may not be clear about what's important and meaningful to us (spiritual area). If we fail to build our personal capacity in these areas, we quickly become "dulled," and worn out from the imbalance. We're unable to move forward as effectively in the other roles of our lives.

We often hear stories of Olympic athletes who have spent years in vigorous training and preparation for their event. They mentally rehearse their performance, envisioning over and over the details of execution. They create in themselves the strength that allows them to compete successfully. These athletes can't train only when it's convenient or easy and expect to come out winners. Neither can we expect to have the capacity to enjoy life fully without caring for and conditioning the sources of strength in our lives.

You may find that this "role" of sharpening the saw overlaps with a personal development role you already defined. That's not a problem. The important thing is that none of the four areas is neglected. Some people use their "sharpen the saw" role for organizing weekly "investment" activities such as daily exercise or personal reading, and use one of their other roles for long-term issues such as career planning or continuing education. It's really a matter of what works best for you.

It's also important to realize that all of these roles are not distinct "departments" of life. They form a highly interrelated whole. By identifying your roles, you're not trying to break your life down and fit it into neat little boxes on a planning page. You're creating a variety of perspectives from which to examine your life to ensure balance and harmony. The paradigm is always one of importance, interdependence, and relatedness.

> If you haven't done so, write your roles on your worksheet now.

Now consider these questions:

- *Do I often find that I'm consumed by one or two roles in my life, and that the others do not receive the time and attention I'd like to give them?*
- *How many of my "first things" are in roles other than those that receive most of my time and attention?*
- *Do the roles I've selected work together to contribute to the fulfillment of my mission?*
- *What difference would it make in the quality of my life to consider these roles on a weekly basis, and ensure that my activities are appropriately balanced?*

We'll address these and other role-related issues in Chapter 6.

STEP THREE: SELECT QUADRANT II GOALS IN EACH ROLE

With your framework of roles identified, ask yourself:

What is the most important thing I could do in each role this week to have the greatest positive impact?

As you pause to consider this question, consult the wisdom of your heart as well as your mind. What do you feel would make a significant difference in each role? What about your role as a spouse? As a friend? As a parent? As an employee? As you consider the most important activities in each role, begin to use your compass instead of the clock. Listen to your conscience. Focus on importance rather than urgency.

If one of your roles deals with your own development, your goals might include such things as planning time for a personal retreat, working on a mission statement, or gathering information about a speed reading course. If you are a parent, your goal might be to spend some one-on-one time with your child. If you're married, it might be to go on a date with your husband or wife. Job-related goals could include setting aside time for some long-range planning, coaching a peer or subordinate, visiting customers, or working on shared expectations with your boss.

In the "sharpen the saw" area, physical goals might include regular exercise or proper diet. In the spiritual area, you might choose meditation, prayer, or the study of inspiring literature. In the mental area you might set a goal to attend a class or pursue your own reading program. For social development, you might work on principles of effective interdependence such as empathic listening, honesty, or unconditional love. The key is to consistently do whatever builds your strength in these areas and increases your capacity to live, to love, to learn, and to leave a legacy. An hour a day spent "sharpening your saw" creates the "private victory" that makes public victories possible.

You'll probably be aware of several goals you could set in each role. But for now, limit yourself to the one or two goals that are *most* important. You may even feel, based on your inner compass, that you should not set goals in every role this week. The Quadrant II process allows for that flexibility and encourages you to use your compass in determining what's most important for you to do. In Chapter 7, we'll look at how you can use your endowments to make those choices and to set and achieve principle-based goals that create quality-of-life results.

> Write your goals in the "goals" area or on the weekly worksheet.

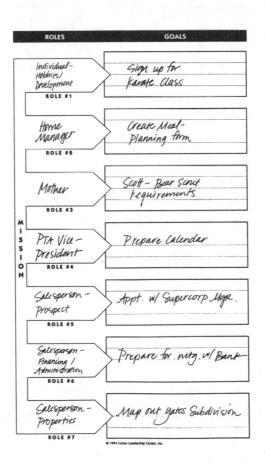

ROLES	GOALS
Individual-Hobbies/Development ROLE #1	Sign up for Karate Class
Home Manager ROLE #2	Create Meal-Planning form
Mother ROLE #3	Scott – Bear Scout Requirements
PTA Vice-President ROLE #4	Prepare Calendar
Salesperson - Prospect ROLE #5	Appt. w/ Supercorp Mgr.
Salesperson - Financing / Administration ROLE #6	Prepare for mtg. w/ Bank
Salesperson - Properties ROLE #7	Map out Yates Subdivision

MISSION

© 1994 Covey Leadership Center, Inc.

If you've considered carefully, your goals will represent those activities that you feel are truly important to fulfillment in your roles.

Now ask yourself these questions:

- *What would happen if I did these things during the coming week?*
- *How would I feel about the quality of my life?*
- *What if I did only some of them?*
- *Would it make a positive difference in my life?*
- *What if I did this every week?*
- *Would I be more effective than I am now?*

STEP FOUR: CREATE A DECISION-MAKING FRAMEWORK FOR THE WEEK

Effectively translating high-leverage Quadrant II goals into an action plan requires creating a framework for effective decision making throughout the week. Most people are constantly trying to find time for the "important" activities in their already overflowing Quadrant I/III schedules. They move things around, delegate them, cancel them, postpone them—all in the hope of finding time for first things. The key, however, is not to prioritize your schedule, but to schedule your priorities.

One of our associates shared this experience:

I attended a seminar once where the instructor was lecturing on time. At one point, he said, "Okay, it's time for a quiz." He reached under the table and pulled out a wide-mouth gallon jar. He set it on the table next to a platter with some fist-sized rocks on it. "How many of these rocks do you think we can get in the jar?" he asked.

After we made our guess, he said, "Okay. Let's find out." He set one rock in the jar . . . then another . . . then another. I don't remember how many he got in, but he got the jar full. Then he asked, "Is that jar full?"

Everybody looked at the rocks and said, "Yes."

Then he said, "Ahhh." He reached under the table and pulled out a bucket of gravel. Then he dumped some gravel in and shook the jar and the gravel went in all the little spaces left by the big rocks. Then he grinned and said once more, "Is the jar full?"

By this time we were on to him. "Probably not," we said.

"Good!" he replied. And he reached under the table and brought

out a bucket of sand. He started dumping the sand in and it went in all the little spaces left by the rocks and the gravel. Once more he looked at us and said, "Is the jar full?"

"No!" we all roared.

He said, "Good!" and he grabbed a pitcher of water and began to pour it in. He got something like a quart of water in that jar. Then he said, "Well, what's the point?"

Somebody said, "Well, there are gaps, and if you really work at it, you can always fit more into your life."

"No," he said, "that's not the point. The point is this: if you hadn't put these big rocks in first, would you ever have gotten any of them in?"

With the "more is better" paradigm, we're always trying to fit more activities into the time we have. But what does it matter how much we do if what we're doing isn't what matters most?

Our Quadrant II goals are like the "big rocks." If we put other activities—the water, sand, and gravel—in first, and then try to fit the big rocks in, not only will they not fit, we'll end up making a pretty big mess in the process.

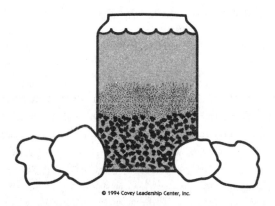

© 1994 Covey Leadership Center, Inc.

But if we know what the big rocks are and put them in first, it's amazing how many of them we can put in—and how much of the sand, gravel, and water fits in between the spaces. Regardless of what else actually does fit in, the key point is that the big rocks—our Quadrant II goals—are in first. (See the illustration on page 90.)

As you look at your weekly worksheet, put your Quadrant II goals in place. You'll notice that there are two kinds of areas on the weekly worksheet for each day. One is divided into the hours for specific appointments; the other provides space to list priorities for the day. To

© 1994 Covey Leadership Center, Inc.

schedule your Quadrant II goals, either set a specific time during the day to work on the goal, or list it as a priority for the day. (See page 91.)

Usually, the specific appointment is the most effective. You may feel your most important goals for the week include doing some long-range planning, exercising, and preparing a major project proposal. Make specific appointments with yourself to work on these goals, and treat an appointment with yourself as you'd treat an appointment with anybody else. Plan around it. Channel other activities and requests to different time blocks. If that appointment has to be changed, reschedule it immediately. Give yourself the same consideration you would give anyone else.

In some cases, it may be more effective *not* to schedule a goal at a particular hour of the day, but to list it as a priority instead. For example, if your goal is to improve your relationship with your teenage daughter, it's important to realize that the opportunity may not surface at a predictable time. Rather than planning a specific activity together during the week, you may find it more effective to simply put her name at the top of your list of "other priorities" and watch for an opportunity. If you do this on Monday and nothing develops, draw an arrow on that line across to Tuesday. If nothing happens on Tuesday, draw it across to Wednesday. This way, the priority is on your mind. You're looking for the right occasion. And you can see what's happening in your week with regard to it.

OTHER PRIORITIES	OTHER PRIORITIES	OTHER PRIORITIES
Time w/ Sharrie	→ →	→ →

© 1994 Covey Leadership Center, Inc.

1 Connect to Mission   3 Identify Goals

2 Review Roles

4 Organize Weekly

5 Daily: Exercise Integrity in the Moment of Choice

6 Evaluate

ROLES	GOALS
SHARPEN THE SAW	
Physical	Exercise three times
Social/Emotional	Practice listening in meetings
Mental	Read chap in "Habits Psych."
Spiritual	Work on Mission Statement
Individual – Hobbies/Development ROLE #1	Sign up for Karate Class
Home Manager ROLE #2	Create Meal-planning form
Mother ROLE #3	Scott – Bear Scout requirements
PTA Vice-President ROLE #4	Prepare Calendar
Salesperson – Prospect ROLE #5	Appt. w/ SuperCorp. Mgr
Salesperson – Financing/Administration ROLE #6	Prepare for mtg w/ Bank
Salesperson – Properties ROLE #7	Map out Yates Subdivision

MISSION

REMINDERS		MONDAY	TUESDAY	WEDNESDAY	THURSDAY
	7	Exercise		Exercise	
	8		Create Meal Form		
	9	Sign up for Karate Class		Prep to SuperCorp	
	10				SuperCorp Mtg
	11				
	12				
	1				
	2	Bank Proj Prep	Bank Proj Prep	Bank Proj Prep	
	3				
	4				Yates Division
	5		Scott: Bear Scout Mtg		
	6				
	7				
	8				
	9				
OTHER PRIORITIES		OTHER PRIORITIES	OTHER PRIORITIES	OTHER PRIORITIES	OTHER PRIORITIES
		PTA Calendar		Reading	

© 1994 Covey Leadership Center, Inc.

Then, on Wednesday evening, when you're reading the paper and she comes in and wants to talk, you have the motivation to push your paper—not your daughter—aside.

Of course, specific activities with your children are also very valuable. It's often the time spent bowling or watching a movie together that allows the spontaneous conversations to occur. The important thing is to be sensitive to both the need for the goal and the nature of the goal when determining what's most appropriate.

> If you're planning your week as you go through this chapter, take some time now and schedule your Quadrant II goals.

Scheduling important Quadrant II goals is a big step toward putting first things first. If we don't put the Quadrant II activities in place first, it's easy for the week to be filled by the flood of activities from Quadrants I and III that constantly clamor for our attention. It's hard to "fit in" those important Quadrant II activities that would make such a significant difference.

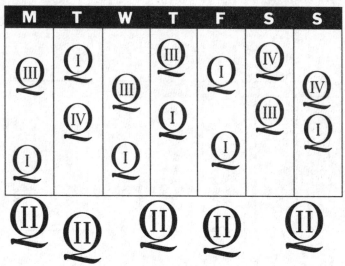

© 1994 Covey Leadership Center, Inc.

But if we put the "big rocks" in first, we reverse that tendency. We create a framework to accomplish what we feel is important, around which we can then "fit in" other activities.

With the big Quadrant II rocks in place, you can comfortably start adding other activities—either as appointments or priorities for the day. It pays to examine each activity carefully and determine which quadrant it's really in. It may *feel* urgent. Is it? Or does it just seem

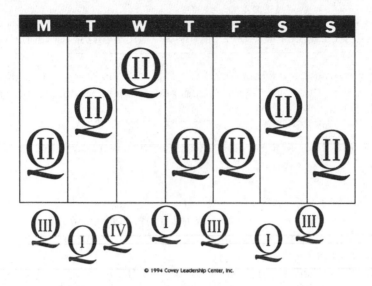

© 1994 Covey Leadership Center, Inc.

that way because someone or something else is creating pressure? Is it really important? Or has the feeling of urgency made it only *seem* important?

As we observed earlier, if you're addicted to living in a crisis mode, it's easy to think that almost everything you do is in Quadrant I. But careful analysis will probably reveal a great deal of time spent in Quadrant III. If you're struggling to find time to invest in Quadrant II, Quadrant III is the primary place to get it.

Once you start to invest time in Quadrant II, it significantly impacts the amount of time you spend in each of the other quadrants. As you plan, prepare, build relationships, or enjoy quality re-creation, you'll find that you spend far less time picking up the broken pieces in Quadrant I or reacting to the urgent demands of others in Quadrant III. The ideal to work toward is eliminating III and IV. It's spending time on important Quadrant I and II activities, and shifting more and more to the preparing, prevention, and empowering activities of Quadrant II.

As you look at your week, it's important to realize that it's critical *not* to fill every moment of every day with time-sensitive appointments. Allow for flexibility. While you do your best to plan what's important based on available knowledge, the fact is that life is not the automatic incarnation of a planning page, no matter how well that page is written. To ignore the unexpected (even if it were possible) would be to live without opportunity, spontaneity, and the rich moments of which "life" is made.

The object of Quadrant II organizing is not to set a schedule in cement. It's to create the *framework* in which quality decisions based on importance can be made on a day-by-day, moment-by-moment basis.

> If you're working on your week now, plan your other key activities around your Quadrant II goals and schedule them as appointments or as daily priorities.

Consider the value of such a weekly framework by asking yourself the following questions:

- *How do I feel about my week as I have it planned?*
- *What difference would it make if I planned Quadrant II goals in each role (either as appointments or as daily priorities) each week, and carried them out?*
- *Do I see the logic in putting the "big rocks" in first? How will this help me to get those important things done?*

In Chapter 8, we'll take a closer look at three "operating perspectives" we gain as we move from the daily to the weekly focus.

STEP FIVE: EXERCISE INTEGRITY IN THE MOMENT

With important Quadrant II goals in place for the week, the daily task is to keep first things first while navigating through the unexpected opportunities and challenges of the day. Exercising integrity, or integratedness, means translating the mission to the moment with peace and confidence—whether putting first things first means carrying out your plan or creating conscience-directed change. All the steps we've taken so far in the process are designed to enhance your character and competence, your judgment, your ability to access that inner compass in decision-making moments where the rubber meets the road.

There are three additional things you can do at the beginning of the day that will enhance your ability to put first things first:

1. *Preview the day.* This is a much different process from the "daily planning" of traditional time management. It's spending a few moments at the beginning of the day to revisit your schedule, enabling you to get your bearings, check your compass, look at the day in the context of the week, and renew the perspective that empowers you to respond in a meaningful way to unanticipated oppor-

tunity or challenge. At this point, some people prefer the room for greater detail available on a daily page.

2. *Prioritize.* Before you begin to prioritize in the traditional sense, you may find it helpful to identify your activities as QI or QII. This gives you an additional opportunity to ensure that Quadrant III activities haven't slipped into your schedule in disguise. It also helps you keep a *kairos* or compass context to the day—which is normally more *chronos* or clock-focused. And it helps reinforce the importance paradigm and make you more aware of the nature of the choices you make.

If further prioritization is helpful, you can give some indication of the status of each QI or QII activity. Some people prefer to use the ABC method, assigning each item an A, B, or C, depending on importance, and always working on A's. Others prefer a simple numbering system that requires more specific priority decision. (See pages 96 and 97.)

Whether or not you use the more detailed priority indication, we highly recommend that you highlight, circle, or mark with an asterisk your most important priority. This may require deciding between two Quadrant II activities you have scheduled for the day. If the nature of the day is such that nothing else gets done, you still have the satisfaction of knowing you did the one thing that mattered most.

As you prioritize, it's critical to remember that your prioritization only includes the items you've put into your framework for the week. It does not take into consideration the priority of unexpected opportunities or challenges. If you've given careful consideration to your roles and goals, what's in your framework will reflect your best effort to determine what's first for the week. But none of us is omniscient. Things can come up that are genuinely more important than what you have planned. Keep connected with your inner compass so that you can act with integrity to what's important; not necessarily to your schedule.

3. *Use some form of T planning for the day.* On the daily sheet, the basic structure allows you to list "time sensitive" activities on the left and activities that can be done at any time of the day on the right. This technique is often called "T planning." By separating the time-sensitive activities from the rest, you're able to make more effective scheduling decisions and remain sensitive to

5	Exercise Integrity in the Moment of Choice

MAR

S	M	T	W	Th	F	Sa
					1	2	3
4	5	6	7	8	9	10
11	12	13	14	15	16	17
18	19	20	21	22	23	24
25	26	27	28	29	30	31

MONDAY
DAY 71, 294 LEFT

12 APR

APPOINTMENTS	IMPORTANCE / ACTION ITEMS
Morning Walk	QI: Bank Deposit!
	Return Call: State
7 Office	PTA Board (555-7362)
↓	Contact city for Yates
8	Sub. Div. Contract
	Prepare Sales Report
9 Collins House:	for Team mtg.
Show team	Pay Registration fees
	for Karate class
10	Pick up lumber (3 2x4s)
	for Scott's project
11	
12 Lunch - Jared	
	QII: Get city zoning maps
1	for Cindy
	Get video tape
2 Bank Project	for Scott's game
	Send Marsha's
3	Birthday card
	Drop off Tim's shirts
4 Initial Contact:	Confirm Dinner date
Mel & Tisha Bared	w/ Paul and Kate
5 Errands	
6 Dinner	
7 PTA task committee	
8	
9 Reading	
	EXPENSES	AMOUNT

© 1993 Covey Leadership Center, Inc. ::::::

5	Exercise Integrity in the Moment of Choice

MAR

S	M	T	W	Th	F	Sa
				1	2	3
4	5	6	7	8	9	10
11	12	13	14	15	16	17
18	19	20	21	22	23	24
25	26	27	28	29	30	31

MONDAY
DAY 71, 294 LEFT

12 APR

APPOINTMENTS	IMPORTANCE / ACTION ITEMS
Morning Walk	QI: A1 Bank Deposit!
	A2 Return Call: State
7 Office	PTA Board (555-7362)
↓	B1 Contact city for Yates
8	sub. Div. Contract
	B2 Prepare Sales Report
9 Collins House:	for Team mtg.
Show team	C1 Pay Registration fees
10	for Karate class
	C2 Pick up lumber (3 2x4s)
11	for Scott's project
12 Lunch — Jared	
	QII: A1 Get city zoning maps
1	for Cindy
	B1 Get video tape
2 Bank Project	for Scott's game
	B2 Send Marsha's
3	Birthday card
	B3 Drop off Tim's shirts
4 Initial Contact:	C1 Confirm Dinner date
Mel & Tisha Bared	w/ Paul and Kate
5 Errands	
6 Dinner	
7 PTA task committee	
8	
9 Reading	

EXPENSES	AMOUNT

5	Exercise Integrity in the Moment of Choice

MAR

S	M	T	W	Th	F	Sa
					1	2
3						
4	5	6	7	8	9	10
11	12	13	14	15	16	17
18	19	20	21	22	23	24
25	26	27	28	29	30	31

MONDAY

DAY 71, 294 LEFT

12 MAR

7

8

9

10

11

12

1

2

3

4

5

6

7

8

9

	EXPENSES	AMOUNT

MONDAY	TUESDAY	WEDNESDAY	THURSDAY	

important commitments. The more condensed Weekly Worksheet puts these same areas above and below. (See pages 98 and 99.)

An activity is considered "time-sensitive" if its value is attached to a specific time of the day. A doctor's appointment, for example, may have high value at 10:00 in the morning, but no value at all at 4:00 in the afternoon (unless you're still waiting in the doctor's office). Because an activity is scheduled in the "time sensitive" area does not automatically mean when the time arrives you quit what you're doing and shift focus. You may be involved in something genuinely more important and need to reschedule. The key is your ability to discern between the two activities and determine which is more important at the time.

As you live through the day, factors will undoubtedly come up that cause you to reevaluate the activities you've planned—your boss calls a meeting, somebody offers you two tickets for the symphony, your daughter calls from school with a broken arm, a client cancels an appointment.

Quadrant II organizing empowers you to look at the best use of your time through the paradigm of importance rather than urgency. As situations change, you can pause and connect with your inner compass to determine the "best" use of your time and energy. When the unexpected is less important than what you had planned, Quadrant II organizing gives you perspective and the power to keep on track. When the unexpected is more important, it empowers you to adapt and change with confidence, knowing that you're acting on the truly important and not just reacting to the urgent.

In Chapter 9, we'll take an in-depth look at how to access that inner compass in any moment of choice. We'll talk about how to be strong in hard moments, how to know when the unexpected opportunity or challenge is more important than what you've planned, and how to either stay with what you've planned or change with confidence and peace.

STEP SIX: EVALUATE

The Quadrant II process would be incomplete without closing the loop—without turning the experience of one week into the foundation for the increased effectiveness of the next. Unless we learn from living, how are we going to keep from doing the same things—making the same mistakes, struggling with the same problems—week after week?

At the end of the week—before you review your mission statement to begin organizing the next week—pause to ask questions such as:

- *What goals did I achieve?*
- *What challenges did I encounter?*
- *What decisions did I make?*
- *In making decisions, did I keep first things first?*

In Chapter 10, we'll suggest more specific questions that draw on the power of the four human endowments to help us learn from living. With this final step, the Quadrant II process becomes a living and learning cycle that creates an upward spiral of growth.

Now suppose you were to spend thirty minutes a week for the next fifty-two weeks of your life going through this process. Suppose you only accomplished half of the Quadrant II goals you set. Would that represent more time in Quadrant II time than you're now spending? A little or a lot? If you were able to invest that much more time in Quadrant II, *what difference would it make in the quality of your personal and professional life?*

THE PARADIGM AND THE PROCESS

Quadrant II is not a tool; it's a way of thinking. We recognize that many people using second- and third-generation planning tools use them essentially in a fourth-generation way. On the other hand, some people using fourth-generation tools—including our own organizing system—use them in second- or third-generation ways with significantly less effective results.

The paradigm is obviously most essential. But we do need to recognize that a tool that's not in alignment with the paradigm can create ineffectiveness and frustration. If you're trying to create a fourth generation lifestyle based on importance, and you're using a tool that's focused on daily prioritization of the urgent, it's like trying to make progress along a path while someone is dropping boulders in front of you every step of the way. The system may even threaten to overpower the paradigm so that you end up serving the system to your disadvantage instead of having the system serve you in helping you accomplish what you're trying to accomplish.

The Quadrant II organizing process reinforces the "importance" paradigm. The greatest value of the process is not what it does to your schedule, but what it does to your head. As you begin to think more in terms of importance, you begin to see time differently. You become empowered to put first things first in your life in a significant way.

If you're like most of the people we've had the opportunity to work with, you've probably been able to see some of the immediate benefits of this Quadrant II organizing process—the shift from urgency to importance thinking, the greater perspective of the week, increased flexibility, getting the "big rocks" in first.

But the journey has just begun. This chapter has provided an overview of the Quadrant II organizing process. The next six chapters contain the depth and richness of this process that will empower you, over time, to "keep the main thing the main thing" in your life.

5: *The Passion of Vision*

It's easy to say "no!" when there's a deeper "yes!" burning inside.

VIKTOR Frankl, an Austrian psychologist who survived the death camps of Nazi Germany, made a significant discovery. As he found within himself the capacity to rise above his humiliating circumstances, he became an observer as well as a participant in the experience. He watched others who shared in the ordeal. He was intrigued with the question of what made it possible for some people to survive when most died.

He looked at several factors—health, vitality, family structure, intelligence, survival skills. Finally, he concluded that none of these factors was primarily responsible. The single most significant factor, he realized, was a sense of future vision—the impelling conviction of those who were to survive that they had a mission to perform, some important work left to do.[1]

Survivors of POW camps in Vietnam and elsewhere have reported similar experiences: a compelling, future-oriented vision is the primary force that kept many of them alive.

The power of vision is incredible! Research indicates that children with "future-focused role images" perform far better scholastically and are significantly more competent in handling the challenges of life.[2] Teams and organizations with a strong sense of mission significantly outperform those without the strength of vision.[3] According to Dutch sociologist Fred Polak, a primary factor influencing the success of civilizations is the "collective vision" people have of their future.[4]

Vision is the best manifestation of creative imagination and the primary motivation of human action. It's the ability to see beyond our present reality, to create, to invent what does not yet exist, to become what we not yet are. It gives us capacity to live out of our imagination instead of our memory.

In this chapter, we'd like to explore the impact of personal vision on our time and our lives. We'll look at how we can create an empowering vision and integrate it into the fabric of everyday living.

We all have some vision of ourselves and our future. And that vision creates consequences. More than any other factor, vision affects the choices we make and the way we spend our time.

If our vision is limited—if it doesn't extend beyond the Friday night ball game or the next TV show—we tend to make choices based on what's right in front of us. We react to whatever's urgent, the impulse of the moment, our feelings or moods, our limited awareness of our options, other people's priorities. We vacillate and fluctuate. How we feel about our decisions—even the way we make them—changes from day to day.

If our vision is based on illusion, we make choices that aren't based on "true north" principles. In time, these choices fail to create the quality-of-life results we expect. Our vision becomes no more than platitudes. We become disillusioned, perhaps cynical. Our creative imagination withers, and we don't trust our dreams anymore.

If our vision is partial—if we focus only on our economic and social needs and ignore our mental and spiritual needs, for example—we make choices that lead to imbalance.

If our vision is based on the social mirror, we make choices based on expectations of others. It's been said that "when man discovered the mirror, he began to lose his soul."[5] If our self-vision is no more than a reflection of the social mirror, we have no connection with our inner selves, with our own uniqueness and capacity to contribute. We're living out of scripts handed to us by others—family, associates, friends, enemies, the media.

And what are those scripts? Some may seem constructive: "You're so talented!" "You're a natural ball player!" "I always said you should be a doctor!" Some may be destructive: "You're so slow!" "You can't do anything right!" "Why can't you be more like your sister?" Good or bad, these scripts can keep us from connecting with who we are and what we're about.

And consider the images the media project—cynicism, skepticism, violence, indulgence, fatalism, materialism. "Important news" is bad news.

If these images are the source of our personal vision, is it any wonder that many of us feel disconnected and at odds with ourselves?

VISION THAT TRANSFORMS AND TRANSCENDS

When we talk about "the passion of vision," we're talking about a deep, sustained energy that comes from a comprehensive, principle-based, need-based, endowment-based *seeing* that goes beyond chronos and even kairos. It deals with an *aeon* concept of time, from the Greek *aion*, meaning an age, a lifetime or more. It taps into the deep core of who we are and what we are about. It's fueled by the realization of the unique contribution we have the capacity to make—the legacy we can leave. It clarifies purpose, gives direction, and empowers us to perform beyond our resources.

We call it "passion" because this vision can become a motivating force so powerful it, in effect, becomes the DNA of our lives. It's so ingrained and integrated into every aspect of our being that it becomes the compelling impetus behind every decision we make. It's the fire within—the explosion of inner synergy that happens when critical mass is reached in integration of the four fundamental needs. It's the energy that makes life an adventure—the deep burning "yes!" that empowers us to say "no"—peacefully and confidently—to the less important things in our lives.

This passion can empower us to literally transcend fear, doubt, discouragement, and many other things that keep us from accomplishment and contribution. Consider Gandhi, for example, who came from a background of timidity, scarcity, jealousy, fear, and insecurity. He basically didn't even want to be with people; he wanted to be alone. He didn't like working as a lawyer until he gradually began to find some satisfaction in hammering out win-win relationships between opposing people.

But as he began to see the injustices against the Indian people, a vision was born in his mind and heart. Out of that vision grew the idea of creating an experimental community—an ashram—where the people could practice egalitarian values. He saw how he could help the Indian people transform their image of themselves as inferior to their British overlords and develop a sense of self-worth.

As he focused on his vision, his personality weaknesses were essentially eclipsed. Vision and purpose created personality growth and development. He wanted to love people, to serve people, to be with people. His highest wish was to help redeem a nation. As a result, he eventually brought England to its knees and freed three hundred million people.

Near the end of his life, he remarked, "I claim to be no more than an average man with below average capabilities. I have not the shadow of a doubt that any man or woman can achieve what I have if he or she would put forth the same effort and cultivate the same hope and faith."[6] The power of transcendent vision is greater than the power of the scripting deep inside the human personality and it subordinates it, submerges it, until the whole personality is reorganized in the accomplishment of that vision.

The passion of *shared* vision empowers people to transcend the petty, negative interactions that consume so much time and effort and deplete quality of life.

Stephen: I recently spent two days working with the faculty and administration of a college in one of the provinces in Canada. They were dealing with very divisive issues, and they were totally caught up in scarcity thinking. The environment was inundated with smallness, pettiness, and accusation.

They had spent some time thinking around a mission statement, and as we worked together, they came to a sense of closure. They finally determined that their mission was "to become a mentoring educational college" for their province. They wanted to be an organization that cares about and mentors other organizations in becoming principle-centered.

As they came to that decision, the smallness and pettiness evaporated. These people became energized by something more important, by a transcendent purpose that made other things irrelevant.

This is what happens when people have a real sense of legacy, a sense of mattering, a sense of contribution. It seems to tap into the deepest part of their heart and soul. It brings out the best and subordinates the rest. Petty things become unimportant when people are impassioned about a purpose higher than self.

The passion of the kind of vision we're talking about has a transforming, transcending impact—probably the greatest impact of any single factor on time and quality of life.

CREATING AND LIVING AN EMPOWERING MISSION STATEMENT

One of the most powerful processes we've found to cultivate the passion of vision is creating and integrating an empowering personal mission statement.

You may already be aware of the concept of a personal mission statement. The idea isn't new. People from a variety of cultures have created statements of belief, personal creeds, and similar statements throughout time. You may have already written your own as part of a corporate personal development program or in some other capacity.

But as we've become involved in mission statement work worldwide, we've found that some statements are significantly more empowering than others. People attempting to write a mission statement for the first time often write to please or impress somebody else. They don't go the distance or pay the price to create a deep inner connection. Their mission statements become a potpourri of platitudes, a "to do" checked off the list and filed somewhere for occasional inspiration.

On the organizational level, this is what happens when mission statements come down from the executive "Mount Olympus" and are wordsmithed by the PR department. There's no significant involvement, and, therefore, no buy-in. The statement ends up hanging on the wall instead of living in the hearts and minds and lives of the people who work there.

What we're talking about here is not simply writing a statement of belief. We're talking about accessing and creating an open connection with the deep energy that comes from a well-defined, thoroughly integrated sense of purpose and meaning in life. We're talking about creating a powerful vision based on the true north principles that ensure its achievability. We're talking about the sense of excitement and adventure that grows out of connecting with your unique purpose and the profound satisfaction that comes in fulfilling it.

AN EXERCISE OF CREATIVE IMAGINATION

If you've never attempted to write a personal mission statement—or even if you have one but you'd like a different perspective—we invite you to take a few minutes now and exercise your endowment of creative imagination. Visualize your eightieth birthday or your fiftieth wedding anniversary. Try to imagine a wonderful celebration where friends, loved ones, and associates from all walks of your life come to honor you. Imagine it in as much detail as you can—the place, the people, the decorations.

See these individuals in your mind's eye as they stand, one by one, to pay tribute to you. Assume they represent roles you are now fulfilling in life—perhaps as a parent, teacher, manager, or community servant. Also assume that you have fulfilled these roles to the utmost of your potential.

ROLES

TRIBUTES

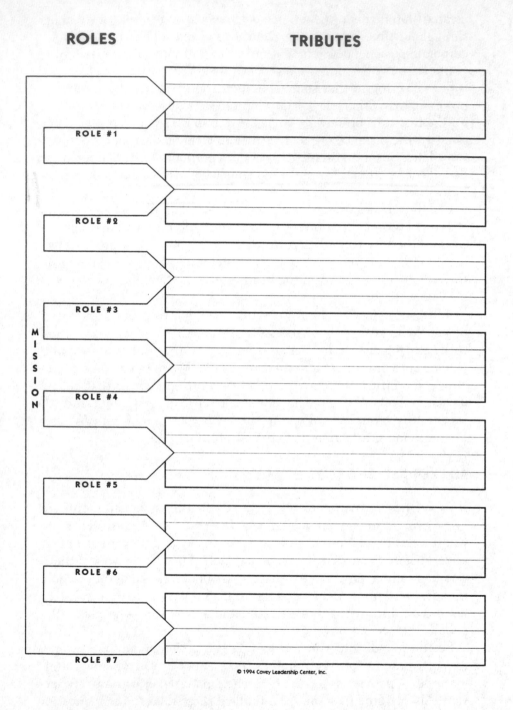

ROLE #1

ROLE #2

M
I
S
S
I
O
N

ROLE #3

ROLE #4

ROLE #5

ROLE #6

ROLE #7

© 1994 Covey Leadership Center, Inc.

What would these people say? What qualities of character would you be remembered for? What outstanding contributions would they mention? Look around at the people there. What important difference have you made in their lives?

As you ponder, try writing down your roles, and beside each, the tribute statement you would like to be said of you on this occasion.

How do you feel when you look at this vision of what your life could represent? Now what if you were able to take that vision, ensure that it was principle-based and connected with your deepest inner imperatives, translate it into words, thoroughly refine it, use it as the basis for weekly Quadrant II organizing, memorize it, envision its fulfillment, write it in your mind and heart so that every moment of your life was touched by it?

This quick exercise will give you some insight into the potential power and passion of vision. Actually creating and integrating an empowering mission statement takes time and earnest investment. In order to do it, we have to get into and create an open connection with our deep inner life.

GETTING INTO OUR DEEP INNER LIFE

In a sense, we each live three lives. We have our public life, where we interact with other people at work, in the community, at social events. We have our private life, where we're away from the public. We may be alone or we may choose to be with friends or family.

But our most significant life is our deep inner life. This is where we connect with our unique human endowments of self-awareness, conscience, independent will, and creative imagination. Without these endowments, it's impossible to create the kind of empowering vision that will create quality-of-life results.

Self-awareness

In our deep inner life, we can use our endowment of self-awareness to explore our needs and capacities and integrate them on a very essential level. We can examine our paradigms, look at the roots and fruits in our lives, explore our motives. One of the most powerful uses of self-awareness is to become aware of conscience and how it works within us.

Conscience

Conscience puts us in touch with both the unique and the universal.

Only as we tap into our conscience can we discover our unique purpose and capacity for contribution. Think deeply about the people represented by each of the roles in the birthday or anniversary exercise you just went through and of the unique opportunity you have to influence their lives. No one else can be the mother or father you are to your children. No one else can be the husband or wife you can be to your spouse. No one else can be the doctor you can be to your patients, the teacher you can be to your students, the sister, the friend, the community volunteer you can be to the people whose lives you can touch. What you alone can contribute, no one else can contribute. Viktor Frankl said we don't invent our mission; we detect it. It's within us waiting to be realized.

> Everyone has his own specific vocation or mission in life; everyone must carry out a concrete assignment that demands fulfillment. Therein he cannot be replaced, nor can his life be repeated. Thus, everyone's task is unique as his specific opportunity to implement it.[7]

Nineteenth-century social reformer and writer William Ellery Channing had this to say:

> Every human being has a work to do, duties to perform, influence to exert, which are peculiarly his, and which no conscience but his own can teach.[8]

Only as we connect with our conscience in this deep inner life can we create the fire within. Mission statements that come out of public or private life thinking will never access that deep inner core of personal empowerment.

As explorer, writer, and filmmaker Sir Laurens van der Post put it:

> We have to turn inwards, to look into ourselves; look into this container which is our soul; look and listen to it. Until you have listened in to that thing which is dreaming through you, in other words—answered the knock on the door in the dark, you will not be able to lift this moment in time in which we are imprisoned, back again into the level where the great act of creation is going on.[9]

Roger: Some years ago, I met Tom at a seminar for university students. When I asked him to introduce himself and tell a little about his goals, he indicated that he was majoring in civil engineering. Later during the seminar, I asked him to share with others what he would do if he had a month with no demands on his time and unlimited funds.

THE PASSION OF VISION 111

His face lit up like a Christmas tree. "That's easy!" he replied enthusiastically. "I'd buy a table saw, a planer, and . . . oh, lots of other tools. I'd set them up in my garage, get all the kids in the neighborhood together, and we'd build things—tables, playhouses, furniture. It would be great!"

As I noticed the shining eyes, I couldn't help but remember the apathy with which he had announced his college major a few moments before.

"You really like to teach, don't you?" I asked.

"I love it!" he said simply.

"And you enjoy working with tools?"

"Oh, you bet!"

"How are you enjoying your classes in civil engineering?"

"Oh, I don't know. There's good money in engineering . . ."

His voice dropped off.

"Tom," I said, "did it ever occur to you that they pay people to teach kids how to build things with tools?"

It was fascinating to watch his face. It was obvious that his decision to major in civil engineering was not the result of a deep inner connection with his own talents and a conscience-inspired sense of contribution. But when he touched that connection, even briefly— when he suddenly saw the possibility of fulfilling his own uniqueness—he became totally energized.

While Tom might have been an adequate civil engineer, it was easy to see he would be a phenomenal wood shop instructor, and that his love for woodworking and for young people would empower him to make a difference.

Conscience not only puts us in touch with our own uniqueness; it also connects us with the universal true north principles that create quality of life. We can use conscience to align our values and strategies with principles, ensuring that both the ends and the means of our mission statement—both the contribution and the methods used in making the contribution—are principle-based.

Creative Imagination

Once we tap into conscience, we can use our endowment of creative imagination to envision and give meaningful expression to conscience-inspired vision and values by creating an empowering personal mission statement. It's the blueprint before the construction; the mental before the physical creation.

After writing a mission statement, we can use our creative imagination to visualize ourselves living it—today at work, tonight when we come home, when we're tired, when our expectations haven't been met, when we're disappointed. We can use our minds to face and creatively solve the most difficult challenges to our integrity. We can live out of our imagination instead of our memory.

Independent Will

When living our mission statement means swimming upstream, going against the environment or our own deeply ingrained habits or scripts, we can use our endowment of independent will. We can act instead of being acted upon.

The passion of vision gives us a new understanding of independent will. Without the passion of vision, "discipline" is regimentation and restraint—control yourself, grit your teeth, white-knuckle your way through life. The basic paradigm is that without some form of tight control, we'll mess up. We don't have trust in ourselves that, left to our own internal motivation, we would moment by moment make effective choices.

But the passion of vision releases the power that connects "discipline" with its root word, "disciple." We become followers of our inner imperatives, voluntarily subordinating the less important to that deep burning "yes!" Instead of "control," we're focused on "release."

The key to motivation is motive. It's the *why*. It's the deeper "yes!" burning inside that makes it easier to say no to the less important.

CHARACTERISTICS OF EMPOWERING MISSION STATEMENTS

As we've had the opportunity to read hundreds of mission statements from around the world, we've found it to be a humbling experience to see so clearly into the deep inner lives of other human beings. As we read each expression, we feel we stand on sacred ground.

These statements are incredibly diverse. They range from a few words to several pages. Some are expressed in music, poetry, and art. Each person's personal vision is unique.

But one of the greatest validations of the reality of true north is in the almost universal expression in these statements of the basic Laws of Life. The foundational principles and the recognition of the four needs and capacities—to live, to love, to learn, to leave a legacy—are transcultural, transreligious, transnational, transracial. Regardless of who or where they are, when people get into their deep inner lives, they sense true north.

Those mission statements people have found to be most empowering seem to have several other characteristics in common as well. You may find this list helpful to you in writing your own mission statement, or in evaluating one you've already written.

An empowering mission statement:

1. represents the deepest and best within you. It comes out of a solid connection with your deep inner life.
2. is the fulfillment of your own unique gifts. It's the expression of your unique capacity to contribute.
3. is transcendent. It's based on principles of contribution and purpose higher than self.
4. addresses and integrates all four fundamental human needs and capacities. It includes fulfillment in physical, social, mental, and spiritual dimensions.
5. is based on principles that produce quality-of-life results. Both the ends and the means are based on true north principles.
6. deals with both vision and principle-based values. It's not enough to have values without vision—you want to be good, but you want to be good for something. On the other hand, vision without values can create a Hitler. An empowering mission statement deals with both character and competence; what you want to be and what you want to do in your life.
7. deals with all the significant roles in your life. It represents a lifetime balance of personal, family, work, community— whatever roles you feel are yours to fill.
8. is written to inspire you—not to impress anyone else. It communicates to you and inspires you on the most essential level.

A mission statement with these characteristics will have the comprehensiveness, depth, and principle-based foundation to make it empowering. If you'd like more specific help in creating a personal mission statement, we've included a mini-mission statement workshop with detailed exercises, instructions, and sample mission statements in Appendix A.

FROM THE MISSION TO THE MOMENT

Even with a powerful written document, it's vital to realize that it's impossible to translate the mission to the moment in our lives without weekly cultivation—pondering over it, memorizing it, writing it in our heart and in our mind, reviewing it, and using it as the basis for weekly Quadrant II organizing. You may also find it helpful to go on a personal retreat—perhaps yearly—to evaluate and update it.

Unfortunately, many people living with the efficiency paradigm of third-generation time management tend to see "writing a personal mission statement" as another "to do" to be checked off a list. As one woman observed:

I wrote my mission statement—I actually felt really good about it. But then I filed it in my organizer and mentally checked it off as "done."

I went along for months—successful in business, setting goals, moving ahead with my life. I became increasing focused on the "have's"—I want to have a new car. I want to have a new house.

I wrote down goals—"We want to build this house." So what do we need to do? Save this amount of money, qualify for this loan—all those kinds of things. I thought I was doing everything right.

And then late one night, I found myself sitting alone in my beautiful new house thinking, "Why am I not happy?" I'd thought once we closed on the loan, once we signed the papers, all of a sudden I'd have what I was working for. But I just felt lonely. I thought, "There's something missing." I didn't feel the happiness I thought would come from these things.

As I was thinking, I saw my organizer, and so I opened it up and read my mission statement. Never once in all the time we were building our house had I even looked at that statement.

As I read, I realized that there was nothing materialistic in it. Everything was "be"—I want to be a good person . . . I want to be a good example . . . eventually, I want to be a good mother.

I found myself crying. I sat in my beautiful new house with the lights off thinking. I had thought this would make me happy . . . as soon as I had this car or this house or whatever it was, then I'd be happy. But I looked at all I had and I wasn't anything I wanted to be.

An empowering mission statement is not a "to do" to be checked off. To be empowering, it has to become a living document, part of our very nature so that the criteria we've put into it are also into us, into the way we live our lives day by day. Another individual shared this experience:

A short time after I wrote my personal mission statement, my wife and I had a falling out with some really close friends of ours. We didn't really know why it happened. All we knew was that it was something that had come over a matter of time and suddenly, there was some straw that broke the camel's back, and we were no longer friends.

We lived with the pain of this for two months. We would be in situations where we were with other friends, and we would not even talk to each other. My wife and I would lie in bed and talk about it. There wasn't a day that went by that I didn't think about my friends and how I could bridge this gap that was between us.

One night I was driving home and it suddenly dawned on me—is the way that I have handled this whole scenario from start to finish in harmony with my mission as an individual? As a friend? Part of my mission deals with learning some of the lessons of life and being able to understand and mature through them so that I can teach them to others—not only to my family, but also to friends and whoever else might have the same problem at some point in their lives.

I suddenly realized that the way I had acted was not consistent with my mission, and in that instant—I know this might sound strange—I was liberated from the guilt and the pain. I knew I needed to really understand this whole experience and learn from it—what had gone wrong, how it had happened—and then to make reconciliation. I was able at that point to take my mission and overlay it onto the problem and say, "This is what my mission is and this is how I choose to handle this situation." I went home and outlined in my mind how I would bridge the gulf. And at that point, my mission became real to me.

I went to my friend and told him how deeply sorry I was about the whole situation and how painful it had been for my wife and me. I felt humble and teachable. I really, deeply wanted to understand how he felt and what had gone wrong.

At that point, he was softened and he was willing to talk about what he felt had been the problem, and how he and his wife might have been wrong. We were able to communicate deeply and work things out. Then we got together with our wives and they were able to have a similar experience.

That was such a liberating experience. I was even grateful for the pain! And it was powerful for me to realize how important and how real a mission statement can be. It was alive at that point. It was a living document.

From that experience I've been able to take other experiences in different roles and responsibilities and say, "Is this really part of my mission?" And this whole thing—this whole notion of Quadrant II time management and putting first things first—has come to life. I have been able to make this document almost a transparent overlay, to put it over any situation and decide how I choose to respond.

Most people who feel empowered by their mission statement find that there seems to be some point at which their statement "lives." They own it. It's theirs. The vital connection is made between the mission and the moment in life. Then, with nurturing and continuing cultivation, the mission statement becomes the primary factor that influences every moment of choice.

A LEGACY OF VISION

Creating and living an empowering mission statement has a significant impact on the way we spend our time. When we talk about time management, it seems ridiculous to worry about speed before direction, about saving minutes when we may be wasting years. Vision is the fundamental force that drives everything else in our lives. It impassions us with a sense of the unique contribution that's ours to make. It empowers us to put first things first, compasses ahead of clocks, people ahead of schedules and things. Creating and integrating an empowering personal mission statement is one of the most important Quadrant II investments we can make.

And as we live, love, and learn with greater meaning in our lives, we begin to realize that perhaps the most important legacy we can leave is vision. What our children and others see of themselves and of their future has a profound effect on quality of life for us all.

QUADRANT II GOALS TO CULTIVATE THE PASSION OF VISION:

- Set Quadrant II time each week to cultivate a rich inner life, to nurture a quiet place within yourself where you can connect with your own inner compass.
- Schedule a personal retreat to go through the Mission Statement Workshop (Appendix A) and write a personal mission statement.
- Schedule time to evaluate and revise your current mission statement.
- Commit your mission statement to memory.
- Set a daily "sharpen the saw" goal to visualize yourself living your mission statement.
- Review your mission statement each week before you begin to organize.
- Keep a daily journal record of how your experiences, your choices, and your decisions are affected by your personal mission statement.
- Read mission statements written by other people throughout history. Consider the impact of these statements on their lives and on society.
- Help your children or others whose lives you touch to create their own mission statements. Nurture vision in others.

6: *The Balance of Roles*

Balance isn't either/or; *it's* and.

PROBABLY the deepest and most often expressed pain we hear in the area of "time management" comes from imbalance.

Many people who go through the mission statement experience come to a stark and painful awareness of important areas of their lives they've been neglecting. They realize they've invested tremendous time and energy in one area of their lives—such as business, athletics, or community service—at the expense of other vital areas such as health, family, or friends. Others are more aware of their various roles, but they feel torn between them. Their roles seem to be in constant conflict and competition for their limited time and attention.

We frequently hear comments such as this:

I want to provide for my family and be successful in my career. But my company doesn't think I'm serious about advancement unless I get to the office early and work late and on weekends.

By the time I get home, I feel exhausted. I have more work to do, and no energy or time to give to my family. But they need me. There are bikes to fix, stories to read, homework assignments to help with, things to talk over. And I need them. What is quality of life if it isn't spending time with the people you love most?

And that doesn't even get into my other roles. I want to be a good neighbor. I want to help in the community. And I need some time for myself to exercise, to read—time just to think once in a while.

I'm being pulled in so many directions—and they're all important! How can I possibly do it all?

The most frequently mentioned conflict is between work and family roles. The most often expressed pain is in relationships and lack of personal development. People are saying, "I can't run fast enough to touch all the bases in my life every day. Some important things in my life just aren't getting done. The faster I run, the more out of balance I feel."

If you've seen the movie *The Karate Kid* you may remember the scene at the ocean where the elderly Miyagi sends his young student Daniel out into the pounding surf. "Learn balance! Learn balance!" he calls.

Time after time, as the boy struggles against the crashing waves, he's knocked off his feet. Finally, he turns to see his mentor in the distance, poised atop a single post. From this position, Miyagi executes the intricate movements of the crane technique, demonstrating perfect balance as he easily shifts midair between one foot and the other.

We may hear our own deep inner voice telling us, "Learn balance! Learn balance!" But for the most part, many of us feel like Daniel out in the pounding surf, getting knocked off our feet by powerful forces that seem to come at us from every direction.

WHAT IS BALANCE?

Obviously, balance is a "true north" principle. We see manifestations of it all around us—the balance of nature, balance of trade, balance of power, well-balanced meals. As with any principle, one of the most powerful witnesses of its reality is the consequence of living with its opposite—imbalance. An inner ear infection that causes us to lose our balance, being knocked off our feet in a basketball game, or just living with the discomfort of an out-of-balance life validate the reality and importance of the principle.

But how do we nurture balance in our lives? Is it simply a matter of running between bases fast enough to touch them all every day? Or is there some other, more effective way to see it that creates a powerful impact on the results we're getting in our lives?

Take a moment and look back at the roles you listed when we went through the Quadrant II organizing process.

How do you see these roles? Many of us in the Western world are programmed from an early age to see them as separate "compartments" of life. We go to different classes in school, we have separate subjects, we have separate textbooks. We get an A in biology and a C in history and it never crosses our mind that there's any relationship

ROLES

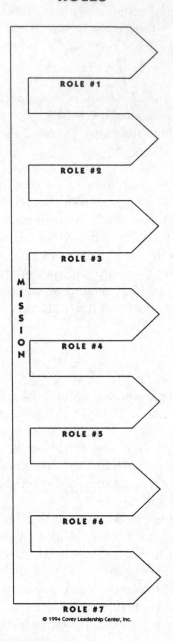

© 1994 Covey Leadership Center, Inc.

between the two. We see our role at work as completely separate from our role at home, and neither as having much to do with other roles such as personal development or community service. As a result, we think in terms of "either/or"—we can focus either on one role or another.

This compartmentalization translates into our character. What we are at work is somehow separate from what we are at home. What we do in our private life is detached from what we do in our public life.

In *The Unschooled Mind*, Howard Gardner shows the impact of compartmentalized thinking.[1] People with advanced academic degrees perform well as long as they work in the way they were trained. But give them a test where you change the situation or the circumstance and they not only do worse—they flunk! They can't do it. They can't think across borders.

The way we see the problem *is* the problem. This compartmentalization is based on illusion, and to try to live the illusion is incredibly strenuous.

In reality, these roles are parts of a highly interrelated whole, a living ecosystem in which each part impacts every other part. As Gandhi observed, "One man cannot do right in one department of life whilst he is occupied in doing wrong in any other department. Life is one indivisible whole."[2]

This more holistic paradigm is foundational to Eastern wisdom, where balance is considered essential to life and health.

As Chinese-trained physician Dr. David Eisenberg observes:

> We [in the Western world] invented the notion that "biology" and "physics" and "psychology" and "psychiatry" are separate. If we want to deal with health, and we're looking only at the chemistry or the emotional state, we have an imperfect glimpse. The patient sitting before me brings with him or her not only chemistry, but also family, relationships, emotions, and character. The distinctions we bring to a hospital in terms of mind and body are abstractions that we make. The patient is still a whole person, and to help him or her get better, ideally we would deal with all of these aspects—the balance of a person's life."[3]

The essence of this more holistic paradigm of balance is captured in the words of the ancient Sufi teaching: "You think because you understand *one* you must understand *two*, because one and one makes two. But you must also understand *and*."[4]

When we begin to apply this paradigm on a personal basis, we see that balance in our lives isn't a running between compartments; it's a dynamic equilibrium. It's all parts working synergistically in a highly interrelated whole. Balance isn't "either/or" it's "and."

CREATING SYNERGY AMONG ROLES

What an incredible difference this makes in our lives! The personality ethic literature of the past seventy years would have us believe that "success" in some roles means putting on a different personality—like putting on a sweater or a pair of shoes. It creates fragmentation, duplicity. But the reality is that the same person who gets up, showers, and eats breakfast in the morning is also the person who interacts with clients at the office, makes presentations to the board, coaches the Little League team, cleans out the garage, and goes to church. Whatever we are we bring to every role in our life.

And what's true of character is also true, to a large extent, of competence. Although there are certain specific competencies attached to each role, true north principles empower us with competencies basic to every role, creating a powerful synergy among roles.

Rebecca: I remember when Roger was in graduate school and I was at home with small children. As we talked in the evenings about what he was working on in his classes, it became more and more apparent to us that the same principles that worked in a business setting could be applied in the leadership and management of a home. It was thrilling to discover that the principles of empowerment that developed responsible, competent employees could be translated to empower three- and four-year-old children to clean their rooms.

We also found that many of the principles that created strong, positive relationships in the family could be applied with significant results in a business setting. We realized that trust was the foundation for effective corporate synergy; integrity was essential to lasting corporate influence.

It seemed that once we focused on principles, our different roles were no longer compartments that segmented and separated our lives. They became avenues of application for universal principles. It became an exciting challenge to see how many ways we could apply the same principles in the different arenas of our lives.

This inter-role synergy saves incredible problem-solving time and energy. A principle such as a proactivity—accepting personal responsibility for your own life—is just as empowering in dealing with a disgruntled spouse or a rebellious teenager as it is in dealing with an irate customer, a demanding boss, or a frustrated direct report. Empathy—seeking first to understand—creates the same kind of trust and empowerment in work teams as it does in friendships, families, and community service organizations.

This synergy empowers us to look at our roles with a MacGyver mentality. We can think in terms of fulfilling a personal development goal to exercise and a parenting goal to build a relationship with a teenage daughter by taking that daughter out for a game of tennis. If we need to inspect a factory and train a new assistant, we can see inspecting the factory together as a way to train that assistant.

Understanding this synergy helps us to transcend either/or dichotomies. A woman who chooses to have children and to be with them can transcend the painful chronos mentality dichotomy of children or career. She becomes energized by the vision of her mothering role as a significant contribution to society. She develops character and competence that empower her to fulfill other roles as well.

Rebecca: I'm often troubled by the stigma attached to women who choose to focus their time and effort primarily on motherhood. It is as if society somehow deems it less valuable to raise competent children than to raise the profit on a company's product line.

A woman who chooses to focus on motherhood, and does so out of a clear sense of her own personal vision, becomes truly energized in her role. She recognizes the value of her efforts in shaping the characters of future leaders in society. And in the process, she develops competence and character to fulfill other roles. Perhaps a second career or another degree are in the plans, but that doesn't distract from the task at hand. It's not a matter of capacity, but of chosen contribution.

There are women who choose motherhood for a season who don't earn the character and competence because they aren't deeply connected to a vision of the role and don't fully apply their creative energy to it. But those who do are empowered to fulfill other roles with excellence.

The transcendence of either/or thinking is becoming critical for our contemporary organizations. In a segmented society that's sometimes slow to appreciate and translate the skills of the competent home manager—man or woman—to the job market, it is society itself that suffers. Current research indicates that the so-called feminine attributes (well exercised in parenting) are the critical capacities required to effectively manage in the emerging democratic cultures of our organizations.[5] But why are we just coming to this realization?

In the fifth century B.C., Xenophon records that Nicomachides, a professional soldier, was disgruntled when another man—with no more to recommend him than his excellence in managing a home and chorus—was selected to be a general instead of himself. In response, Socrates observed that "over whatever a man may preside, he will if he knows what he needs, and is able to provide it, be a good president, whether he have the direction of a chorus, a family, a city, or an army. . . . Do not, therefore . . . despise men skillful in managing a household; for the conduct of private affairs differs from that of public concerns only in magnitude."[6]

When we see our roles as segmented parts of life, we develop a scarcity chronos mentality. There's only so much time. Spending it in one role means we can't spend it in another. It's win-lose—one role wins, the other roles lose. We're in competition with ourselves. We get involved in a self-fulfilling prophecy and go about gathering evidence to justify the position we find ourselves in.

But principles empower us with an abundance mentality. There's more of everything. We can think win-win with all the roles in our lives, to see them as parts of a highly interrelated whole.

THREE PARADIGMS THAT NURTURE BALANCE

Most of us, when going through the Quadrant II organizing process for the first time, look at roles as a great way to organize information and tasks. While we receive some benefit from that new perspective, we benefit far more by gaining a deeper understanding of our roles that empowers us to create synergy and balance in our lives. We'd like to suggest three fundamental paradigms that create that deeper understanding.

1. Our "Natural" Roles Grow Out of Our Mission

Where do we get our roles? If we haven't paid the price to work them out in our deep inner life, they're probably a combination of feelings we have about ourselves and the social mirror.

But if we have paid the price, our roles are like the branches of a living tree. They grow naturally out of a common trunk—our mission, the unique fulfillment of our needs and capacities—and common roots—the principles that give sustenance and life. Our roles

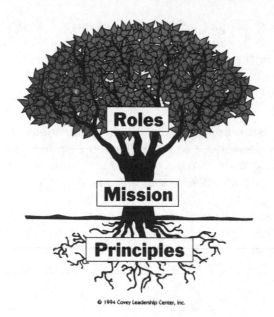

© 1994 Covey Leadership Center, Inc.

become the channels through which we live, love, learn, and leave a legacy.

This deep connection with vision gives passion and energy to our roles. For example, when parents begin to detect the powerful uniqueness of their role—their singular opportunity to enhance the growth and development of a new life and the generative force that new life represents in affecting future generations—they become energized and liberated to transcend bad scripts, old baggage, the weaknesses of prior generations. Instead of passing them on, they change them. They become *transition* instead of *transmission* figures. A sense of legacy empowers them to deal with themselves in transformational rather than transactional ways.

On the other hand, roles that are truncated from needs, principles, and mission—a work role that has no meaning except economic security; a relationship based on illusion instead of principle; or community service based on the expectations of others instead of inner conviction—have no sustaining power because they don't tap into that deep burning "yes!"

Each role is vitally important. Success in one role can't justify failure in another. Business success can't justify failure in a marriage; success in the community can't justify failure as a parent. Success or failure in any role contributes to the quality of every other role and life as a whole.

Without this "big picture" awareness of our roles, we can easily become consumed by some roles to the neglect of others. That's why we take the time in the Quadrant II organizing process each week to write down our roles.

As one busy executive expressed:

In the last seventeen years of being a business executive, I've taken a lot of people out to lunch. But as I wrote out my roles and came to "husband," I realized that I hadn't been taking my own wife out for lunch. And my relationship with her is one of the most important relationships in my life.

So, as a result of weekly organizing, we started doing that, and it's brought us much closer. Our communication has increased, which has led me to discover other ways I can be a better husband. As I review my role as a husband each week, I believe I'm doing a much better job.

Writing our roles each week keeps them in our awareness and helps us pay attention to all the important dimensions of our life. But that does not necessarily mean that we set a goal in every role every week. Nor does it mean that our roles are necessarily the same each week, or that we address all roles every week. The balance of nature itself teaches us the principle of times and seasons. There are times in our lives when imbalance is balance, when a short-term focus contributes to our overall mission in life.

A mother with a new baby, for example, spends an incredible number of hours loving, serving, and caring for that baby. For a time, her life seems out of balance. But to look at life from the aeon perspective—to realize that balance is living, loving, learning, and leaving a legacy over a lifetime—gives context and meaning to her seasonal imbalance. Other times when short-term imbalance creates long-term balance might include involvement in a meaningful project of contribution, caring for an elderly parent, or starting a new business. There are seasons when intense investment can make the difference between success and failure, between mediocrity and excellence. And that investment, or lack of it, has tremendous implications for others down the road—for spouse, children, employees, associates, the community as a whole. During times of chosen imbalance, we may feel more comfortable listing only one or two roles during weekly organizing. Some feel this frees them for greater focus; others feel a sense of context in having their roles in front of them even though they don't set goals in each one.

The vital factor in any choice concerning balance in our lives is a deep connection with our inner voice of conscience. Because we live in an environment inundated by human *doing*, more than human *being*, it's easy to get caught up in imbalance to the point that it no longer reflects mission or principles. Rather than being mission-driven, we become urgency-driven.

As Carol Orsborn, founder of Overachievers Anonymous, points out:

> There are periods when producing at the outer reaches of endurance and ability for an extended period of time is necessary and even nurturing. I do not, for instance, regret the long hours I invested in the early years of building our business. I have no problem burning the midnight oil while driven by inspiration to capture some exciting new thought for this book.
>
> The real problem comes, however, when I—or any of us—go into unconscious overdrive, forgetting to shift back out of high gear after such a bout with adrenaline has served its purpose.[7]

Only as we keep an open communication with our deep inner life will we have the wisdom to make effective choices. As psychologist Dr. Barbara Killinger observes:

> Wisdom comes from . . . balance. Workaholics are very intelligent, interesting, often witty and charming people, but they lack this inner wisdom. The crises in their lives attest to this. Good judgment comes when your logical and rational thoughts and ideas are supported by a gut reaction that the decision "feels" right, and you can live comfortably with the consequences of your action. Inner wisdom goes even farther because the decision not only feels right, but it also fits in with your values and beliefs. Something deep inside you can answer "Yes!"[8]

We've known people with incredible careers who have walked away from them for a time to focus on a son or daughter who was on drugs. We've seen people with six- and seven-figure incomes retire early to coach a neighborhood soccer team. We've seen people marshal tremendous energy and support from the family and friends who had to do without them as they've spent incredible time and energy on projects they felt would contribute to humanity as a whole. And these people all felt wonderful about their choices! They were mission-driven. They were firmly connected to their deep inner lives.

One woman who seems to have created this inner connection shares this experience:

I sit on a board of a residence for pregnant teenagers. It's a wonderful organization, very dear to my heart. I chaired the public relations committee for some time.

We had a hiatus of two months during which I tried to get a handle on my new business. I also spent some important time with my family. Everybody took for granted that I would be heading up the board again. But I had to say, "No, I'm not going to serve on the committee this year. I don't want to build your expectations and then not be able to fulfill them." It was painful.

I discovered the anchor is trusting myself a lot more and knowing that I can walk away from situations—and it's okay. Realizing that has been liberating. I've learned to say no in deference to a larger "yes" in my life.

I get out of sync with it and fall back into some old habits sometimes. There are rushes. There are work crunches that just won't wait. But with the internal knowledge and comfort that I'm anchored, I can readjust quickly and come back into balance.

When following our inner voice leads us into times of short-term imbalance, we can involve others whose lives are affected by the focus and work out an interdependent balance together.

Rebecca: As we considered working on this book, I felt very uncomfortable about the imbalance I thought it would create in my life. Although I've been involved in a number of community service efforts and in other writing projects, my family has been my major passion and area of contribution for the past twenty-five years. The choices I've made through the years to "be there" for my husband and children have been mission-driven. But I also felt a sense of passion about this work. It tied into other values and other roles that are also a vital part of my life.

I thought about what I couldn't do for my family if I chose to write. I still have three children at home who need help with music practice and homework, transportation to lessons, nutritious meals, and a listening ear. I feel a great desire to strengthen our association and build deeper bonds with our married children living nearby. Wanting to do these things, I was feeling pain because I knew that, for a time, I could not do them, at least not to the extent that was important to me in my role as a mother.

Roger and I worked together for a time writing and parenting so that we could provide for the basic needs of our children living at home, and grandparents provided wonderful help with music practice and transportation. But the real breakthrough came as we created a synergy between this project and our children's need to leave a legacy. Part of our family mission is "to wisely use our time, talents, and resources to bless others." As we sat down with the children and involved them in the purpose of this book, we created a shared vision that tapped into the power of that part of our mission. They became excited and willing to help in whatever way they could. Several of our married children became involved in the project itself. Others helped out in other ways. One Saturday, several of them and their spouses showed up to help with outdoor projects that had been preempted by our writing.

We had to make sacrifices, but the children were willing to work together and help in countless ways that made the project possible. Instead of taking us away from our family, in many ways it's brought us closer. It's something we've done together. And we've all grown in the process.

When our roles grow out of mission, vision, and principles, "balance" is a deeper issue than spending time in compartmentalized boxes of life. Balance is in living, loving, learning, and leaving a legacy, and our roles create the synergistic, sometimes seasonal avenues through which we do it.

2. Each Role Is a Stewardship

Nature teaches us of a larger interdependent balance. A tree itself is part of a huge ecosystem. Its well-being affects and is affected by the well-being of other living things around it. The reality of this interdependence makes it vital to recognize each role as a stewardship.

A stewardship is a trust. A steward is "one called to exercise responsible care over possessions entrusted to him or her." We're stewards over our time, our talents, our resources. We have stewardships at work, in the community, and at home.

Stewardship involves a sense of being accountable to someone or something higher than self. Whether we think of that someone or something as a Creator, future generations, or society in general—this is an idea whose time has critically come. That fact has been dramatically brought to our attention by such issues as the environment, the national debt, and AIDS. "Ownership" implies "I can do what I want without consequence to anyone else." But the idea that we can destroy or misuse any resource with impunity is an illusion. We're creating results that impact quality of life for future generations.

ROLES   **PERSON(S)**

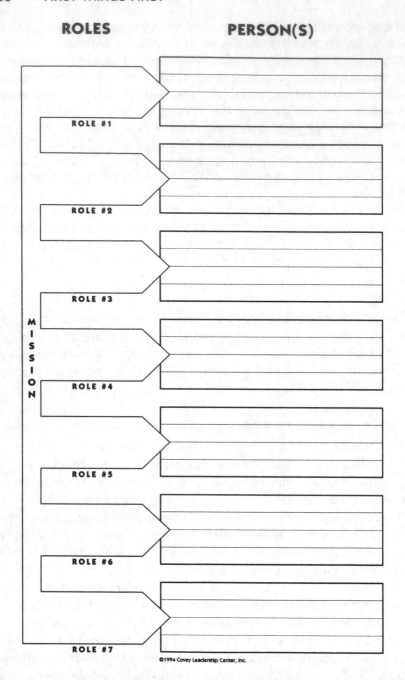

ROLE #1

ROLE #2

ROLE #3

M
I
S
S
I
O
N

ROLE #4

ROLE #5

ROLE #6

ROLE #7

©1994 Covey Leadership Center, Inc.

There's no way we can escape accountability. We *do* make a difference—one way or the other. We *are* responsible for the impact of our lives. Whatever we do with whatever we have—money, possessions, talents, even time—we leave behind us as a legacy for those who follow. And regardless of our own scripting, we can exercise our unique human endowments and choose the kind of stewards we want to be. We don't have to pass on abuse, debt, depleted natural resources, self-focus, or illusion to future generations. We can pass on a healthy environment, well-cared-for possessions, a sense of responsibility, a heritage of principle-based values, and the vision of contribution. By doing so, we improve quality of life both now and in the future.

You may find it helpful to use the chart on the opposite page to look at your own roles in terms of stewardships and identify to whom you feel a sense of accountability in each role.

In Section Three, we'll take an in-depth look at how we can create stewardship agreements with others that deal with the full reality of the interdependent nature of our roles.

3. Each Role Contains All Four Dimensions

Each role in our lives has a physical dimension (it requires or creates resources), a spiritual dimension (it connects to mission and principles), a social dimension (it involves relationships with other people), and a mental dimension (it requires learning).

Let's consider the social and mental dimensions in more detail. Every role has a relationship with family members, work associates, relatives, or friends. Even the work role of the janitor who cleans the building alone at night involves his relationship with the people he works for and those who benefit from his labors.

To see this vital social dimension empowers us to put people ahead of schedules. Executives who see their role in terms of *tasks* are easily frustrated by "interruptions" from employees; those who see their role in terms of *people* find deep fulfillment in opportunities to meet needs, to empower, and to help. Homemakers who see their role in terms of making beds, cleaning, and preparing meals have difficulty dealing with a child who doesn't want to do his work. Those who see their role in terms of the family members they love and serve find joy in a teaching moment with a child.

Instead of a task orientation that gets in the way of relationships, awareness of the social dimension of each role helps us develop a people orientation that creates rich, rewarding relationships with the people with whom we live and work.

Each role also has a mental dimension of learning, growing, increasing understanding, and skill. A significant part of effectiveness in any role is in the balance between developing and doing, between production (P) and increasing our production capability (PC). We see it in the executive who goes to a seminar to learn things that will help her be more effective in her business role. We see it in the teacher who spends part of his summer taking a class to improve his teaching skills. We see it in the mother or father who reads or takes classes to improve parenting skills.

Looking at our lives as a whole, the P/PC balance involves renewal in all four dimensions on a regular basis. It's taking time to exercise, to read, to connect with our deep inner life so that we increase the character and competence, the energy and wisdom we bring to every role in our lives.

QUADRANT II ORGANIZING NURTURES BALANCE

Natural balance is a dynamic equilibrium that manifests itself in three important ways in our lives.

- Primary balance is the inner balance between our physical, social, emotional, and spiritual dimensions. There's no balance in life without balance in our inner life—without the synergy created when living, loving, learning, and leaving a legacy coalesce.
- Secondary balance is in our roles. It's a synergistic balance, a sometimes seasonal imbalance, as the parts work together to create a greater whole.
- The P/PC balance is the balance between developing and doing that empowers us to do more effectively by increasing our capacity to do.

Let's look at how the Quadrant II process nurtures abundance and balance in our lives.

As we review our mission each week, we connect with passion and perspective. We focus on the fundamental inner balance of our physical, social, mental, and spiritual dimensions that gives meaning to outer balance in our lives.

As we review our roles, we see them as the avenues through which we can accomplish our mission. We see their social, mental, and spiritual as well as their physical dimensions. We look for ways to create synergy between them and with the needs and capacities of others.

The first role on the weekly worksheet, "sharpen the saw," is the only role that has a printed title. All the rest are blank. That's because "sharpen the saw" is our personal PC role. It reminds us not to be so busy sawing that we don't take time to sharpen the saw. Through this role, we renew each of the four dimensions on a daily basis and we increase the character and competence, the energy and wisdom we bring to every other role in our lives.

We can further nurture the balance of roles in the Quadrant II process by organizing and clarifying expectations around roles.

Organizing Information by Roles

Filing notes by a particular role—rather than chronologically or alphabetically—makes retrieval quick and easy because of the mental association.

In your organizer, you can create a section for each role. Then when you take notes, you can file them under the appropriate role. If you get prices for new siding for your home, put it under the role that includes home management. If you get an idea for a new product, put it in the job role that reflects product development. If you receive information for the charity drive, put it in your community leadership role. If you have information on your spouse's birthday, your children's shoe sizes, or the dog's vaccination schedule, put it in your family role.

Some people even find it handy to keep a list of phone numbers and addresses under each role. For example, they keep phone numbers for work associates under a work role, and phone numbers for services such as carpet cleaning or window washing under home management.

When you no longer need immediate access to your notes, you can transfer them to a file set up according to your roles. Professional information can be filed in a file drawer set up according to your job roles. There might be a folder for each role (perhaps even color-coded for faster identification), and then subdivided for more specific information within each role. Projects in process can also be organized by role and then transferred to the file drawer when completed. Family information, such as gift ideas, clothing sizes, or parenting goals can be organized in a file drawer, three-by-five card file, or in your personal planning tool under the appropriate role. Your own plans for personal development such as a list of books to read, a record of your exercise, or a "wish" list, can be filed under your role as an individual. Your computer screen can also be organized according to role, giving ready access to electronic information.

Organizing information according to roles is consistent with your own mental process. Often trying to follow elaborate filing systems that someone else has devised almost defeats the purpose, unless you happen to have the same mental framework as the system developer.

Organizing information by role also reinforces a focus on Quadrant II, thinking more about the important but not necessarily urgent things. Every time you take a note, look up a phone number, file information, or use your computer, you're thinking in terms of the important relationships and stewardships in your life.

Clarifying Expectations around Roles

Many people find it helpful to create a more detailed definition of a particular role than they have in their personal mission statement. Creating a mission statement or stewardship agreement for a particular role provides that definition and also creates shared expectation for others involved in fulfilling the role with you.

If you're a husband or wife and a parent, for example, you and your spouse may want to express your shared vision and values of parenting. On the job, you may want to create a clear agreement with your boss concerning your role in the business. We'll look at shared vision and stewardship agreements in depth in Chapter 12. Such agreements can be filed under the appropriate role in your organizer for ready access and frequent review.

BALANCE LEADS TO ABUNDANCE

Understanding "balance" and "roles" in a holistic way empowers us to transcend the conventional constraints imposed by chronos time. With a chronos mentality, we see our roles as segmented compartments of life conflicting and competing for our limited time and energy. This paradigm creates a scarcity mentality. There's only so much time. It's "either/or." We can't possibly do it all.

But with these more holistic paradigms, we look at our roles through the lens of "and." We see a deep connection between the roles in our lives and incredible opportunity for synergy. It creates an abundance mentality. Time may be a limited resource, but we aren't. As we create synergy among the roles of our lives, there's more of us to put into the time we have.

QUADRANT II GOALS TO CULTIVATE THE BALANCE OF ROLES

• Evaluate your mission statement and your roles to make sure that your roles grow out of your mission and that your mission includes all the important roles in your life.
• Analyze each of your roles in terms of relationships, and stewardships. You might find it helpful to use the chart on page 130.
• Organize your planner or organizer around your roles.
• Organize your file or computer screen around your roles.
• Work on mission statements or stewardship agreements for each of your roles.

7: *The Power of Goals*

*You can want to do the right thing,
and you can even want to do it for the right reasons.
But if you don't apply the right principles,
you can still hit a wall.*

ONE of the most common elements of all self-help and management literature is the idea of the power of goals. We've been told to set long-term goals, short-term goals, daily goals, monthly goals, personal goals, organizational goals, ten-year goals, lifetime goals. The virtues of "measurable, specific, and time-bound" goals have been preached from the pulpit of self-help books for generations.

Goal setting is obviously a powerful process. It's based on the same principle of focus that allows us to concentrate rays of diffused sunlight into a force powerful enough to start a fire. It's the manifestation of creative imagination and independent will. It's the practicality of "eating our elephants one bite at a time," of translating vision into achievable, actionable doing. It's a common denominator of successful individuals and organizations.

But despite their obvious value, our experience with and feelings about goals are mixed. Some of us can set heroic goals, exercise tremendous discipline, and pay the price for incredible achievement. Others can't keep a New Year's resolution to pass up dessert two days in a row. Some see goals as the primary factor shaping the destiny of individuals and nations. Others see them as superficial, pie-in-the-sky idealism that has no staying power in the "real" world. Some of us stick to a goal, no matter what. And some goals stick to us, no matter what. Some authors tell us that if we think positively, we can do anything; others tell us to stop beating ourselves up when we find out we can't.

TWO AREAS OF PAIN

In all our experience around goal setting, there seem to be two major areas of pain: 1) the blow to our integrity and courage when we don't achieve our goals; and 2) the sometimes devastating results when we do.

Withdrawals from the "Personal Integrity Account"

As we said earlier, we each have what we might call a "Personal Integrity Account" that reflects the amount of trust we have in our ourselves. When we make and keep commitments, such as setting and achieving goals, we make deposits. We increase our confidence in our own trustworthiness, in our ability to make and keep commitments to ourselves and to others. A high balance in this account is a great source of strength and security.

But when we don't achieve our goals, we make withdrawals, and this becomes a source of great pain. Over time, frequent withdrawals cause us to lose confidence in our ability to make and keep commitments and to trust ourselves and others. Cynicism and rationalization follow, and these attitudes sever us from the power of setting and achieving meaningful goals. Then, when we need strength of character to meet critical challenges in our lives, we find it just isn't there.

Stephen: Once I served as an assistant in a survival camp and led a group of students on an overnight hike. We ended up in a valley where we had to cross a river hand-over-hand on a rope. We were exhausted, fatigued, and dehydrated. We'd had no food or water for about twenty-four hours. But we knew that across that raging, forty-foot-wide river was breakfast.

As one of the leaders of the group, I was supposed to go first. I started out with determination and even a little arrogance. I started bouncing around on the rope and showing off. But by the time I got halfway over, I felt my strength starting to go. I tried every technique I knew—from sheer will power to visualizing myself making it across and eating that food—but I reached the point where I was afraid even to take my hand off the rope to move forward. I didn't have the confidence my other hand could continue to hold up my body weight.

Right in the middle of the river, I fell. The strength just wasn't there. I was dangling on my safety rope on top of this churning water. The students loved it! "Pride goeth before the fall." As it turned out, most of them had the same experience. Only a few had the strength to make it.

Building character strength is like building physical strength. When the test comes, if you don't have it, no cosmetics can disguise the fact that it just isn't there. You can't fake it. It takes strength to set a heroic goal, to work on chronic problems instead of going for the "quick fix," to stay with your commitments when the tide of popular opinion turns against you.

There are many reasons why we don't achieve our goals. Sometimes the goals we set are unrealistic. We create expectations that don't reflect any sense of self-awareness. New Year's resolutions are typical examples. Suddenly, we expect to change the way we eat, the way we exercise, or the way we treat people simply because the calendar has changed from December 31 to January 1. It's like expecting one of our children to learn to crawl, eat with a fork, and drive a car all in the same day. Our goals are based on illusion, with little self-awareness or regard for the principles of natural growth.

Sometimes we set goals and work to achieve them, but either the circumstances change or we change. A new opportunity surfaces; there's a shift in the economy; another person comes into the picture; we get a different perspective. If we hold on to our goals, they become masters instead of servants. But if we let them go, we often feel uneasy or guilty that we didn't keep our commitment. We find it hard to maintain a high balance in our Personal Integrity Account when we constantly change our goals or fail to achieve our goals.

Ladders Against the Wrong Wall

While failing to achieve our goals creates painful problems, accomplishing them can as well. Sometimes the goals we achieve are at the expense of other more important things in our lives. It's the "ladder against the wrong wall" syndrome, meaning we climb the proverbial ladder of success only to find that it's leaning against the wrong wall for us.

One of our associates shared this story:

Several years ago, a man announced to his friends and neighbors that his goal for the year was to earn a million dollars. He was an entrepreneur who believed, "Give me a good idea and I can sell a million." He developed and patented a state-of-the-art recreational product, and then drove around the country selling it.

Occasionally he would take one of his kids with him on the road for a week or so. His wife complained to him about taking the kids, saying, "When they come back, they stop saying their prayers and doing their homework. They just party the whole week. Don't take the kids if you aren't going to help them do the things they ought to be doing."

Well, at the end of the year, the man announced that he had met his goal: he made a million dollars. Shortly after, however, he and his wife divorced. A couple of his kids wound up on drugs. Another went off the deep end. Basically the whole family disintegrated.

This man was focused on a single goal and measured everything against it. But he failed to count the total cost. That million dollars cost him a lot more than it was worth.

When we become consumed by a single goal, we're like a horse with blinders, unable to see anything else. Sometimes our goals are "hit-and-run" goals that leave bodies strewn along the way. At other times, our goals may be well intended, but accomplishing them creates other undesirable results. A program participant from Russia shared this experience:

Gorbachev wanted to restrict the use of alcohol and not allow the Russian people to drink as much. It was like the American Prohibition, with similar results. Rather than turning to more productive activities, as was hoped, people went from drinking alcohol to using narcotics instead. The government achieved their goal of dramatically reducing the consumption of alcohol, but it didn't bring them what they wanted.

We typically set a goal with the expectation that meeting it will create positive change and quality-of-life results. But often the change isn't so positive. Accomplishing one goal impacts other areas of life in a negative way. When we come face-to-face with the results, we become disillusioned.

In light of this "disillusioned if we do, and doomed if we don't" dilemma regarding goals, is it any wonder that many of us feel uncomfortable with the goal-setting process?

Is it possible to have the power without the problems? To build a strong Personal Integrity Account by setting and achieving meaningful goals on a regular basis? To be able to let go of or change or even partly reach a goal and still maintain, or even add to, our Personal Integrity Account? To ensure that our ladders are leaning against the right walls?

We affirm that it is possible—even that we can access a significant increase in the power of goal setting. The key is in using our four human endowments in a synergistic way in setting and achieving principle-based goals.

USING OUR FOUR HUMAN ENDOWMENTS

Done well, traditional goal setting is powerful because it accesses the power of two of our unique endowments: *creative imagination* and *independent will*.

We use our creative imagination to visualize, to conceive of possibilities beyond our direct experience. We use our independent will to make choices, to transcend background, scripting, and circumstance. When we set a goal, we're saying, "I can envision something different from what is, and I choose to focus my efforts to create it." We use our imagination to keep the goal in mind, and our independent will to pay the price to achieve it.

The power of these two endowments is formidable—it's the power of purposeful living, the fundamental process of conscious change. But it's only a small part of the power available to us.

What's often missing in the goal-setting process is the power of two other endowments:

- **conscience**—the deep connection of goals to mission, needs and principles; and
- **self-awareness**—the accurate assessment of our capacity and the balance in our Personal Integrity Account

Let's take a closer look at these two endowments to see how they can empower us to set and achieve meaningful goals.

Conscience Creates Alignment with Mission and Principles

Conscience is powerful because it creates alignment between mission and principles and gives guidance in the moment of choice. The moment we set a goal—the moment we consciously decide to focus our time and energy toward a particular purpose—is a moment of choice. What determines that choice? Is it the social mirror, the agendas of others, values that are truncated from fundamental principles, needs, and capacities? Or is it a deep, principle-based, conscience-connected, contribution-focused fire within?

Goals that are connected to our inner life have the power of passion and principle. They're fueled by the fire within and based on "true north" principles that create quality-of-life results.

One of the best ways to access this power is to ask three vital questions: *what? why? and how?*

What?

What do I desire to accomplish? What is the contribution I want to make? What is the end I have in mind?

A principle-based "what" focuses on growth and contribution. It isn't just setting and achieving goals that creates quality of life. Hitler set and achieved goals. So did Gandhi. The difference is what they chose to focus on. What we seek, we generally find. When we set goals that are in harmony with conscience and the principles that create quality of life, we seek—and find—the best.

Why?

Why do I want to do it? Does my goal grow out of mission, needs, and principles? Does it empower me to contribute through my roles?

In the context of mission and vision, the "what" may be easier to identify than the "why" and "how."

Roger: After speaking on the importance of mission and roles in a recent seminar, I asked one of the participants if he would be willing to go through the goal-setting process with me in front of the group. He agreed.

I said, "Okay, choose a role—any role you'd like."

"Father."

"What do you feel is the most important goal you could work on in this role?"

"To improve my relationship with my fourteen-year-old son."

"Why?"

"Well, our relationship's not that good."

"So why do you want to improve it?"

"He's having a lot of challenges at school with friends and peer pressure. He's being pulled in directions that are not productive. I feel it's important to be close to him at this time in his life."

"Why?"

"So I can help him stay on the right path and be productive."

"Why?"

"Because he needs it."

"So why do you want to do it?"

"To help him."

"Why?"

He was beginning to get a little flustered. "Because I'm his father! It's my responsibility!"

"So why do you want to do it?"

Frustration was evident on his face. "Well, because . . . because . . ."

There were two people at his table who absolutely could not sit still a minute longer. At the same instant, they both almost shouted, "Because you love him!"

It was written all over his face. It was reflected in his words. It was so evident that people around him could sense the deep love he had for his son. Maybe he couldn't say it because of the seminar environment, or maybe he hadn't made the connection with that fire within.

The moment these two people said the words, his face broke into a sheepish grin. "That's right!" he said. "I love him." Everyone could feel the strength and peace that flooded over him.

Without this deep connection, we go through life feeling duty-bound to develop sufficient self-control to achieve our goals, to endure to the end, to crawl battered and bruised over the finish line, if it's the last thing we do. There's no connection to our deep energy sources, our convictions, our experiences. We're working against ourselves, not sure why (or even if) we want to accomplish a particular goal. The commitments we make in a moment of enthusiasm don't have the sustaining power to carry us all the way to successful achievement of our goals.

The key to motivation is motive. It's the "why." It's what gives us the energy to stay strong in hard moments. It gives us the strength to say "no" because we connect with a deeper "yes!" burning inside.

If a goal isn't connected to a deep "why," it may be good, but it usually isn't best. We need to question the goal. If it is connected, we need to push our thinking and feeling until we break through and create an open flow between the passion of vision and the goal. The stronger the connection, the stronger and more sustained the motivation.

How?

How am I going to do it? What are the key principles that will empower me to achieve my purpose? What strategies can I use to implement these principles?

Once we create alignment between the "what" and the "why," we're ready to look at the "how." The choice of how often boils down to a choice between "control" and "release" styles of thinking and managing. If our paradigm is one of control, we assume that people have to be tightly supervised if they're going to produce or perform well. If our paradigm is one of release, our assumption is that, given the freedom, opportunity, and support, people will bring out the highest and best within them and accomplish great things.

The way we see others in terms of control or release generally reflects the way we see ourselves. If we have a control perspective, we assume we have to exercise strict control over ourselves if we want to accomplish anything. If we have a release perspective, we see our primary leadership task as creating optimal conditions for releasing inner capacities. If our focus in goal setting is on the endowment of independent will—gut it out, discipline ourselves, do it no matter what—that's a good indication that our basic paradigm is one of control.

Roger: I said, "Okay, how are you going to show your love?"

"I don't know. I guess I'll just look for opportunities."

"How else?"

"I'm going to invest the time."

"How else?"

He sighed. "I don't know. To tell you the truth, I'm scared. I've tried before, and it hasn't worked. Sometimes it seems like the harder I try, the worse it gets."

We then began to talk about some of the principles that could be applied in his relationship with his son. We talked about trustworthiness—if you want to build a trusting relationship, be trustworthy. Make and keep commitments. Be loyal to those not present. We talked about empathy—seek first to understand. Give respect.

He began to realize that, no matter how desperately he wanted to help his son, his efforts would never be effective as long as he was building the relationship on the illusion that he could control him with good intent—not on the reality that he could release him with principle-centered leadership and love.

Often in a seminar situation, people choose a business instead of a family role. Most have an immediate sense of "what" they feel they should do:

"Increase sales 5 percent this month."

"Reduce operating costs 3 percent by the end of the quarter."

"Improve office morale."

But when we go through the "why" process, the motivations people recognize at first are usually negative, economic, extrinsically focused, or urgent: "If I don't do it I'm going to lose my job."

"If I don't accomplish it, I'm going to lose credibility, and I'll feel terrible."

"We have a real problem here that has to be fixed before it spreads."

As we press for deeper answers, we often begin to hear a different story:

"If I do it, I'm going to feel like I really did my job and earned my pay."

"I enjoy feeling like I did something and provided a quality service to the customer."

"I really care about trying to make this world a better place."

Many businesses are so focused on the economic or physical dimension that they never tap into the deeper motivations. They fail to recognize or address social, mental, and spiritual needs. They don't let people connect naturally with what they feel in their hearts—their need to love, to learn, to live for something higher than self. And yet this connection is the very source of the energy, the creativity, the loyalty employers seek.

When we get to the "how," people who choose a business role usually think they just have to "gut it out."

> *"I just have to get in there and do it."*
> *"Have you tried that before?"*
> *"Yes."*
> *"Did it work?*
> *"No."*

We then talk together about some of the "true north" principles that could make a difference. We look at principles of interdependence—empathy, honesty, making and keeping commitments, building relationships. We look at principles of shared vision, win-win agreements, and systems alignment. It soon becomes apparent that knowing what to do and even deeply wanting to do it are not enough. The doing has to be based on the principles that create quality of life. Doing the right thing for the right reason in the right way is the key to quality of life, and that can only come through the power of an educated conscience that aligns us with vision, mission, and true north.

Self-Awareness Empowers Us to Build Integrity

Our trustworthiness is only as high as the balance in our Personal Integrity Account. Because our integrity is the basis of our confidence in ourselves and the confidence we inspire in others, one of the greatest manifestations of effective personal leadership is the exercise of care and wisdom in building a high positive balance in that account.

Primarily, we build it through the exercise of independent will in making and keeping commitments. But without self-awareness, we don't have the wisdom necessary to manage such an account. We may set our goals too high, turning potential deposits into huge withdrawals when we fail to achieve them. We may set our goals too low, depositing pennies when we could be depositing dollars. We may pass up daily, weekly, moment-by-moment opportunities to make deposits because we're too busy blaming circumstances or other people for our own failure to achieve our goals.

Self-awareness involves deep personal honesty. It comes from asking and answering hard questions:

Do I really want to do it?
Am I willing to pay the price?
Do I have enough strength to do it?
Do I accept the responsibility for my own growth?
Am I settling for mediocrity when I could be achieving excellence?
Am I blaming and accusing others for my own inability to set and achieve goals?

Self-awareness prompts us to start where we are—no illusions, no excuses—and helps us to set realistic goals. On the other hand, it also doesn't allow us to cop out with mediocrity. It helps us recognize and respect our need to stretch, to push the limits, to grow. Since much of our frustration in life comes as a result of unmet expectations, the ability to set goals that are both realistic and challenging goes a long way toward empowering us to create peace and positive growth in our lives.

Self-awareness is ear to the voice of conscience. It helps us to recognize that there are principles independent of us, to understand the futility of trying to become a law unto ourselves. It helps us to be humble and open to growth and change, to realize that we are neither omniscient nor omnipotent when we set a goal. To the best of our awareness at the time, out of all the good things we could do, we choose the best thing, for the best reason, and we plan to do it in the best way.

But the situation may change. We may change. *And we can't act with integrity without being open to that change.*

Self-awareness empowers us to ask: Am I allowing the good to take the place of the best? The best may be the goal we set. The best may be in the unexpected opportunity, the new knowledge, the new options created by increased understanding. If change is driven primarily by urgency, mood, or opposition, it takes us away from the best. If change is driven by mission, conscience, and principles, it moves us toward the best. To have the self-awareness to know the difference between the good and the best and to act based on mission, conscience, and principles is to make the most significant deposits in our Personal Integrity Account.

Integrity means more than sticking to a goal, no matter what. It's integrity of system, an integrated process that creates an open connection between the mission and the moment.

HOW TO SET AND ACHIEVE PRINCIPLE-BASED GOALS

Without principles, goals will never have the power to produce quality-of-life results. You can *want* to do the right thing, and you can even want to do it for the right reasons. But if you don't apply the right principles, you can still hit a wall. A principle-based goal is all three: **the right thing, for the right reason, in the right way.**

Principle-based goal setting involves the full, synergistic use of all four human endowments:

- Through conscience, we connect with the passion of vision and mission and the power of principles.
- Through creative imagination, we envision possibility and synergistic, creative ways to achieve it.
- Through self-awareness, we set goals with realistic stretch and stay open to conscience-driven change.
- Through independent will, we make purposeful choice and carry it out; we have the integrity to walk our talk.

The principle-based goal-setting process is most effective when it includes: 1) setting "context" goals, 2) keeping a "perhaps" list, and 3) setting weekly goals.

1. Setting "Context" Goals

Most people find it helpful to connect weekly goals with the context provided by their mission statement through the use of long-term and mid-range goals. But the terms "long-term" and "mid-range" put these goals into a chronos framework.

While timing may be an important issue, we suggest that other issues such as relationships with people and with other goals and events are better recognized through "context" goals. The term "context" reminds us that personal leadership is not just having a long-range view—it's having broad-range understanding.

If you organize around your roles, you could keep a page of context goals under each role in your organizer for easy access. The what/why/how format is an effective way to capture these goals. For example, a context goal in your "sharpen the saw" role might look like this:

WHAT:
My goal is to maintain a healthy, well-disciplined body.

WHY:
So that:
- I can have the strength, endurance, and physical presentation necessary to effectively fulfill my missions.
- I can be an example to my children and to others in effective health maintenance.
- I can build my personal character strength.

HOW:
- *Good nutrition.* I will increase my intake of fresh fruits and vegetables, complex carbohydrates, whole grains, poultry, and fish; I will decrease my intake of sugars, fats, salt, and red meats; and I will eat smaller meals more frequently.
- *Physical maintenance.* I will do thirty minutes of aerobic exercise four times a week; I will join a basketball league; and I will get seven hours of sleep a night by retiring and rising early.
- *Mind/body connection.* I will think positive thoughts about my body and health; I will read and attend seminars and workshops to learn more about health.
- *Focus.* I will attend to specific health problems.

This "what/why/how" format creates an open connection between mission, principles, and goals. As you prepare to set your weekly goals, you can review these context goals to immediately tap into that connection and select a bite-sized actionable piece that will move you toward them.

Looking at a goal in this way reaffirms the interconnectedness of our lives. Although this goal might be considered a "physical" goal and filed under the "sharpen the saw" role, think of how interrelated it is with each of the other dimensions and with all other roles.

For example, most people report that one of the greatest benefits of regular physical exercise is not in the physical, but in the spiritual dimension—the increase in integrity and character strength. The mental dimension—learning more about health, thinking healthy thoughts, and reducing stress—powerfully impacts the effectiveness of this "physical" goal. Exercising with friends or family members can create a rich social as well as physical experience. Increased health empowers us in the physical, mental, social, and spiritual dimensions of all our other roles.

An awareness of this interconnectedness keeps us open to abundance thinking and empowers us to create a powerful synergy among our goals.

2. Keeping a "Perhaps" List

One problem we have in dealing with goals is that often we read a book, attend a seminar, or have a conversation with someone and come away from the experience with an idea of something we really want to do. We're not ready to set a goal, but we don't want to lose the idea.

Most of the time, we let it wander around in an already overcluttered cerebral waiting room, floating in and out of awareness, distracting us from the task at hand and causing a vague uneasiness of something not yet done. Or we write it down on a generic "to do" list that collects items faster than they can ever be accomplished, mingles top-priority items with things that don't matter much, and constantly reminds us of all we haven't done.

Far more effective is the "perhaps" list, a list kept under each role of things you might want to do. Whenever an idea occurs to you, write it on the "perhaps" list under the appropriate role for future consideration. Writing it here does not mean it's a goal or a commitment. *Perhaps you'll do it; perhaps you won't.* It's simply input to be considered for future organizing. Your integrity is not on the line.

Noting ideas on a "perhaps" list diffuses the anxiety and distraction and makes them accessible for future consideration. During weekly organizing, you can look over the list, translate any item you wish to a goal for the week, keep it on the list for future reconsideration, or discard it as not really that important.

3. Setting Weekly Goals

When we set our weekly goals, the "what/why/how" format becomes more a way of thinking about our roles and goals. As we set our goals, we look at each role, and then we pause in that space between stimulus and response to ask:

What are the one or two most important things I could do in this role this week that would have the greatest positive impact?

The answer to this question may be in a feeling or impression that comes as we review our mission and roles. One man shared this experience:

When I review my roles each week, I often get impressions of specific things I need to do, especially in my role as a father. Something will come to my mind regarding a particular child. I find I'm more aware of my children's individual needs, more sensitive and open to opportunities to make a difference.

The answer may come as a result of reviewing our context goals in each role, or from an insight or idea we put on our "perhaps" list in a particular role during the week. As we review these things, we create an open connection between our deep inner life and our current situation. We create the context that gives meaning to our goals.

CHARACTERISTICS OF EFFECTIVE WEEKLY GOALS

As you set your goals, keep in mind five characteristics of effective weekly goals:

1. *They're driven by conscience.* An effective goal is in harmony with our inner imperatives. It's not driven by urgency or reaction. It's not a reflection of the social mirror. It's something we feel, deep inside, we need to do, and it's in harmony with our mission and with true north principles. We need to be sensitive to our inner

voice of conscience, especially as we select goals in our most unique roles, where we can have the greatest influence. We also need to maintain balance. It's important to remember that we don't necessarily need to set a goal in each role each week. There are times of short-term imbalance when wisdom suggests that we make the conscious choice not to set goals in some roles.

2. *They're often Quadrant II goals.* The Quadrant II organizing process automatically creates a connection between the "what" and the "why." As a result, the goals that we select are typically important, but not necessarily urgent. We may also select some Quadrant I goals that are both urgent and important, but we select them primarily because they're important.

3. *They reflect our four basic needs and capacities.* Good goals can be about doing in the physical dimension, but they can also be about understanding and being (the spiritual dimension), relating (the social dimension), and growing or learning (the mental dimension). Many of us feel dissatisfied and imbalanced because the goals we pursue are essentially time-bound and physical. To ignore the reality of other vital dimensions is to severely limit our capacity to create meaningful quality of life. It's also to deprive ourselves of the incredible synergy that can be created among goals.

4. *They're in our Center of Focus.* We each have what we call a Circle of Concern that encompasses everything we're concerned about—our health, a meeting with the boss, a teenage son's plans for the weekend, offensive magazines on display in a neighborhood convenience store, the President's foreign policy decisions, the threat of nuclear war.

We also have another circle that usually falls within this Circle of Concern called the Circle of Influence. This circle defines the area of concern where we can actually make a difference. We may not be able to influence the President's foreign policy decisions or the threat of nuclear war, but we can do something about our health. We may also be able to influence our son's weekend plans or the neighborhood store's magazine display.

But the most effective use of our time and energy is generally in a third circle—the Center of Focus.

In this circle are the things we're concerned about, that are within our ability to influence, that are aligned with our mission,

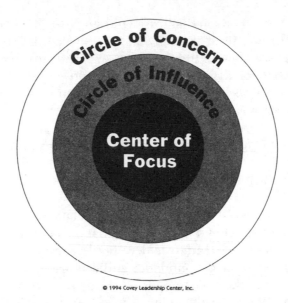

© 1994 Covey Leadership Center, Inc.

and are timely. To spend time and effort in any other circle diminishes our effectiveness. When we operate in our Circle of Concern, we basically waste effort on things we have no ability to control or affect. When we operate within our Circle of Influence, we do some good, but what we do may be at the expense of something better. When we set and achieve goals that are in our Center of Focus, we maximize the use of our time and effort.

Interestingly, we find that as we do this over time, our Circle of Influence automatically increases. We find positive ways to influence more people and circumstances.

5. *They're either determinations or concentrations.* You may find it helpful to distinguish between *determinations*—things you're determined to do, no matter what—and *concentrations*, areas of pursuit you focus your efforts around. When you set a determination, you put your integrity on the line. This is when it's vital to follow through, to keep your commitment, to do what you said you were going to do. The only valid reason for not sticking to a determination would be if you became thoroughly convinced—through conscience and deep self-awareness—that the "best" goal you set had for some reason become only "good." Then, and only then, could you change with integrity.

When you set a concentration, you identify an area where you desire to focus time and energy. You seek opportunities to do it. You move toward it. But you don't risk your integrity. If you don't do it, you lose the benefit of the time and energy you invested, but you don't make withdrawals from your Personal Integrity Account.

Remember, you don't have to put your integrity on the line every time you set a weekly goal. In fact, it's important to manage your actual commitments with great care, being sensitive and wise in building the balance in your Personal Integrity Account. But your caution should not keep you from moving forward with purpose.

CONFIDENCE AND COURAGE

To set and work toward any goal is an act of courage. When we exercise the courage to set and act on goals that are connected to principles and conscience, we tend to achieve positive results. Over time, we create an upward spiral of confidence and courage. Our commitment becomes stronger than our moods. Eventually, our integrity is not even an issue. We build the courage to set increasingly challenging, even heroic goals. This is the process of growth, of becoming all we can become.

On the other hand, when we exercise courage in setting goals that are not deeply connected to principles and conscience, we often get undesirable results that lead to discouragement and cynicism. The cycle is reversed. Eventually, we find ourselves without the courage to set even small goals.

The power of principle-based goal setting is the power of principles—the confidence that the goals we set will create quality-of-life results, that our ladders are leaning against the right walls. It's the power of integrity—the ability to set and achieve meaningful goals regularly, the ability to change with confidence when the "best" becomes the "good." It's the power of the four human endowments working together to create the passion, vision, awareness, creativity, and character strength that nurture growth.

To access this power is to create the upward spiral that empowers us to continually put first things first in our lives.

QUADRANT II IDEAS TO NURTURE THE POWER OF GOALS

- Use the what/why/how format to set context goals in each of your roles.
- Set up a "perhaps" list under each role in your organizer. During the week, write down ideas that come to you for goals you may want to set under the appropriate role. Notice how you feel about putting these ideas on "perhaps" lists. As you plan your next week, refer to the lists for goal ideas.
- As you set your weekly goals, pause and connect with conscience. Act on what you feel is most important for you to do in each role.
- Think about how you're using each of your endowments as you set and achieve goals for the week.
- Identify each of your goals for the week as a "determination" or "concentration." At the end of the week, analyze how this differentiation affected your attitude toward the goal, your progress in achieving it, and the balance in your Personal Integrity Account.

8: *The Perspective of the Week*

Priority is a function of context.

PROFESSIONAL photographers work with a variety of lenses. They use ultra-wide-angle and wide-angle lenses to capture the big picture. They use a telephoto lens to bring an object closer. They use a normal lens to capture the view that most closely resembles what's seen by the human eye. They use a micro lens for close-up work. Part of their expertise is in knowing when to use each lens to create the desired result.

Like the photographer, part of our expertise in personal leadership is knowing when to focus in the most effective way. Most time management tools and techniques focus on daily planning, and there seems to be good rationale for the focus. The day is the smallest complete natural unit of time—the sun rises and sets, and we face a new agenda every twenty-four hours. We can plan the day, set daily goals, schedule appointments, and prioritize activities. And when one day is over, we can take what's left and plan, schedule, and prioritize it all over again tomorrow. Nothing gets lost in the cracks.

But the problem with focusing on daily planning is that it's like trying to walk down the street while looking through the telephoto lens of a camera. It keeps us focused on what's right in front of us—what's pressing, proximate, and urgent. So we're essentially into prioritizing crises. While the objective of most daily planning approaches is to help us put first things first, the reality is that daily planning keeps us focused on doing urgent things first. The perspective is insufficient to accomplish the result.

Of course, we can't just be focused on the big picture either. If we don't translate vision into action, we lose touch with reality, become idealistic dreamers, and lose credibility with ourselves and with others. We all face this apparent dilemma.

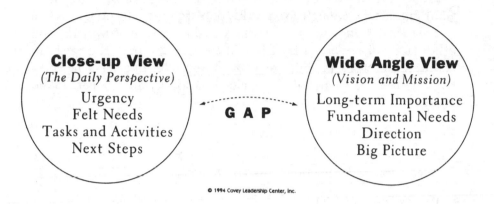

Close-up View
(The Daily Perspective)

Urgency
Felt Needs
Tasks and Activities
Next Steps

G A P

Wide Angle View
(Vision and Mission)

Long-term Importance
Fundamental Needs
Direction
Big Picture

© 1994 Covey Leadership Center, Inc.

So, how do we resolve this dilemma and keep things in focus and in perspective?

The perspective of the week provides a synergistic third-alternative solution that links the big picture to the day in a balanced, realistic way.

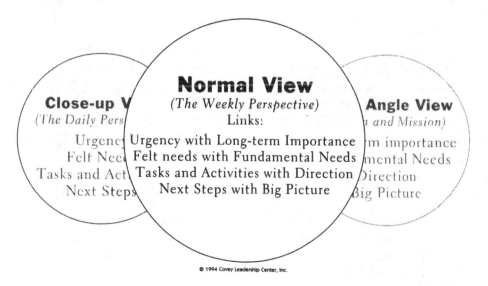

Close-up V
(The Daily Pers

Urgenc
Felt Nee
Tasks and Act
Next Steps

Normal View
(The Weekly Perspective)
Links:

Urgency with Long-term Importance
Felt needs with Fundamental Needs
Tasks and Activities with Direction
Next Steps with Big Picture

Angle View
a and Mission)

m importance
mental Needs
Direction
Big Picture

© 1994 Covey Leadership Center, Inc.

Because it creates these vital connections, the week becomes the "normal lens" that gives the most accurate perspective for creating a balanced quality life.

THREE OPERATING PERSPECTIVES

The week represents a complete patch in the fabric of life. It has the workdays, evenings, the weekend. It's close enough to be highly relevant, but distant enough to provide context and perspective. It's the international standard: many business, education, government, and other facets of society operate within the framework of the week. In addition, the week provides us with three useful operating perspectives: 1) balanced renewal, 2) whole-parts-whole, and 3) content in context.

1. Balanced Renewal

The perspective of the week prompts us to plan for renewal—a time for recreation and reflection—weekly and daily.

Weekly Renewal

Most cultures support the notion of weekly renewal. The Judeo-Christian world, for example, honors a weekly Sabbath—one day in seven expressly devoted to reflection and recommitment. The academic world expands this concept to include the sabbatical, the one year in seven devoted to the personal development of the instructor. The most common examples of weekly renewal are found in weekend activities that may include recreational sports or social events with family and friends.

Quadrant II organizing helps us to make weekly renewal part of a balanced lifestyle. Instead of living day after day pressed up against the urgent until we feel we have to break out and escape to Quadrant IV, we can proactively plan genuine re-creation and renewal as a needed change of pace between creative periods. Renewal is not mindless, purposeless escape activity. It includes such valuable Quadrant II activities as:

- Building, repairing, or renewing relationships with family and friends
- Recommitting to deep values through religious activities
- Restoring energy through rest and recreation
- Developing talents through special interests and hobbies
- Contributing through community service

Experience teaches us the immense value of weekly renewal. When we're pressed by urgency and we work day after day and into the weekends without any change of activity or pace, we feel ourselves losing our edge, our energy, and our perspective in every area of life. It's like reading a run-on sentence that goes on for pages without a comma or period, or like listening to a piece of music without any phrasing. When we finally do escape to Quadrant IV, the change of pace gives some relief, but we generally feel empty and dissatisfied, neither renewed nor re-created.

Personal leadership is cultivating the wisdom to recognize our need for renewal and to ensure that each week provides activities that are genuinely re-creational in nature.

Quadrant II weekly organizing itself is a renewing activity. Through it, we renew our awareness of our needs and capacities and true north principles. We renew our connection with our four human endowments and our commitment to a path of contribution, of living for purposes higher than self. We renew the passion of vision, the balance of roles, the power of goals in our lives. After experimenting with weekly organizing, one man wrote to say:

I used to spend Sunday evenings in Quadrant IV watching TV. But I've found it's the point in the week when I have the most peace of mind. I've attended church services. I've spent time with my family. That creates an excellent frame of mind for reviewing my mission, roles, and goals. So I now block out time on Sunday evenings to plan the upcoming week.

Some people prefer to organize on Friday afternoon before they leave the office. Others prefer Sunday morning or first thing Monday morning. The important thing is to do it when you can be alone to connect with your deep inner life. Without regular renewal, people are generally pushed in other directions. Instead of acting, they're constantly being acted upon.

Daily Renewal

The perspective of the week provides context for balance in daily renewal. If you were to devote an hour a day to renewal, for example, you might interpret "balance" to mean that you exercise for fifteen minutes, listen to your teenage daughter for fifteen minutes, study for fifteen minutes, and meditate for fifteen minutes.

But consider the increased possibilities when you expand your perspective to the week. Health experts say that to achieve the "training effect," you need to invest at least thirty minutes three times a week in vigorous exercise, and rest the body between workouts. Emphasizing physical renewal on those three days will have a more positive effect than faithfully spending fifteen minutes a day doing light exercise. On the days you don't do vigorous resistive exercise, you could stretch or go for a walk—perhaps increasing the value of that activity by doing it with your spouse or listening to tapes at the same time. On those days, you could spend more time on in-depth educational or inspirational reading. Though the nature and timing of each activity varies over the week, you're sharpening the saw in a balanced, optimal way.

2. Whole-Parts-Whole

As we review our mission statement, we see the whole—the big picture, the end in mind, the meaning in what we do. But to get lost in the whole is to become an idealistic dreamer. So we then move to the parts—our roles and goals. We take a "close-up" look at each part of our lives. But to get lost in the parts is to make our life more mechanical, compartmentalized, or fragmented.

So as part of the process, we bring them together again into the whole, marrying the strengths of both perspectives through the normal lens of weekly organizing.

As we bring them together, we can see the interrelatedness of the parts. We see how each part of life—work, family, personal development, community activity—empowers us to contribute and fulfill our

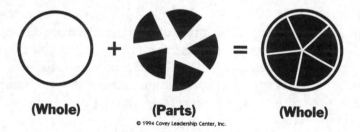

(Whole)   **(Parts)**   **(Whole)**

© 1994 Covey Leadership Center, Inc.

mission. We see how each part contributes to every other part, how character and competence in any role benefit us in all roles.

This "whole-parts-whole" perspective enables us to create synergy and to remove artificial barriers among roles and goals.

Creating Synergy among Goals

Whole-parts-whole thinking empowers us to create synergy among roles and goals. We recognize that some activities can be combined and accomplished in ways that are actually better than if each activity were pursued separately. We also recognize that some activities should not be combined—they need exclusive focus. We can then adjust the rest of our activities with wisdom, knowing how each impacts the other.

For example, as we do our weekly organizing, we might combine a parental goal "to build my relationship with my son" with a sharpen-the-saw goal "to exercise my body" by planning a time to take that son for a swim. We might combine a goal to learn a new language with a community service goal by volunteering to work with minority groups in need of social support. As we really begin to develop an abundance mentality, we find ways to synthesize even more goals. We could fix a gourmet meal, meet the new neighbors, and prepare for next month's service club meeting by cooking enough for three meals at once—serving one to the family, taking one to the new neighbors, and freeing one so we don't have to spend time preparing dinner on the night of the service club meeting. The possibilities are endless. There are an infinite number of ways we can create synergy in our lives that we might never see with a segmented, linear perspective.

The objective, however, is not to cram as many activities as possible into our schedule or to try to do everything at once. We're not trying to be Superman or Superwoman. The objective is to use our creative imagination to come up with synergistic, principle-based ways to accomplish goals that create even greater results than would be achieved if the goals were accomplished separately.

A good test is to see how you feel inside as you make the connections. If it feels forced or contrived, you may be violating a principle—perhaps spreading yourself too thin—and the activities would be better approached separately. When activities naturally go together, you'll feel a sense of peace and increased capacity, because you're operating in harmony with principles. Instead of conflicting and competing, the parts of your life are working together in beauty and harmony.

There are several ways to capture this synergy on the weekly worksheet. One way is to simply draw lines that join goals and transfer the synergistic activity to the appropriate day of the week.

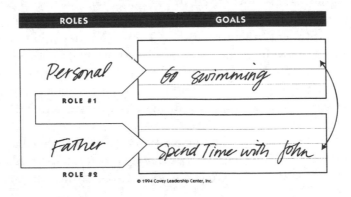

ROLES	GOALS
Personal ROLE #1	Go swimming
Father ROLE #2	Spend Time with John

© 1994 Covey Leadership Center, Inc.

Another way is to write the synergistic activities in the column labeled "Reminders" and put an asterisk or some other defining mark by those activities that represent your goals.

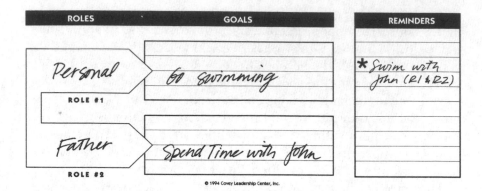

ROLES	GOALS	REMINDERS
Personal ROLE #1	Go swimming	* Swim with John (R1 & R2)
Father ROLE #2	Spend Time with John	

© 1994 Covey Leadership Center, Inc.

Once we've created the synergy, we can translate our chosen activities into the week, either as appointments or priorities for the day.

Removing Artificial Barriers

We often tend to build walls between work, family, and personal time. We act as if what we do in one area doesn't affect what we do in the others. Yet, we all know that these barriers are artificial. A bad day at the office may create a sense of hopelessness, a lack of contribution, that affects us in our personal and family lives. Personal and family struggles can affect the quality of our work. On the other hand, a quality family relationship can create positive impact on our work, and when something wonderful happens at work, we often want to share it with family and friends.

Life is one indivisible whole. As we make connections between the various aspects of our lives and our overall sense of purpose, we discover that renewal in any role creates renewal in other roles as well. At work, we may connect with some of the purposes of the organization, and find fulfillment by contributing to them. We may find fulfillment in the service we provide for our customers or in the growth and development of the people we train or work with. As we invest and connect in ways that bring growth and contribution, we discover that the person who comes home from work at night is stronger and better than the one who left for work in the morning.

At home, we may invest in personal renewal that strengthens us in all of our roles. Family time can create deeper relationships as we contribute to our loved ones. We can work with our family to contribute to our communities and friends. As we invest in a rich personal, family, and social life, we find that the person who goes to work in the morning is stronger and better than the one who left the night before.

Whole-parts-whole thinking empowers us to see relationships and create the connections that lead to growth, contribution, and fulfillment instead of fragmentation, discouragement, and self-focus. It becomes a subconscious way of thinking that empowers us to integrate our lives and weave elements together in a beautiful pattern. It's the abundance "seeing" that leads to abundance doing and abundance living.

3. Content in Context

Priority is a function of context, or the "bigger picture" in which something occurs. For example, if you were told right now that someone close to you was having a serious problem and needed assistance, you'd probably put down this book and go to help. Why? Because the context for deciding how to best spend your time had changed.

Weekly organizing puts *content*—the activities of our lives—into the *context* of what's important in our lives. It's big-picture renewal that puts us in touch with the purposes and patterns of life. It creates a powerful framework that represents our best thinking around what first things are and how we can put them first during the next seven days of our lives. When urgency pushes us, moods pull us, or unexpected opportunities beckon, we have something solid against which we can weigh the value of change. We can put content in context and choose the "best" over the "good."

As one individual noted:

Before I practiced weekly organizing, I would jump whenever the telephone would ring. If someone told me of a committee meeting, I would go. Now I can say, "I'd love to be there, but I have a commitment at that time with my daughter." Sometimes I have to cancel an appointment with a friend because of responsibilities at work, but I reschedule the appointment for another time if it's important. Nothing goes on the schedule unless it's important.

Quadrant II organizing is not prioritizing what's on the schedule; it's scheduling priorities. It's not filling every time slot with scheduled activity; it's putting the "big rocks" in first and filling in with whatever sand, gravel, and water we need to add.

The objective is not to fill the container to the brim, but to make sure that the big rocks are there and that the container is not so full it can't accommodate conscience-directed change.

To help keep content in context, many people find it helpful to create time zones and preserve time for preparation.

Creating Time Zones

Time zones are large, interchangeable blocks of time set aside for specific important activities. If family activity is a high value for you, you might want to regularly block out Saturday mornings for family activities as you organize your week. In doing this, you're not making an appointment or a firm commitment that every Saturday morning, without fail, you'll do some family activity. But as you plan other activities and goals, you tend to keep that time reserved for family activities.

If you're active in a local community project or a service club that meets on Thursday evenings two weeks out of the month, you might block out every Thursday evening for that service activity. When no meeting is held, you could use the time to work on the membership roster or do whatever else you may need to do to fulfill that role.

In your job, you may want to block out one morning a week for one-on-one staff interviews. When people want to see you, you can channel your appointments toward that established time zone. You might set aside another block of time during the week to prospect for new clients, read trade journals, or work on long-term planning.

Time zones can provide a template for more effective weekly organizing. The idea is not to fill the entire week with time zones, but to set aside a few specific time periods to provide focus for high-priority activities.

There are a number of advantages in using time zones. To begin with, you have the time blocked out for high-priority, often Quadrant II, activities. It also gives a sense of order to your life that other people become aware of and respond to. If they know you set aside Thursday nights for club work, rather than interrupting you throughout the week, they know they can probably reach you on club matters then, when you're available and focused.

Since time zones are often interchangeable, you gain flexibility in your schedule without sacrificing the time you allocated in the week. For example, if some friends suddenly find they are unable to attend a concert on Thursday night and they offer you their tickets, you might switch your family time to Thursday, take your family to the concert, and do your club work on Saturday morning. In the course of the week, you still accomplish what's most important in both roles.

Time zones also help clarify expectations with other people. If you

	MONDAY	TUESDAY	WEDNESDAY	THURSDAY	FRIDAY	SATURDAY	SUNDAY
7							
8							
9		Staff interviews				Family time	
10							
11							
12							
1	New client prospecting						
2							
3							
4							
5							
6							
7				Service club work			
8							
9							
OTHER PRIORITIES	OTHER PRIORITIES	OTHER PRIORITIES	OTHER PRIORITIES	OTHER PRIORITIES	OTHER PRIORITIES	OTHER PRIORITIES	OTHER PRIORITIES

have an assistant who schedules appointments for you, time zones can empower you both. Given time zones on Monday, Wednesday, and Friday between 10:00 and 4:00 to schedule appointments for you, your assistant knows that you won't schedule anything during those times without checking first. At the same time, you know your assistant won't schedule appointments for you at other times without checking with you first.

Setting Aside Time to Prepare

Much of our frustration and anxiety come from the feeling of being unprepared. Many activities become urgent as a result of lack of proper preparation. Through weekly organizing, we create a framework that allows for and encourages preparation.

For example, if you're supposed to make an important presentation at a meeting set for Friday morning, you may need to set aside some time on Wednesday to prepare and on Thursday to practice. If you plan to work in your garden on Saturday morning, you may need to go to the store on Friday to purchase seeds or tools.

The successful experiences most of us would like to have in life are rarely an accident. They are almost always an achievement, the result of careful planning and thorough preparation. The moment of clarity when we organize the week gives us the perspective to set aside the time necessary to make that preparation possible. Obviously, when things go as planned, we're generally much more effective when we're prepared. But even if things change, time spent in preparation empowers us to more quickly and effectively recognize the value and cost of change and to move in the right direction.

Once you gain the perspective of the week, you'll find it hard to limit yourself to the myopic view of the day. Content in context empowers you to make more wise and effective decisions in your moments of choice.

THE QUALITY-OF-LIFE DIFFERENCE

An attempt to put first things first in our lives with a single dimensional chronos paradigm is simplistic. It's saying that what's important in our lives and how well we're doing are functions of mechanical clocks and printed calendars. The tick of the clock determines the pace of our lives.

But the wide-range perspective created through the weekly organizing process creates whole new levels of seeing and being. The best way to understand the difference is to experience it. We often hear comments such as these:

My profession was consuming most of my time, but not any longer. I feel as if a great weight has been lifted off my shoulders and I'm enjoying life again. I'm getting more done at work and still having plenty of time for my other roles. My life is regaining a sense of balance.

I'm discovering a significant amount of quality time. Before, I was always saying, "There just aren't enough hours in the day, enough days in the week. I've got too much to do." I fall back into old habits sometimes, but I have the comfort of knowing that I'm anchored and balanced and I can adjust very quickly. There are rushes, work crunches that just won't wait, but the reward is that I can then block out some time for myself and know, really know, that this is as important as any Quadrant I client emergency or anything else. Before, I thought I had to schedule every hour of the day. Then I realized that the point was not to schedule every little thing, but to work on first things first.

The most noticeable change has been with my children. Mondays were always hectic days, with my daughter going horseback riding and my son off to soccer practice and the whole family trying to get dinner together inbetween events. In organizing my week, I suggested to my wife that we make this a special time with the kids, each taking one child and going out to eat before or after the event, and that we put our focus on the child rather than the rushing around. Last Monday, after working with the plan for two weeks, my son took my hand as we were leaving the fast food restaurant on our way to soccer practice. "Monday's my favorite day of the week, Dad," he said as we walked to the car. "I don't even care which of you is with me. I just like to talk."

There are quality-of-life issues that simply can't be seen through a myopic chronos paradigm. Even the simple addition of a weekly worksheet to a daily planning system creates a significant difference. But there's an even more powerful difference when we add the kairos or abundance paradigm—when we see that all parts of our lives matter to our mission, and that synergy among the parts creates energy in the whole. Life becomes a productive cycle of growth and continuous learning, fulfilling relationships, and meaningful contribution.

The perspective of the week nurtures balance and perspective and provides the context for making effective choices, moment by moment, regarding the things we decide to put first in our lives.

QUADRANT II GOALS TO CULTIVATE THE PERSPECTIVE OF THE WEEK

- Designate a specific time each week to do your Quadrant II organizing. Find a place that's conducive to introspection and contemplation.
- During the week, take note of situations you handle differently because of a weekly perspective. Record these in your organizer. At the end of the week, evaluate your experience.
- If you're not already doing so, set aside a day during the week for renewal, reflection, and recommitment—not just recreation. On this day, don't do the things you normally do on other days. After a month, evaluate the effect in your life.
- If you live or work with other people, have a weekly organizing meeting with them. Look for ways to coordinate your activities to better accomplish everyone's objectives.

9: *Integrity in the Moment of Choice*

*Quality of life depends on what happens
in the space between stimulus and response.*

SUPPOSE that over the weekend you spent a quality half hour going through the Quadrant II process and connecting with your deep inner life. You reviewed your mission and your roles; you identified important goals. You translated them into an action plan for the week. Then, as the day began, you reviewed your plan for the day, quickly reconnected with importance, and made any conscience-directed change you felt you should make. You're convinced that you've identified "first things" and have a good plan to put them first during the next twenty-four hours of your life.

So you start to live through the day you've planned. But somehow the day doesn't go "as planned."

• You're just concluding an interview with one of your employees when he suddenly breaks down and begins to share some deep concerns that affect his work. You care about this employee, but you're scheduled to be at an important meeting in ten minutes, and you also care about the five other people who have arranged their time to be there. What do you do?

• You receive a phone call from the principal at your daughter's elementary school asking you to serve on a special task force committee to secure needed playground equipment for the school. You've recently made the decision not to accept any more commitments because you feel you haven't been spending enough time in personal renewal and with your family. But you value your daughter and what the principal is trying to do for the school she attends, and you know that you have talent, resources, and connections that could make an important difference to the project. What do you say?

• You've been working intensely on a project for several hours and you feel that your effectiveness is dwindling. You have the thought that taking a break to read a little or eating an early lunch might regenerate you. But you have a deadline, and you're not sure whether the break is really renewal or escape. How do you decide?

These examples may not describe your particular situation, but whatever your circumstances, you know that each day brings unexpected challenges, new opportunities, reasons, or excuses for not doing what you planned to do.

How do you respond in such situations?
What choices do you make?
How do you feel about your choices?
How do you feel about making them?
How do you feel by the end of the day? Are you frustrated, feeling inadequate because you can't do it all, exhausted from the effort of running fast enough to try? Or do you feel calm, peaceful, and deeply satisfied that you did, in fact, put first things first?

These challenges aren't fantasy; they're everyday life. And as powerful as Quadrant II organizing is, neither it nor any other planning process can empower us to know everything that's going to happen in advance or to control it. If our idea of effective time management is to bulldoze our way through a list of scheduled appointments and "to do's," no matter what, we're setting ourselves up for almost inevitable frustration. The nature of most days will violate that expectation, in addition to which we'll miss some of the richest, most meaningful dimensions of living. And chances are very good that, for a significant part of the time, we won't be putting first things first.

Any week or day or moment in life is uncharted territory. It's never been lived before. We're parachuted into unfamiliar terrain, and while the road map we've created is helpful, our ability to navigate effectively depends, to a great extent, on the quality of our internal compass, the strength of the four endowments that make it possible for us to detect and align with true north at any time. That's why the purpose of Quadrant II organizing is to empower us to live with integrity in the moment of choice. Whatever detours may come up, whatever new roads may be built after the map is created, we can depend on our internal compass to keep us moving in the right direction.

THE MOMENT OF CHOICE

A moment of choice is a moment of truth. It's the testing point of our character and competence. Consider some of the factors acting on us in the moment of choice:

- urgency (things that are pressing and proximate)
- the social mirror (things that are pleasing and popular)
- our own expectations
- the expectations of others
- our deep values (what we feel is important in the long run)
- our operational values (what we want in the short run)
- our scripting
- our self-awareness
- our conscience
- our fundamental needs
- our wants

With all these factors acting on us, it's important to remember that a moment of choice is just that—a moment of choice. Whether we react automatically to one or more of these influences, empower circumstances or other people to control us, or use our human endowments to make a conscious, conscience-directed decision—it's our choice.

As Viktor Frankl discovered in the death camps of Nazi Germany:

> We who lived in concentration camps can remember the men who walked through the huts comforting others, giving away their last piece of bread. They may have been few in number, but they offer sufficient proof that everything can be taken from a man but one thing: the last of the human freedoms—to choose one's attitude in any given set of circumstances, to choose one's own way.
> And there were always choices to make. Every day, every hour, offered the opportunity to make a decision, a decision which determined whether you would or would not submit to those powers which threatened to rob you of your very self, your inner freedom; which determined whether or not you would become the plaything of circumstance. . . .[1]

We may find it convenient to live with the illusion that circumstances or other people are responsible for the quality of our lives, but the reality is that we are responsible—response-able—for our choices. And while some of these choices may seem small and insignificant at the time, like tiny mountain rivulets that come together to create a mighty river, these decisions join together to move us with increasing force toward our final destiny. Over time, our choices become habits of the heart. And, more than any other factor, these habits of the heart affect our time and the quality of our lives.

THE PRINCIPLE-CENTERED CHOICE

The essence of principle-centered living is making the commitment to listen to and live by conscience. Why? Because of all the factors that influence us in the moment of choice, this is the factor that will always point to true north. This is the one that unerringly leads to quality-of-life results.

To demonstrate the difference of this principle-centered choice, we'd like to ask you to try an experiment. We ask that you invest deeply in this experiment because to experience it is to understand the essence of this chapter.

Think for a moment of some relationship you have that you deeply care about, and you feel really needs to be improved. It could be with a spouse, a parent, a child, a boss, an employee, a friend. As you think about that relationship, try to go into your deep inner life and ask yourself this question:

What is one thing I could do that would significantly improve the quality of that relationship?

As you think about it, does an answer come to mind?

Do you feel confident that doing this thing would improve the quality of the relationship?

How do you know?

Whenever we ask these questions, people almost invariably have an immediate sense of some specific thing they could do that would make a difference. They know it would improve the quality of the relationship.

"How do you know?"

"Well, I just know."

For most people, it's not that they've tried it before in this circumstance or even in other circumstances. It's not necessarily the direct extension of linear thought. It's just a deep inner knowing of the "right" thing to do and a confidence that doing it would produce quality results.

"Is the answer you came up with in harmony with true north principles?"

"Yes."

"Is it in your Circle of Influence?"

"Yes."

"It may be hard, but is it something you can do?"

"Yes."

This deep inner knowing seems to immediately zero in on the most high-leverage, principle-based thing we could do to improve quality of life in the particular situation. It's the same kind of knowing you may have experienced as you worked through your mission statement or did your weekly organizing.

Now, what if, day to day, moment by moment, you were able to access that deep inner knowing? In the heat of the battle of the day, instead of making your decisions based on urgency, social pressure, the expectations of others, pain avoidance, expediency, or quick-fix, what if you were able to make your decisions based on that inner wisdom? What if you were able to execute those decisions effectively? Would that make a difference in your life?

Stephen: Some years ago, I spoke to a group of university students on this subject of listening to and living in harmony with conscience. In the process, we went through a listening exercise where I encouraged them to connect with their deep inner lives and listen to their conscience. "What can you do to be a better student? What can you do to be a better son or daughter, a better roommate? What can you do to live a life of greater integrity?"

Afterward, a young woman came up to me and said, "How do I know if what I'm hearing is really my conscience?" What she was asking was a question many people have asked: "How can I know if what I'm hearing is that deep inner voice of conscience or some other voice—social conscience, scripting, my own wishful thinking?"

I said, "When we went through the listening exercise, did you feel or sense anything?"

"Oh, yes!" she replied. "I know of so many things I need to do to be a better person."

"Then I suggest you forget your question. Just do those things. As you do, you'll become acquainted with that inner voice and that will give you the answer to your question."

I watched her expression. "You didn't like that answer, did you?"

"No," she replied.

"Why not?"

She sighed. "I have no excuse anymore."

A year later, I spoke at the same university on another subject. This same young woman came up afterward and introduced herself again, reminding me of the question she had asked the year before. As the situation came back to my memory, I said, "So what happened?"

"I did those things!" she replied. "I took it seriously."

"What did you do?"

"I really began to study the wisdom literature in a serious way. I made reconciliation with certain individuals I had thought I could just forget because I didn't like them. I became more cooperative at home, more helpful. I stopped procrastinating as a student. I realized I had a stewardship as a student, as well as stewardships for my family and my church. I tried to be more pleasant with my brothers and sisters. I didn't talk back to my parents. I became a less defensive and angry person." She paused a moment, and then she said, "I know very clearly now the difference between that voice and the many other voices within and without."

Several years later, I was speaking to another group—in another state, in fact—and she came up to me once more. "Would you be interested in the third installment?" she asked. I told her I would. She said, "I can't believe the difference in my life once I started to realize that I have my own inner guide. I feel a sense of direction in everything do, and, as long as I'm true to it, everything seems to work together to make it happen."

This is the essence of principle-centered living. It's creating an open channel with that deep inner knowing and acting with integrity to it. It's having the character and competence to listen to and live by your conscience.

This is obviously not a "quick-fix." As this young woman discovered, it takes tremendous effort and investment over time. But the more we're able to do it, the more we experience the quality-of-life fruits that come from a principle-centered life.

HOW WE CAN IMPLEMENT THAT CHOICE

The essential purpose of the Quadrant II process is to increase the space between stimulus and response and our power to act in it with integrity. We do that as we create a personal mission statement. We do it as we organize the week. We pause between stimulus and response to proactively choose a response that is deeply integrated with principles, needs, and capacities.

On a daily, moment-by-moment basis, we increase our ability to act with integrity as we learn to do the same thing—to pause. And in that pause, integrity comes as we use our human endowments to ask with intent, listen without excuse, and act with courage.

1. Ask with Intent

To ask with intent is the essential act whereby we become principle-centered. It is to ask our conscience, not out of curiosity, but out of commitment to act based on the wisdom of the heart.

Asking with intent reaffirms the humility of principles, the acknowledgment that there are principles and that they are in control. It affirms our human endowments—that we have self-awareness to realize that we need to ask, conscience to direct us to true north, independent will to exercise choice, and creative imagination to carry it out in the most effective way. It implies teachability, courage, and confidence. It's the manifestation that our desire to do the right thing is greater than our desire to just do something.

Acting with integrity in the moment of choice begins with asking—much as we ask when we create a personal mission statement or set goals during weekly organizing. As we face the challenges of the day, we need to create a key question that will draw us immediately into the focus of listening to and living by conscience. Because this is such a deeply personal experience, we've concluded that people are more empowered when they use words that most effectively communicate in their own language. Questions some people have asked that have meaning to them include:

> "What's the best use of my time right now?"
> "What's most important right now?"
> "What is life asking of me?"
> "What's the right thing to do now?"

However the question is worded, it needs to be a question of the heart. In addition, there are other questions we can effectively ask in moments of choice.

> Is this in my Circle of Influence?
> Is it in my Center of Focus?

Is there a third-alternative solution?
What principles apply?
What is the best way to apply them?

Let's take one of the situations we introduced at the beginning of this chapter to show how these questions might help us to act in a principle-centered way.

Suppose that an employee opens up and begins to share deeply just a few minutes before you're scheduled to be at an important meeting. A typical reaction would be one of frustration and anxiety, a feeling of being caught in a dilemma, being pulled in different directions. There could be fear of losing face with authority figures at the meeting if you aren't there. The knee-jerk reaction might be to look at your watch and say, "I'm really sorry, but I have to go to a meeting," and to send the employee to personnel with a quick brush-off.

But what would be the cost of that decision in terms of the loyalty and creativity of that employee? In terms of others to whom that employee might talk about his experience? In terms of your own Personal Integrity Account?

Suppose you were to take a deep breath and pause.

What's most important right now?

You're not sure. People are more important than schedules, but this particular scheduled event involves other people as well.

Is this in my Circle of Influence?

Both situations are in your Circle of Influence, both tie to your mission and purposes.

What principles apply?

It may be as you consider the situation that particular principles come to your mind—be honest and open. Involve people in the problem and work out solutions together. You may feel to say to the employee, "I appreciate your willingness to share your deep concerns with me. This is so important that I want to have time to really talk it over with you and help you find solutions. I have a concern because I've made a commitment to some other people to meet with them right now, but I should be through by 3:00. How would you feel about meeting together at that time and seeing what we can come up with?"

Or you may have a different experience. The principle that comes to mind may be the value of the one. You may ask the employee to wait a minute while you request that your secretary walk down to the meeting and explain that something important has come up and you will be a half hour late. You may have her ask that your agenda items be shifted to the end of the meeting, or you may call an associate and ask him or her to represent you at the meeting.

Or you may have yet another experience altogether if, in the pause, you realize that the concerns of this employee are not in your direct area of responsibility. You may feel to walk the employee over to the Human Resources director's office, where his or her needs can be more directly addressed.

The point is that instead of reacting based on your own needs and what you feel are time pressures, you're pausing to think about principles and connect with conscience in a way that empowers you to put first things first in the moment of choice.

It's important as you ask to realize that wisdom is a marriage—a synergy—of heart and mind. Many times what our conscience tells us to do will seem familiar or "common sense." It's something we've read about, thought about, or experienced, so it's part of our rational framework. In these cases, conscience pinpoints or highlights the appropriate application of the knowledge.

At other times, the wisdom of the heart transcends the wisdom of the mind. We may have no direct knowledge or experience in doing what we feel we should do, but somehow, we know it's right. We know it will work. As we learn to listen to and live by our conscience, many of the things it teaches us are transferred through our own experience into our rational framework of knowledge. We learn to reason things out in our minds, but not to get lost in reason. Wisdom is learning all we can, but having the humility to realize that we don't know it all. That's why it's so fundamental to integrity in the moment that we ask with intent.

2. Listen without Excuse

When we hear the first whispering of conscience, we do one of two things—we either act in harmony with it, or we immediately begin to rationalize—tell ourselves "rational lies"—as to why we should make some other choice.

If we choose the first option, we feel peaceful. We create greater alignment with true north. We grow in our ability to recognize that inner voice and in our personal effectiveness.

If we choose the second option, we feel disharmony and tension.

We begin to justify our decision, often on the basis of external factors such as other people or circumstance. We typically begin blaming and accusing others. They may sense our incongruence and respond in kind, creating a negative synergy called collusion, where we're each acting in ways that invoke in others the very negative behavior that becomes the excuse for our own.

Suppose, for example, that you come home, tired after a hard day's work. You're ready to relax and you're looking forward to spending a quiet evening watching a video you rented on the way home. But at dinner, you sense that your teenage son is having some kind of inner struggle and you feel a little twinge inside telling you that the best use of your time is to rearrange your plans and create some quality together time tonight.

Bottom-line, you don't want to do it. You don't consciously admit that to yourself. You really love your son. You want the best for him. But you're so tired. And you've been looking forward to this video and time to relax. After all, you deserve it. You've been working all day to put food on the table for him. You've spent ten hours commuting, dealing with inter-office rivalry and politics, grappling with tough issues and intense interpersonal challenges, slaving over budgets and reports, laboring with irate customers and frustrated suppliers—all so that he could have some of the finer things in life. And all you want is two hours to yourself—just two hours to watch the video you've put off seeing for months because you were so busy.

So you go for a quick fix at the dinner table.

"Hey, you doin' all right?"

He looks up to see if you're serious. You're not. *"Yeah, I'm okay."*

"So, school okay? Homework? Dates?"

"Yeah, everything's fine."

"You working hard on your grades? Scholarship's important, you know."

"Yeah, I know." He gets up from the table and grabs his sweater from the back of the chair.

"Goin' out?"

"Yeah."

"Where?"

"Just around."

"When'll you be back?"

"Later."

"You've got school tomorrow. Be home by 10:30. Okay?"

"Okay."

As he's on his way out the door, you call after him, *"Hey, you know if you've got a problem I'm here for you."*

"Yeah, I know," he calls back.

"So you wanna talk?"

"Naw, I gotta go."

"You ever gonna talk anymore? All I ever get's one-word answers. It's impossible to communicate with you."

"Yeah," he mutters under his breath. *"You're not so easy to get along with yourself!"*

"You'd think teenagers could open their mouths and say something intelligent just once in a while!"

As the screen door slams behind him, you make your way to the easy chair, muttering about teenagers and lack of communication and how hard it is to be a parent these days. You tried! He's just a close-mouthed zombie. He resists any effort to communicate.

Well, teenagers are weird anyway. Right? So, validated in your own mind, you settle down to start your video. And within a few minutes, the lingering discomfort inside you is temporarily drowned out by the VCR.

Meanwhile, your son is struggling even more. He's feeling blamed and accused for the failure to communicate. His problems are compounded. He feels worse than ever and he has no one to talk to about it.

Over time, the cost of withdrawals such as this is enormous. Brick by brick, walls of justification and rationalization begin to surround your heart. Your son builds walls around his own heart to protect his tender feelings and deep needs. Communication becomes superficial, strained, quickly escalating to blaming and accusing in the effort to validate behavior. You live in a complex web of discomfort and pain created by the consequences of not listening to and acting in harmony with that first whisper of conscience.

We exhaust ourselves far more from the tension and the consequences of internal disharmony—not doing what we feel we should—than from hard, unremitting work. And when we seek to escape the tension by filling our lives with Quadrant III activities we've tried to convince ourselves are important or by running to Quadrant IV, we only increase the tension. In fact, many of what we call "time management" frustrations—feeling hassled, pressured, caught in dilemmas—are, at the core, problems of inner dissonance.

Even in the tension of the moment, it seems so much easier to live with the questions than with the answers. As long as we have questions, as long as we're in doubt, as long as we're struggling, we're not responsible to do anything; we're not accountable for results. So we spend days, weeks, months, years wallowing in the mass of rational lies we've created to avoid the simple actions that would put us in harmony with the laws that govern quality of life.

The key to acting with integrity is to simply stop playing the game. Learn to listen—as well as to conscience, to our own response. The instant we feel ourselves saying, "Yes, *but*" change it to, "Yes, *and*." No rationalizing. No justifying. Just do it. Look at every expression of conscience as an invitation to create greater alignment with the fundamental Laws of Life. Then listen, respond . . . listen, respond.

3. Act with Courage

It's easy to think of "courage" in connection with very dramatic, extraordinary events like carrying a message through enemy lines, living with a terminal illness, or running into a burning house to save a child. But some of the greatest acts of courage are in that instant between stimulus and response in our everyday decisions in life.

It takes tremendous courage to be a transition person, to stop transmitting negative intergenerational tendencies such as abuse, and to choose to act based on principles of human dignity and respect. It takes courage to be self-honest, to examine your deepest motives, and to let go of the excuses and rationalizations that keep you from living true to your best self. It takes courage to live a principle-centered life, knowing that the choices you make may not be popular or understood by others. It takes courage to realize that you are greater than your moods, greater than your thoughts, and that you can control your moods and thoughts.

Rebecca: At one time I made the decision to attend a week-long seminar. I had clear expectations around what I was going to accomplish—particularly regarding some personal Quadrant II goals I planned to work on between and after seminar sessions.

But I ran into a conflict the very first day of the seminar when I was asked to coordinate some activities for the seminar participants during the event. At the deepest level, to contribute to the success of others at this conference by fulfilling that responsibility was in harmony with my values and principles. The more I thought about it, the more I realized it was something I felt I really should do. But I also felt very frustrated because I knew the experience would be so different from what I had planned and anticipated.

I accepted the responsibility . . . but I found myself under a lot of pressure and anxiety, running from one thing to another, trying to meet everyone's needs, and feeling more than a little frustrated that I didn't have time to do the things I'd planned to do.

In the midst of these negative feelings, I remember one particular moment when I stopped and said, "Wait a minute! I don't have to live with this frustration. I've made the choice to do what I really felt I ought to do, but that doesn't mean I have to suffer all this anxiety and tension. I can choose differently."

I took a deep breath and decided to choose my own response to the situation. I made the determination to just let go of all the anxiety, the concern about extrinsic pressure, the worry about what wasn't getting done. In my mind, I kept saying the words, "I choose differently! I choose differently!"

As I stood there, I felt all the negative anxiety and frustration leave. In their place, I felt a quiet determination to face my challenges with courage, to do what I could about those things I felt I ought to do something about, and to mentally let go of the rest.

This was not a one-time decision. I had to revisit it several times during the week as I began to feel the pressures and the anxiety creeping back—it was so easy to get sucked into it! But I just stopped each time and said, "I choose differently!" And the more I did it, the more empowered I felt.

For a while, I almost thought it was presumptuous to call these little acts "courageous." But the more I thought about it, the more I realized that it really does take courage to just do what we feel we ought to do in the moment of choice—and to let go of all the reasons, the rationalizations, the justifications, the "if only" thinking that threatens to overpower the peace of that decision.

In looking back, I know that if I had refused that assignment, I would have felt ill at ease and duplicitous all week. As it turned out, the experience was much more satisfying, more powerful, more renewing than I had ever thought it would be.

"That which we persist in doing becomes easier to do," said Emerson, "not that the nature of the thing has changed, but that our ability to do has increased."[2] As we learn to ask with intent, listen without excuse, and act with courage, we build our ability to live a principle-centered life.

Over time, listening to and living by conscience becomes the fundamental habit of the heart. Instead of living with rationalization, fear, guilt, or frustration, we live with the peaceful inner assurance that we're putting first things first on a day-by-day, moment-by-moment basis. Genuine guilt (not social, scripted guilt) becomes our teacher, our friend. Like a homing device that signals when an airplane gets off course, it warns us when our lives are out of alignment with the true north principles that create quality of life. Mistakes also become our teachers. Life becomes an upward spiral of growth as we learn more and more of true north.

EDUCATING THE HEART

Educating the heart is the critical complement to educating the mind. In the words of American educator John Sloan Dickey:

> The end of education is to see men made whole, both in competence and in conscience. For to create the power of competence without creating a corresponding direction to guide the use of that power is bad education. Furthermore, competence will finally disintegrate apart from conscience.[3]

Educating the heart is the process of nurturing inner wisdom. It's learning how to use all four endowments synergistically to act with integrity in the moment of choice.

The Quadrant II process helps nurture this inner wisdom in several important ways:

- One of the highest uses of the space between stimulus and response is creating a personal mission statement. This statement becomes the DNA for every other decision we make.
- Weekly organizing gives us the opportunity to connect the big picture to the reality of the moment with a perspective that keeps the "importance" focus in moments of choice.
- End-of-the-week evaluation helps us see time as a cycle of learning and growth rather than as linear chronos measurement. It empowers us to learn from living, to increase the quality of the decisions we make.
- Sharpening the saw increases the quality of our decisions by providing renewal in all four human dimensions, as discussed below.

The Physical Dimension

Studies repeatedly show the powerful negative effects of fatigue and illness on effective decision making. As Vince Lombardi said, "Fatigue makes cowards of us all."[4] When we're tired or ill, we often tend to be more reactive. In addition, the abuse of chemical substances such as drugs and alcohol can severely diminish the space between stimulus and response.

Sharpening the saw physically—exercising, eating the right foods, getting adequate rest, avoiding harmful substances, having regular physical checkups—significantly increases the likelihood that we'll make good choices in decision moments. It also increases our options, as good health becomes a resource from which we can do so much more. Our body is a fundamental stewardship; it's the instrument through which we work to fulfill all other stewardships and responsibilities.

The Mental Dimension

Quality mental renewal gives us added knowledge and perspective in decision-making moments. Consider the value of something like Stephen's bicentennial review of two hundred years of American success literature.[5] The literature at the time of the review and for the previous fifty years was essentially a reflection of the Personality Ethic—the quick-fix, superficial social-image focus that portrayed "success" as a matter of personality and technique. That literature created an illusory paradigm of success that could never empower people to create long-term quality-of-life results.

But transcending that limited paradigm, we can see that before the Personality Ethic literature were one hundred and fifty years of literature based on the Character Ethic, which said that the most fundamental ingredients to success were such things as honesty, integrity, humility, fidelity, justice, patience, and courage. This Character Ethic literature echoed the wisdom of thousands of years in other civilizations that also acknowledged these true north principles of success. Interestingly, one of the often repeated themes of the time management literature is that "time is life." Yet this literature is filled with techniques, and the idea of character is starkly missing.

As we study civilizations throughout time, we see the consequences in the lives of individuals and societies that lived by these true north principles . . . and those that didn't. We're back to the video of the orange again—the close-up focus creates confusion, disorientation; but as we draw back, the normal lens empowers us to see things "in perspective." And that perspective—that awareness of influences in our environment that pull us away from true north—makes a tremendous difference in the way we make moment-by-moment decisions about the way we spend our time.

- Do I go for the quick-fix solution so I can get more things done now . . . or do I take the time to invest in this relationship and accomplish more important things in the long run?
- Do I try to feed my social need with the cotton-candy satisfaction of confessing my boss's weaknesses to other employees in the hall . . . or do I nurture quality relationships by being loyal to those not present and talking over differences face-to-face?
- Do I automatically say "Yes!" when my boss asks me to work over the weekend . . . or do I look for third-alternative solutions that will meet her need, and mine too?
- Do I push doggedly ahead and work on the independent project I had planned . . . or do I recognize an opportunity to improve the quality of life for someone else and myself as well by helping solve a problem?

Meaningful mental renewal empowers us to transcend the limited wisdom of our environment in decision moments and keeps our minds sharp and clear and well exercised for ready use.

The Spiritual Dimension

Renewal in the spiritual dimension cultivates a sense of meaning and overriding purpose that powerfully impacts our daily decisions. One of the most essential elements of the wisdom literature is the idea that an individual's life is part of a greater whole. And whether people see this greater whole in terms of life after death, recurring cycles of life, or intergenerational legacy, this bigger picture orientation puts the challenges of daily living in a contextual framework of meaning.

As psychologist David Meyers points out in his book *The Pursuit of Happiness*, study after study shows that those who have this bigger picture orientation in their lives are happier, more satisfied, contributing people. He points out that, contrary to popular belief, some form of religious faith or meaning-of-life convictions are characteristic of happy people, and that people involved in religious activity to the point of making financial contributions are by far the biggest contributors to other philanthropic endeavors.

> Religious consciousness, it seems, shapes a larger agenda than advancing one's own private little world. It cultivates the idea that my talents and wealth are unearned gifts of which I am a steward.[6]

But Meyers also notes that many people surveyed in the United States who do not necessarily consider themselves "religious" nevertheless spend considerable time searching for and contemplating the meaning of life. As people see the consequences of living with the illusion of a self-focused, consumer-oriented, materialistic chronos paradigm, many begin to look at their lives more closely and search for ways to contribute that will change the results.

Renewing activities in the spiritual dimension—meditation, prayer, formal religious activity, altruistic service, studying the wisdom and sacred literature, memorizing and reviewing a personal mission statement—nurture the big picture context and the contribution focus of true north. This renewal plays a vital role in the education of the heart. It's the basis for deciding what "first things" are. It gives us the passion and the power to subordinate the less important to the most important. It empowers us to transcend the powerful influences of urgency, expediency, and instant gratification in the moment of choice.

The Social Dimension

As we move into Section Three, the Synergy of Interdependence, we'll take a closer look at the social dimension. But the vital connection we need to make at this point is how our relationship with ourselves affects our relationships with others, and how this can be important to our education of the heart.

Rebecca: I remember an event years ago that brought me to a startling awareness of the effects of violating conscience. At the time, I was a would-be writer as well as a young mother—very busy with preschool-age children and struggling with some health problems and other concerns. I walked into a bookstore one day, and there on the bookshelf was a recently published book written by a woman I had known and had considered a good friend several years before.

My feelings moved rapidly from surprise to disbelief. How in the world could she have written a book? She had a busy public life as well as a home and family to take care of. Where did she get the time to do something like that?

The longer I stared at the book, the more I found myself beginning to rationalize, to justify. "She probably hires a baby-sitter to take care of the children. They must be rolling in money. They probably eat out every night so she doesn't have to fix dinner. And she has so much energy—she's probably never been sick a day in her life. There's no way she could have written that book if she had to handle the challenges I have."

As my thoughts ran on, I began to think of other things I never had time for. Suddenly, every book on that shelf seemed to jump out and yell, "Why haven't you read me?" It wasn't long before I felt like a hopeless, incompetent, victimized, frustrated mess. I felt almost angry at my "perfect" friend and with the people and circumstances I thought were responsible for my own situation.

I went out to the car and sat there for a few minutes just thinking. The experience was shocking to me because my reaction seemed so out of character. I usually found deep joy in the successes and accomplishments of others.

Somewhere deep inside I knew my response was way out of proportion. I knew there had to be some underlying reason for the way I felt, so I decided to sort it all out. I tried to just let go of all the negative, blaming, angry reactions and look honestly into my own heart.

I had one of those wonderful, painful flashes of light that suddenly let you see everything for what it is. I wasn't really angry with my friend. She simply had some things in her life that I didn't . . . some things I knew I needed to have. I was seeing her accomplishments as a mirror of my own weaknesses. And, seeing myself in that mirror, I lashed out at the reflection.

I knew she was a great mother. Mothering was a challenge for me, and I was seeing her tremendous patience and positive attitude as a foil to what I felt was my own incompetence. She managed her time to do meaningful and creative things outside the home. I knew I had a talent for writing too, but I simply had not been efficient enough in my other responsibilities to find the time to develop that talent.

I was assuming financial ease on her part because I felt restricted by a weakness in money management. Some wrong decisions earlier in our marriage had put us in debt. I felt that bondage kept me from doing a lot of things I wanted to do in life.

My friend was healthy, but that wasn't the problem. The problem was that I knew I ought to exercise on a regular basis . . . and I didn't do it.

If I had been doing the things in my own life I knew I ought to be doing, I never would have had those feelings in the first place. My friend's success would have been the joy it should have been to me.

I knew I couldn't snap my fingers and suddenly change all those things in my life. But, at least, I knew the root of the problem was the fact that I wasn't putting first things first in my own life. And that was something I could do something about.

"People seem not to see," said Emerson, "that their opinion of the world is also a confession of character."[7] One of the best ways to educate our heart is to look at our interaction with other people, because our relationships with others are fundamentally a reflection of our relationship with ourselves.

When we don't listen to or live by our conscience, we tend to blame and accuse other people in an attempt to justify our own inner dissonance. If we don't have a sense of mission and principles to measure ourselves against, we benchmark against other people instead of our own potential. We're into comparative thinking and win-lose mentality. We become self-centered and autobiographical. We impose our motives on the actions of others. We see their strengths and weaknesses in terms of how they affect us. We empower their weaknesses to control us.

When we have a family, a work group, an organization, a society that's into blaming and accusing and confessing each other's sins, we have a fairly good indication that people are not living in harmony with their own inner imperatives. For the most part, they're caught up in a rescue fantasy. The problem is "out there" and somebody out there is going to come along and solve it.

As it says in Proverbs, "Keep thy heart with all diligence; for out of it are the issues of life."[8] As we move into the material on the interdependent reality, the most important thing we can take with us is a vivid awareness of the impact of our own integrity on our interactions with others.

THE RESULTS OF LIVING BY CONSCIENCE

People who listen to and live by their conscience do not have the cotton-candy satisfaction of urgency addiction, pleasing other people, or getting their security from being incredibly busy every minute of the day. They do, however, experience deep fulfillment—even in the midst of difficulties and challenges—and they go to bed at night with the confidence that they've done the most important things they could have done that day. They experience a deep level of inner peace and quality of life. They do not waste time rationalizing, fighting themselves, blaming and accusing other people or extrinsic conditions for their own situation. They have an almost sacred sense of stewardship about their roles—a sense of being "response-able" to contribute to quality of life for others in meaningful ways. They're strong in hard moments. They have a high balance in their Personal Integrity Account.

The amazing thing is that, with all the negative consequences of violating conscience, we sometimes make that choice.

Stephen: Recently, as I was getting into a cab in a major Canadian city, the bellman told the cab driver, "Dr. Covey wants to go to the airport." So the cab driver thought I was an M.D., and he started telling me all about his medical problems. I tried to explain to him that I was not that kind of doctor, but his English was limited and he didn't understand me. So I just listened.

The more he described his problems, the more convinced I became that the problems he was describing were basically a function of his lack of integrity. He was leading a life of duplicity—lying and cheating. His biggest worry was being caught by the police. It was affecting his health. I was sitting there in the back seat without a seat belt and he was talking about seeing double as he drove down the highway.

Even as we pulled up to the airport, he said (and I'm paraphrasing his broken English), "I'm gonna be looking for another fare. And I'm not gonna follow their rules and wait for two hours. I know how to get those fares." Then his expression sobered. "But if the policemen find me, I will get in trouble. I will lose my license. What do you think, Doctor?"

Finally, I said to him, "Don't you think that the main source of all these tensions and pressures is that you're not being true to your conscience? You inwardly know what you should do."

"But I can't make a living that way!"

"Where's your faith? Put your faith in the principles of integrity. You'll get peace of mind and wisdom will come to you."

Something seemed to touch him profoundly. He became open and teachable. "Do you think it would?"

"I absolutely know it would. But you've got to make the commitment in your heart. See yourself living by the fundamental Laws of Life that are basic to all civilizations. Don't cheat. Don't lie. Don't steal. Treat people with respect."

"You really think it would help?"

"I know it would."

In the end, he didn't want to take a tip. He just embraced me. "I'm gonna do that. I already feel better!"

People know it. In their deep inner lives, they know what they ought to be doing. And they know it would improve quality of life. The challenge is to develop the character and competence to listen to it and live by it—to act with integrity in the moment of choice.

QUADRANT II GOALS TO CULTIVATE INTEGRITY IN THE MOMENT OF CHOICE

- When you set your goals for the week, really pause and connect with conscience. Observe your own involvement in the process. Think about how it feels to connect when you're not in the pressure of the moment. Work to translate that experience into the decision moments of each day.
- Create a specific question to ask yourself in moments of choice. Review it at the beginning of the day and several times throughout the day so that it's constantly before you. Work toward building the habit of pausing to ask that question in the space between stimulus and response.
- At the beginning of each day, think about your Personal Integrity Account. Jot down deposits and withdrawals as you interact with conscience during the day.
- Think about the three-part process:

  Ask with intent
  Listen without excuse
  Act with courage

  Set a goal to go through the process each time you face a decision moment.
- Be aware of how you typically respond in moments of choice. Keep track of the times during the day that you pause and connect with conscience—and the result.
- In at least one decision moment each day, stop and analyze the factors that are acting upon you, such as urgency, the priorities of others, fatigue, expectations (yours and others'), and scripting. Write them down, then jot beside them some indication of their importance. Notice if you feel your response to these factors changing as you take time to become aware of and think about them.
- Evaluate your experience. One of the most effective ways to build integrity in the moment of choice is to learn from your interaction with conscience. This is a process, a becoming—something you can practice. In the following chapter, we'll give specific ideas about how you can evaluate what's happening in your life as part of the Quadrant II organizing process.

10: *Learning from Living*

As long as you live, keep learning how to live.[1]

—*Seneca*

Roger: In consulting with a large corporation several years ago, I had the opportunity to work and become friends with a psychologist who was raised in New York. As we frequently presented to the same group on the same day, I often heard him tell the story of how he and his professional peers would work with rats in mazes. They put the rat at one end of the maze and a piece of food at the other end, and watched the rat as he bumped around until he eventually found the food. The next time they put him in, he bumped a little less and got to the food a little faster. After a while, he got to where he would zip through the maze and have that tidbit in his teeth within a few seconds.

Then they took the food away. For a little while, each time he was put in, the rat kept making a beeline for the end of the maze. But it wasn't too long before he figured out the food wasn't going to be there and so he stopped going.

"That's the difference between rats and people," my friend would say. "The rats stop!"

Although his comments were made in fun, the point this psychologist made was very real. We often get into ruts, on treadmills, caught up in patterns and habits that aren't useful. We keep doing the same things in our lives week-in, week-out—fighting the same alligators, struggling with the same weaknesses, repeating the same mistakes. We don't really learn from our lives. We don't stop to ask: What can I learn from this week that will keep next week from essentially being a repeat of the same?

EVALUATION: CLOSING THE LOOP

The value of any week is not limited to what we do in it; it's also in what we learn from it and become as a result of it. For this reason, no week's experience would be complete without some kind of evaluation that enables us to process it.

Evaluation is the final step—and the first step—in a living and learning cycle that creates an upward spiral of growth. It takes us back to the beginning of the process again, but with greater capacity. As we learn from living, we're better prepared to review our mission and roles, set goals, create a framework for a new week and act with greater integrity in the moment of choice. As we organize, act, evaluate . . . organize, act, evaluate . . . and organize, act, and evaluate again, our weeks become repeating cycles of learning and growth.

© 1994 Covey Leadership Center, Inc.

"Be observant if you would have a pure heart," said one unknown writer, "for something is born to you in consequence of every action."

"What I like about experience," wrote C. S. Lewis, "is that it is such an honest thing. . . . You may have deceived yourself, but experience is not trying to deceive you. The universe rings true wherever you fairly test it."[2]

This living and learning cycle is in the spirit of *kaizen*—the Japanese word for the spirit of continuous improvement. It's in direct contrast to the Western mentality of "If it ain't broke, don't fix it!" It's following Seneca's advice: "As long as you live, keep learning how to live." It's applying Peter Senge's Fifth Discipline of effective, learning organizations on a personal basis:

Real learning gets to the heart of what it means to be human. Through learning we re-create ourselves. Through learning we become able to do something we never were able to do. Through learning we extend our capacity to create, to be part of the generative process of life. There is within each of us a deep hunger for this type of learning.[3]

Recognition of the importance of the evaluation process is reflected in what's often called the Growth Cycle or the Evaluation Cycle, variations of which are used in the Total Quality Movement and other processes focused on improvement and growth. Through weekly evaluation on a personal basis, we increase self-awareness, educate our conscience, and build effective habits of the heart.

HOW TO EVALUATE YOUR WEEK

Evaluation can be done in a personal journal or on the back page of the weekly worksheet as you wrap up one week and prepare for the next. You may find it helpful to create a checklist of questions to carry with you in your organizer and go through them each week before you begin the Quadrant II organizing process for the following week. You probably won't want to use more than five or six questions. You may want to select some from the following list:

- Which goals did I achieve?
- What empowered me to accomplish these goals?
- What challenges did I encounter?
- How did I overcome them?
- Was accomplishing these goals the best use of my time?
- Did my focus on these goals blind me to unexpected opportunities for better use of my time?
- Did meeting these goals add to my Personal Integrity Account?
- Which goals did I not achieve?
- What kept me from accomplishing these goals?
- As a result of the choices I made, did I use my time in better ways than I had planned?
- Did my choices make deposits or withdrawals from my Personal Integrity Account?
- What unmet goals should I carry into the coming week?
- Did I take time for renewal, reflection, and recommitment?
- Did I take time to sharpen the saw on a daily basis?

- How did the time spent in renewal impact other areas?
- In what ways was I able to create synergy between roles and goals?
- How was I able to apply character and competence gained in one role to other roles?
- What principles did I apply or fail to apply during the week? What was the effect?
- How much of my time was spent in Quadrant II? Quadrant I? Quadrant III? Quadrant IV?
- What can I learn from the week as a whole?

As you go through your questions, it's important to use your compass—to be deeply honest and self-aware, to connect with conscience, to use independent will and creative imagination to consider possibilities and commit to positive change.

THE WEEK AS PART OF A GREATER WHOLE

It's also helpful to see each week as it connects to every other week. You may want to do a monthly or quarterly evaluation and ask questions such as these:

- What patterns of success or failure do I see in setting and achieving goals?
- Am I setting goals that are realistic but challenging?
- What keeps getting in the way of accomplishing my goals?
- What patterns or processes can be improved?
- Am I creating unrealistic expectations? How can I modify them?

Rebecca: At one point some years ago, I felt a deep need to have some personal renewal time. Roger arranged to be home with the children for a few days and I went alone to an inn where I spent hours reading through my personal journals. It was a very enlightening experience. I was able to revisit many moments of living with an increased perspective that gave me deeper understanding. But the most helpful insight came as I was able to see repeating patterns in my life that it was impossible for me to see from day to day. In the overview, I found the personal direction I needed and I came home refreshed and much more connected to what was really important in my life.

I've found that regular personal evaluation and renewal time is a vital part of learning from living. It's a time to review my mission statement, to think about important relationships in my life, and to set context goals in each of my roles. And Roger and I have found that doing it as a couple provides the same sense of renewal in our marriage. When we take time to be together alone on a regular basis, to review our shared mission statement, to set goals as marriage partners and parents, it really improves the quality of our lives, our relationship, and our family.

The repeated process of organizing, acting, and evaluating helps us see the consequences of our choices and actions more clearly. It's the four endowments in action. It empowers us to learn from living and to live what we learn.

THE POWER OF THE PROCESS

As you think back over these last six chapters, can you begin to see why we said that the real power of the process would only be apparent as you became deeply involved in the foundations of it? If you're like many people, your initial experience with the Quadrant II organizing process may well have been essentially a third-generation experience. But as you go back to the process now with deeper understanding, you'll find yourself beginning to have more of a fourth-generation experience. You'll be able to go through each step of the process each week with greater depth of meaning and more powerful results.

Consider how deeply understanding and following these six steps can empower you to put first things first in your life:

- ***Connect to mission*** empowers you to access the deep burning "yes!" created by the awareness of first things in your life, the "yes!" that generates passion and energy and makes it possible for you to say "no"—with confidence and peace—to the less important.
- ***Review your roles*** enables you to reconnect with the avenues through which you can do first things in a balanced, synergistic way.
- ***Identify your goals*** empowers you to focus effectively on the most important thing you can do in each role each week to accomplish your mission. It enables you to set principle-based goals that will create quality-of-life results.

- *Organize the week* enables you to put the "big rocks"—your important Quadrant II goals—in first, and to schedule other things around them.
- *Exercise integrity* in the moment empowers you to pause in the space between stimulus and response and act with integrity to first things in any moment of choice in your life.
- *Evaluate* empowers you to turn your weeks into an upward spiral of learning and living.

The shift is from doing more things in less time to doing first things in an effective, balanced, and synergistic way. It's a holistic, integrated, and aligned approach to living, loving, learning, and leaving a legacy.

But, as far as we've come, there's an even richer experience ahead. It has to do with the synergy of interdependence—with the full reality of our connectedness with others. As we move into the next section, we'll be looking at time and quality of life where we experience it most often and most profoundly.

Section Three

THE SYNERGY OF INTERDEPENDENCE

As we move into the interdependent reality, we'd like to ask you to stop and think how powerfully your relationships with other people affect your time and the quality of your life.

- How much time do you spend in unnecessary Quadrant I crises because of miscommunication, misunderstanding, or lack of clarity around roles and goals in interdependent effort?
- How much time do you spend in Quadrant III scrambling to meet the real or perceived agendas of others that often turn out to be not really important at all?
- How much time in your family or organization is wasted in miscommunication, misunderstanding, politicking, backbiting, blaming, accusing, or confessing each other's sins?
- How much of the potential that could have significant impact on time and quality of life—the talent, creativity, and enthusiasm of others you live and work with—remains untapped?

For most people, the large majority of waking time is spent communicating or interacting with other people—or dealing with the results of poor communication or interaction. Effective interdependence is core to the issue of time management. But the traditional literature essentially ignores it or deals with it in a *transactional* way. This transactional approach grows out of the mechanical, controlling, managing "things" paradigm. People are essentially seen as bionic units to whom we can delegate to get more done, or as interruptions to be handled efficiently so that we can get back to our schedule.

But fourth-generation interdependence is not *transactional*; it's *transformational*. It literally changes those who are party to it. It takes into consideration the full reality of the uniqueness and capacity of each individual and the rich, serendipitous potential of creating synergistic third alternatives that are far better than individuals could ever come up with on their own. Fourth-generation interdependence is the richness of relationships, the adventure of discovery, the spontaneity and deep fulfillment of putting people ahead of schedules, and the joy of creating together what did not exist before. It's the ultimate "moving of the fulcrum"—the exponential increase of creativity, capacity, and production that comes from combining the energy and talents of many in synergistic ways.

In this section, we'll take an in-depth look at the interdependent nature of life and see how our character and competence affect our ability to work with people in every dimension. We'll talk about how to create synergy with others through Quadrant II activities such as creating shared vision and empowering stewardship agreements. We'll show you how to create a common compass that will empower you to form complementary teams that leverage your strengths and make your weaknesses irrelevant. Finally, we'll deal with empowerment—the ultimate Quadrant II preparation/prevention tool. You'll see how creating empowerment from the inside out can increase your capacity and influence everyone around you—families, friends, associates—toward higher performance and greater achievement.

If your lifestyle is essentially independent, or for some other reason you prefer not to enter this level of complexity, feel free to move ahead to Section Four. But we encourage you to explore this vital area which is virtually ignored by traditional time management. You'll be surprised to discover how powerfully the problems and the potential of interdependence affect your time and the quality of your life.

11: *The Interdependent Reality*

Interdependence is and ought to be as much the ideal of man as self-sufficiency. Man is a social being.

—Gandhi [1]

AS we move into the interdependent reality, we'd like to ask you to think about what you've decided are "first things" in your life. How many of these things involve relationships with other people?

It's our experience that, almost without exception, everything people identify as really important has to do with others. Even those who list something such as "health" or "economic security" generally do so because they want to have the resources to enjoy life with their family and friends. Our greatest joy—and our greatest pain—comes in our relationships with others.

The fact is that quality of life is, by nature, interdependent.

Our roles are interdependent—we're husbands, wives, parents, friends, bosses, employees, co-workers, friends, associates, community members, citizens. Quality in almost every role involves a relationship with at least one other individual.

Our accomplishments are interdependent. Although we look back in history and tend to say that one particular person "invented" or "discovered" a particular thing, the reality is that most great achievements were not made in a vacuum. The individual who receives the credit usually stands on the shoulders of many who went before, clearing the path, leading the way, finding the things that didn't work so that eventually someone could find the one thing that would work.

Even the fulfillment of our fundamental needs and capacities is interdependent.

To live is to have physical health and economic security. Where would we be without doctors, hospitals, penicillin, and health insurance? We get our paycheck because what we do in some way affects the lives of others. We spend our paycheck on things that represent the labors of others.

To love is, by definition, interdependent. "Love isn't love till you give it away." It involves relationships with others and belonging, and it's based on one of the major themes of all wisdom literature—reciprocity, or the Golden Rule.

To learn is to grow, to feel ourselves expanding. How often does learning come as we read books written by others, attend seminars given by others, sit in classes taught by others? How many times do we get insights as we interact in group situations with other people? How many of our "own" ideas grow out of the ideas of others?

To leave a legacy is also, by definition, interdependent. It's contributing to society, contributing in meaningful ways to the lives of others. The world we live in is the legacy of those who have gone before us. The choices we make in it create a legacy for those who will follow.

The fact is that we're better together than we are alone. Humility comes as we realize that "no man is an island," that no one individual has all the talents, all the ideas, all the capacity to perform the functions of the whole. Vital to quality of life is the ability to work together, learn from each other, and help each other grow.

THE INDEPENDENT PARADIGM

Despite the obvious interdependent reality of quality of life, we tend to see "success" in terms of independent achievement. And the time management literature essentially reflects this independent achievement paradigm. In one way or another, most of the literature says "time is life," but the skills and techniques have to do with management of "things." People are seen primarily as resources through which we increase our leverage through delegation, or as interruptions to be handled efficiently so that we can stay on schedule.

There's a place for independence. In the space between stimulus and response, independence is having the strength of character to transcend scripting, the social mirror, and other influences that would keep us from a principle-centered response to life. But, as well as a place, there's a purpose for this independence. It's not an end in itself. True independence precedes and prepares us for effective interdependence. It's the personal trustworthiness that makes trust possible.

There's also a role for independence when we're dealing with "things," and here is where we find great value in the time management literature. It's filled with excellent, high-leverage ideas and techniques for the management of "things."

But people aren't things. When we're dealing with people, we're dealing with living, breathing human beings who have their own space between stimulus and response. They also have human endowments and an incredible capacity to act within that space. And a good percentage of our time is spent interacting in this interdependent reality.

Aside from personal integrity, our greatest problems—and our greatest potential for impacting time and quality-of-life issues—are in the interdependent arena.

THE COST OF THE INDEPENDENT PARADIGM

When we try to satisfy needs and fulfill capacities through an independent achievement, linear, chronos-only paradigm, life sometimes seems like an hour in a huge smorgasbord. There's only so much time, so we have to maximize our satisfaction, sample as much as we can. We rush through the line, grabbing as much variety as possible. We become gluttons of experiences and sensations.

We rush to live. Maintaining a healthy lifestyle takes too much time and effort, so we eat what we want, do what we want, burn the candle at both ends, and depend on the medical profession to pick up the pieces. Economic security becomes maximizing the bottom line, regardless of meaning or means.

We rush to love. We have hit-and-run relationships, often leaving broken bodies and broken lives strewn along the path. We want the benefits of marriage, but we don't make the emotional commitment to live a life of rich interdependence, of selfless service, of sensitivity, of continuous improvement of character to make it grow. We bring children into the world, but we're not committed to the tremendous time and effort it takes to teach and train, to love and listen. We sample a few of the fruits from the relationships closest to us, but there's no time to reach out to others and love on a broader basis.

We rush to learn. There's no time for deep conversation, for interacting with others in meaningful ways. Learning is superficial—we're into skills, methods, and techniques without understanding the principles that empower us to act in a variety of situations.

We rush to leave a token legacy. We send in a few dollars here, a few dollars there, and it gives us a "fix" of contribution for a moment or two, but it isn't lasting. There's no real commitment, no overriding sense of deep purpose and contribution in our lives.

As many social scientists and commentators have pointed out, this fast-paced independent paradigm has created a massive imbalance in our society. In order to get more golden eggs, we're killing the very goose that produces them. We're so busy consuming that we don't take care of our capacity to produce, and we see evidence of it all around us—in the national debt, health care problems, the world economy, the lack of willingness of Wall Street to invest in long-term development.

Father of modern stress research Hans Selye compares the independent achievement focus to "the development of a cancer, whose most characteristic feature is that it cares only for itself. Hence, it feeds on the other parts of its own host until it kills the host—and thus commits biological suicide, since a cancer cell cannot live except within the body in which it started its reckless, egocentric development."[2] To some extent, as a society, we're on a ladder that's leaning against the wrong wall. We're living with the illusion of independence, but the paradigm is not creating the quality-of-life results we desire.

To change the results, we need to change the paradigm.

THE INTERDEPENDENT PARADIGM

As true north teaches us, the reality is that we're part of a vast, highly interrelated living ecology. Quality of life is interdependent. It's a 360-degree, totally integrated view, as illustrated in the diagram on the following page.

At the center is the personal dimension. Each of us is an individual. We have unique human endowments and some degree of character and competence in using those endowments to fulfill our fundamental needs and capacities. As individuals, we enter into relationships with other individuals. This is the interpersonal dimension. In our relationships, we work with others to accomplish tasks, represented by the managerial dimension. We align systems and coordinate work for collective purposes, which is the organizational dimension. All of these dimensions are in the context of and affect the society in which we live.

Let's look at some of the implications of this interdependent reality.

© 1994 Covey Leadership Center, Inc.

1. All Public Behavior Is Ultimately Private Behavior

The problems we see in families, organizations, and societies are the result of individuals making choices in their space between stimulus and response. When those choices come out of reactivity, scripting, or urgency response, it impacts time and quality of life for families, organizations, and society as a whole.

Look at a marriage, for example. If marriage partners haven't paid the price in their deep inner lives, things may begin wonderfully, but when the hard issues come up—child discipline, finances, in-laws—they won't have the character and competence to interact in synergistic, positive ways. They fall back on their scripting—which may be very different—and if they aren't principle-centered, this difference can lead to positioning and polarization, eventually even bitterness and alienation.

On the other hand, if marriage partners are principle-centered, they tend to value differences and work together to understand their scripting and true north principles. They seek synergistic third-alternative solutions to meet their challenges. They see each other's weaknesses as opportunities to help. They're less concerned about *who* is right than *what* is right. They see their family as the fundamental unit of society and realize that one of the most important ways they can contribute to society is to create a strong home and raise their children to be responsible members of society. They also support and help each other in other ways to contribute to society as a whole.

The same thing is true in organizations. One of the reasons we have difficulty with total quality initiatives and empowerment programs is that many of the people who try to create these things in organizations haven't paid the price to work things out in their own deep inner lives. Often, they've been scripted toward independence and competition through love given conditionally when they were a child, the normal distribution curve of academics, the win-lose paradigm of athletics, or a forced ranking system on the job. They may be very sincere in their effort, but they can't sustain action outside their deep paradigms.

The late W. Edwards Deming, considered by many to be the leading voice of the Total Quality Movement, said that the majority of the problems in organizations are with systems, not people.[3] But people create systems. If people are scripted in competitive, scarcity mentality, independent, chronos-only paradigms, and if they aren't aligned with true north, the results in organizations and society will reflect it. Total quality and empowerment take on dimensions of the "flavor of the month" instead of creating deep, sustained quality change, and people become cynical about the effort.

Total quality begins with total personal quality. Organizational empowerment begins with individual empowerment. That's why work in our deep inner life and integrity are so important.

Stephen: Recently in a large group a man said to me, "Stephen, how do we get principle-centered leadership into the Congress?"

I said, "How do you treat your wife?"

"What's that got to do with it?" he demanded.

I said, "Ultimately, public policy is private morality writ large."

He flushed at that and didn't say another word. Thinking I had offended him, I went up to him afterward to apologize. "I'm sorry if I offended you. I didn't mean to do that. But I really believe in the inside-out approach."

"It's not that you offended me," he said. "But what you said hit home! All my life I've tended to blame other people out there for injustices. And I know I've taken out my frustrations on my loved ones. For you to put your finger on that problem hit me hard. But I needed to hear it."

Ultimately, there's no such thing as "organizational behavior"; it's all behavior of the people in the organization.

2. Life Is One Indivisible Whole

As we mentioned earlier, Gandhi once observed that "a person cannot do right in one department of life whilst attempting to do wrong in another department. Life is one indivisible whole." An associate shared this story:

> At one time I worked for a large aerospace company. I was part of a key marketing team whose assignment was to prepare "executive summary" presentation materials to help sell multibillion-dollar defense programs and products.
>
> One day a new member of the team was hired and introduced. We could tell by the way management rolled out the red carpet that he was considered a prized recruit. He was very bright and came with ten years of related experience in the industry.
>
> He was appointed team leader on the company's most important new business proposal. I was assigned to work with him and to occupy the open office space next to his.
>
> As work progressed on the project, I soon came to know this person very well. Because of our close proximity, I could overhear all of his telephone calls and conversations. These calls began to reveal a very sordid and disorganized private life. Aware that I was picking up signals, he would explain away the calls and then say, "But this won't affect my work." He repeated that line day after day.
>
> As the intense proposal effort peaked, the hours and pressure at work doubled. Now, in the pressure cooker, the private life of this team leader had its ugly effects. Working on little sleep and peace, he became impossible to work with—short-tempered, unreasonable, argumentative, imbalanced. It affected everyone. In spite of his considerable knowledge, he became an obstacle to the project and was fired, only six months after he was brought on with such high expectations.

We may think we're fooling others. We may even be fooling ourselves. But if we're duplicitous or dishonest in any role, it affects every role in our lives.

3. Trust Grows out of Trustworthiness

Trust is the glue of life. It's the most essential ingredient in effective communication. It's the foundational principle that holds all relationships—marriages, families, and organizations of every kind—together. And trust grows out of trustworthiness.

Stephen: At one time, my little boy saw me speaking harshly about someone. He instantly came up to me and said, "Do you love me, Dad?" He was so authentic, so tender, so vulnerable. He could see in my nature the possibility of not loving someone, and he immediately applied it in our relationship. He was questioning my trustworthiness. He wanted to know if it was safe for him to trust my love.

I had a completely opposite experience myself one time when I was asked to teach as a visiting professor for a year at a university in Hawaii. When we arrived, we found that the housing situation was not what we expected. So I went in and complained to the university president about his housing director. I was critical and upset. I told him what the agreement and expectation had been and how things weren't working out.

He listened to me with respect, and then he said, "Stephen, I'm so sorry to hear about this, but the housing director is such a fine, competent person. . . . Let's have him come over here and we'll solve it together."

That was not what I'd expected to hear. I hadn't wanted to get involved. I just wanted to complain and moan and have him fix it. I'll never forget the few minutes it took for the housing director to come over to the president's office, and what was going through my mind and heart. "What have I gotten myself into? I'm probably partly responsible for this mess. I'll bet my own communications weren't that clear." By the time he got there, my whole spirit was subdued. I was humbled. I was also a little chastened and embarrassed for my arrogance.

As the housing director walked in, I said, "Hi! How are you? Nice to see you." I was very aware of my own duplicity. But, oh, what respect I felt for that president who sustained his people, who spoke positively about them and wanted them involved in the process of resolving any negative issues!

That president was principle-centered. I knew if someone were ever to complain about me in his presence—in any capacity—he would treat me with the same respect. This man was loyal to those who were absent.

I never played fast and loose with anyone's reputation around him again. I knew what kind of person he was.

Trust is something you can't fake or quick-fix. It's a fundamental function of character—of personal trustworthiness.

Without a foundation of essential trustworthiness, trust is tentative at best. There are no reserves. There's no confidence in basic motive.

Communication is guarded, full of posturing and positioning. On the other hand, trustworthiness creates flexibility and emotional reserve in relationships. You might even mess up occasionally, but it doesn't ruin the relationship. You have the reserves to draw on. People will trust your basic intent. They know what you are inside.

INTERDEPENDENCE REDEFINES "IMPORTANCE"

Switching from an independent to an interdependent paradigm creates a whole new way of seeing that powerfully impacts the decisions we make concerning the best use of our time—and the results we get. It literally redefines "importance." Think back to the Time Management Matrix.

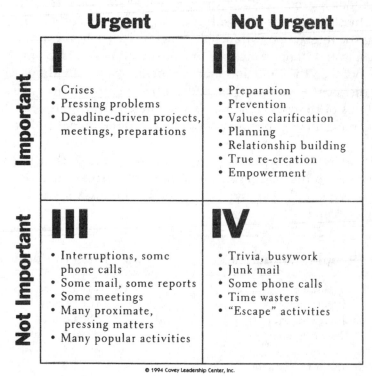

	Urgent	**Not Urgent**
Important	**I** • Crises • Pressing problems • Deadline-driven projects, meetings, preparations	**II** • Preparation • Prevention • Values clarification • Planning • Relationship building • True re-creation • Empowerment
Not Important	**III** • Interruptions, some phone calls • Some mail, some reports • Some meetings • Many proximate, pressing matters • Many popular activities	**IV** • Trivia, busywork • Junk mail • Some phone calls • Time wasters • "Escape" activities

© 1994 Covey Leadership Center, Inc.

As you look through the lens of the interdependent reality, consider these questions:

- Is it more important to get the job done efficiently . . . or to take the time to empower an employee or a child to do it, both now and in the future? Which choice will have greater impact on the quality of your time, the time of others, the time of the organization?

- Is it more important to spend time supervising and controlling others, or to release the tremendous creative potential in others so that they govern themselves?
- Is it more important to schedule your time to efficiently solve the problems created by conflicting expectations . . . or to take the time to work with others and clarify expectations up front?
- Is it more important to spend time trying to solve problems created by lack of communication, or to build the relationships that make effective communication possible?

The fourth generation is a "people" paradigm. More than the efficient, mechanical management of "things," it's focused on effective, synergistic interaction with people. The difference between the focus on people and things represents one of the deepest underlying differences between the third and fourth generations. In the third generation, the focus is on managing and controlling. It relegates people to the status of things. People finally become efficient even with themselves in organizing, planning, prioritizing, disciplining, and controlling.

But the fourth-generation paradigm is people first, things second. It's leadership first, management second. It's effectiveness first, efficiency second. It's purpose first, structure second. It's vision first, method second.

The "People" Paradigm	The "Things" Paradigm
Leadership	Management
Effectiveness	Efficiency
Spontaneity/Serendipity	Structure
Discernment	Measurement
Causes	Effects/Symptoms
Release/Empowerment	Control
Programmer	Program
Transformation	Transaction
Investment	Expense
Customer service	Administrative efficiency
Principles	Techniques
Synergy	Compromise
Abundance	Scarcity

This people focus creates an entirely different way of seeing and a different approach to life, as shown on the chart opposite.

Obviously, the "things" paradigm is appropriate *when we're managing things*. But it's inappropriate—and ineffective—when we try to apply it to people. It's like trying to play tennis with a golf club—the tool isn't suited to the reality.

The people paradigm is vital to success in families, organizations, and groups of all kinds. Japanese industrialist Konosuke Matsushita points out that many of the failures and challenges in business in the West are due to this essential paradigm:

With your bosses doing the thinking while the workers wield the screwdrivers, you're convinced deep down that it is the right way to run a business—getting the ideas out of the heads of the bosses and into the hands of labor.

For us, the core of management is the art of mobilizing and pulling together the intellectual resources of all employees in the service of the firm. We have measured the scope of the technological and economic challenges—we know that the intelligence of a handful of technocrats, however brilliant, is no longer enough to take them up with a real chance of success.

Only by drawing on the combined brain power of all its employees can a firm face up to the turbulence and constraints of today's environment.[4]

When we "see" in terms of the interdependent reality, we quickly recognize the importance of time spent in Quadrant II activities such as building relationships, creating shared vision, and clarifying expectations. We also see that much of what we do in traditional time management is efficiently hacking at the leaves instead of effectively working at the interdependent root.

TRUE INTERDEPENDENCE IS TRANSFORMATIONAL

Interdependence in traditional time management is essentially *transactional*. This kind of transactional interdependence takes place in day-to-day delegation, and it usually involves good human relations principles. It can be done in ways that are efficient and smooth and satisfying to both parties. But it's a low level of interaction. The parties involved are not transformed. They're not altered or changed. Nothing truly synergistic takes place. Nothing new is created.

But the fourth generation is different in kind. It moves from *trans-action* to *transformation*, where the true synergy of interdependence is created in the very nature of the interaction itself. People are altered. They are transformed. They are truly changed. They do not know when they begin the transaction what kind of dynamic is being un-leashed inside the communication process. Something new is being created and neither party is controlling it. Neither could have antici-pated or predicted it. It's people interacting in a state of release rather than control. This kind of transformational interdependence is a whole new world, and is the very essence and core of the fourth gener-ation. In transformational interaction, the third-generation approach of control, efficiency, independent achievement, and chronos is eclipsed by this fourth-generation concept of synergy around a bal-anced set of natural laws or principles that are operating and ulti-mately controlling.

The whole idea of synergy is thrilling and exciting, but at the same time scary. When you go into synergistic communication, you're really not sure how it will end up. And if you've been deeply scripted and trained in independence and in the third-generation philosophy of control and efficiency, you may feel very vulnerable and inexperi-enced, doubting and fearful.

Stephen: I remember the first time I went rappelling on a survival program. I was an assistant instructor, dealing not so much with the survival skills, but with the human interaction. But I had to go through what the students were going through in learning these survival skills. I'll never forget standing on the top of a cliff knowing that it was my turn to literally fall backward over the sheer precipice. I had seen the other instructors do it just before me. I was intellectually convinced that all the safety elements were present and that even if I blacked out, there would be a safety rope to catch me. But all this did not give me peace. I still felt anxious and fearful and vulnerable. I didn't want to say anything because I knew it would stir up a reaction in the students. But I'll never forget the feeling that went through my heart and mind as I actually fell backward into space.

These feelings are akin to what this whole idea of the synergy of in-terdependence is all about. You're truly vulnerable. You're letting go. You're putting your faith in a process and in principles. You do not know what will result. You are truly at risk.

Control is such an illusion. People who are into control have basi-cally internalized sufficient principles or natural laws of life so that they think they are the ones making things happen. But it's really their obedience to those natural laws and principles that makes things happen. This may work at a fairly low level of contribution and in transactional partnership networking and interdependencies.

But when you want to have an enlarged contribution, and to get into transformational interdependency that's truly synergistic and creative and becomes a force in its own right—then you leave the safe haven of superior control and become vulnerable. You have to exercise faith in these principles at a higher level. And you're not sure what's going to happen. Life then becomes a real adventure. You're not sure what's around the next bend. You're not sure how the other person will respond. You're at risk. This is why it takes such courage. You have to go way outside your present comfort zone, way outside your past experience or your present mentors. There may be quite a few models out there that inspire you, that have done it before and encourage you on. But you still have to take that first step. You still have to let go and "fall backward."

THE FOUR ENDOWMENTS IN INTERDEPENDENCE

The reason we can do it—and can create that synergistic whole that's far greater than the sum of its parts—is because of our unique human endowments.

In the interdependent reality, we're dealing with the space between stimulus and response in others as well as ourselves. As we do, we find that we can use our unique human endowments to interact with others with integrity—in an integrated way.

• *Self-awareness* empowers us to have *other awareness*. Because we know how to listen to our own heart, we can listen to the hearts of others. We can step out of our autobiography and seek to understand. We can stop seeing people as a reflection of ourselves, looking at everything they do in terms of how it affects our time and our world. We can stop seeing them merely as resources to get done what we want to get done. We can progress beyond the narcissistic stage, value the difference, be willing to be influenced. Because we have a changeless core, we can be willing to be changed. We can have humility, respect for others. We can see their weaknesses as opportunities to help, to love, to make a difference.

• Because we understand *conscience*, we can know what it is to be part of the *collective conscience*. We value working together to discover true north, having the humility to realize that our own understanding may be limited by our scripting and that others may have insight and experience we don't have. We find deep satisfaction in creating shared vision and values that empower us to achieve first things together.

• Through our *independent will*, we can work to achieve *interdependent will*. We can agree to work together in win-win ways to accomplish worthwhile purposes. We can create structures and systems that support interdependent effort. As truly independent individuals, we can come together to accomplish common purposes that benefit the family, the group, the organization, and society as a whole.

• We can contribute our own *creative imagination* to the incredible process of *creative synergy*. We can help unleash the tremendous creative potential in others and be open and ready to be surprised by the synergistic results. We can create third alternative solutions that are far more creative, more appropriate, more workable, more rewarding than any solution we could ever come up with on our own. Our input can become part of a kaleidoscope that creates dramatic new results as we interact with others in the problem-solving process.

These interdependent endowments empower us to create rich relationships, to be a friend, to give honest feedback, to communicate in authentic ways. Instead of dependence, co-dependence, or counterdependence, we can exercise effective, synergistic interdependence. We can work effectively together to accomplish common goals. We can create powerful teams that build on the strengths of each individual and make weaknesses irrelevant. We can do first things first together in powerful and effective ways.

This is the ultimate fulcrum. It empowers us to take time, energy, and human creativity that's typically wasted in unnecessary Quadrant I crises and unimportant Quadrant III activities, and combine it in ways that create whole new dimensions of effectiveness. In the following chapter, we'll look at two high-leverage Quadrant II activities through which we can use our combined endowments in ways that are truly transformational.

12: *First Things First Together*

Difference is the beginning of synergy.

SUPPOSE one of us were to challenge you to an arm wrestle. The objective is to win as much as you can. The time limit is 60 seconds, and we have an observer who has agreed to give the winner a dime whenever one of us gets the other one down. We're poised and ready for action.

Now suppose, for the sake of the example, that we immediately get you down. But instead of keeping you there, we immediately release the pressure and let you get us down. We quickly respond and go for another down. Out of habit, you resist. You want to *win*. Your muscles are strained, your brows are furrowed in concentration. But in the midst of the struggle, it suddenly occurs to you that each of us now has a dime. If you were to give us another win, and we gave you another win, and you gave us another win . . . we'd both end up winning a whole lot more. So we work together, going back and forth, back and forth quickly—and in 60 seconds we each make three dollars instead of one of us settling for ten cents.

This is the essence of win-win: in almost all situations, cooperation is far more productive than competition. The lesson isn't that we take turns losing—you're on top one minute; we're on top the next. It's that between us is the ability to work together to achieve far more than either of us could on our own.

When we do this little exercise in group situations, we often hear comments such as these:

"I started out thinking this was an adversarial thing. But then I began to figure out that if we had give-and-take on both sides, we'd both be winners."

"There's some symbolic value of prevailing and staying in the upper position. That meant more to me at the moment until I figured out, 'Wait a minute! We're both losing here.' "

"My ego was invested in this. Everyone was watching. I felt I had to win—I had to get you down."

"What I finally realized was that I was fighting myself."

Most of us approach situations with the win-lose mentality. "Winning" means somebody else loses. We're scripted with a scarcity mentality by win-lose athletics, academic distribution curves, and forced ranking systems. We look at life through the glasses of win-lose, and if we fail to develop self-awareness, we spend our lives competing for "dimes" instead of cooperating for "dollars."

So who's winning in your marriage—you or your spouse? Who's winning when your kids take you on, testing their identity? Who's winning on your work team when you have people competing against each other for the recognition, the trip to Hawaii, the cash bonus? What's the cost of this win-lose mentality in terms of time and quality of life?

Contrary to most of our scripting, "to win" does *not* mean somebody else has to lose; it means we accomplish our objectives. And so many more objectives can be accomplished when we cooperate rather than compete.

In the interdependent reality, win-win is the only long-term viable option. It's the essence of the abundance mentality—there's plenty for both of us; plenty in our combined capacity to create even more for ourselves and everyone else. In some respects, it's really what some refer to as "win-win-win." By working together, learning from each other, helping each other grow, everyone benefits, including society as a whole.

THE WIN-WIN PROCESS

In *The 7 Habits of Highly Effective People,* we introduced a simple three-step principle-based process to create win-win:[1]

- *Think win-win* (based on principles of see/do/get, mutual benefit, and cooperation).
- *Seek first to understand, then to be understood* (based on principles of respect, humility, and authenticity).

- *Synergize* (based on principles of valuing the difference and searching for third alternatives).

Let's look at this three-step process more closely in terms of what it is, how we can apply it, and the impact it has on our time and the quality of our lives.

Think Win-Win

Like Quadrant II, win-win is primarily a way of thinking. It's a fundamental paradigm based on what is probably the most often mentioned theme in all wisdom literature—the principle of mutual benefit or reciprocity, often referred to as the "Golden Rule."

As we learn to think win-win, we seek for mutual benefit in all our interactions. We start thinking in terms of other people, of society as a whole. It profoundly affects what we see as "important," how we spend our time, our response in the moment of choice, and the results we get in our lives.

Seek First to Understand, Then to Be Understood

For many of us, communication is first and foremost seeking to be understood, to communicate our ideas and opinions to others in an effective way. If we listen at all, it's usually with intent to reply.

When we're convinced we're right, we don't really want other people's opinions. We want submission. We want obedience to our opinions. We want to clone other people in our image. "If I want your opinion, I'll give it to you!"

But the humility of principles removes this kind of arrogance. We become less concerned about *who* is right and more concerned about *what* is right. We value other people. We recognize that their conscience, too, is a repository of correct principles. We realize that their creative imagination is a rich source of ideas. We appreciate the fact that through their self-awareness and independent will, they may have gained insight and experience we don't have. So when they see things differently, we seek *first* to understand. Before we speak, we listen. We leave our own autobiography and invest deeply in genuinely understanding their point of view.

We look at our differences as though we stand on opposite sides of the same huge lens. From one side, it's concave; from the other, it's convex.

© 1994 Covey Leadership Center, Inc.

Both perspectives have value, but the only way to really understand the other perspective is to go and stand where the other person is standing, to see as that person sees.

© 1994 Covey Leadership Center, Inc.

As Gandhi said, "Three-fourths of the miseries and misunderstandings in the world will disappear if we step into the shoes of our adversaries and understand their standpoint."[2] As we really understand the other point of view, we often find our own point of view changed through increased understanding.

In the words of Martin Buber, "Only men who are capable of truly saying *Thou* [an attitude of deep respect] to one another can truly say *we* with one another."[3] Real listening shows respect. It creates trust. As we listen, we not only gain understanding; we also create the environment to be understood. And when both people understand both perspectives, instead of being on opposite sides of the table looking across at each other, we find ourselves on the same side looking at solutions together.

© 1994 Covey Leadership Center, Inc.

Synergize

Synergy is the fruit of thinking win-win and seeking first to understand. It's the combined power of synergistic creative imagination, the almost magical math where $1 + 1 = 3$ or more. *It's not compromise. It's not $1 + 1 = 1\frac{1}{2}$.* It's the creation of third alternatives that are genuinely better than solutions individuals could ever come up with on their own.

Let's look now at specific ways we can apply this win-win process in families, groups, and organizations to create positive quality-of-life results. Just as we did in the personal section of this book, we'll look at vision, roles, and goals. But this time, we'll do it on an interdependent basis—we'll look at *shared* vision and *synergistic* roles and goals. We'll also look at the empowered culture they create.

THE IMPORTANCE OF SHARED VISION

If you want to have an interesting experience sometime, ask people you work with if they know what "true north" is for your organization—what is its essential purpose for being? Say to the members of your family, "Just tell me in one sentence—what is the purpose of our family?" Ask your spouse, "What is the purpose of our marriage? What is its essential reason for being?" When you go to work, take out your clipboard and ask the first ten people you meet, "Could you help me? I'm doing a little survey. One question: What is the purpose of our organization?" Ask your group, "What is the purpose of this work group?" "What is the purpose of this board of trustees?" "What is the purpose of this board of directors?" "What is the purpose of this executive committee?"

We've done this with the executive cabinets of many companies including some of the Fortune 100—big companies, sophisticated organizations. And in many cases, the top executives are absolutely surprised, chagrined, embarrassed. They cannot believe the different descriptions that are being given as to purpose and vision. This even happens sometimes when there's a mission statement hanging on the wall—a statement that came down through the organization from the executive offices. There's no sense of shared vision. There's no passion, no deep burning "Yes!" in the organization.

And what's the cost?

Roger: Several years ago, I was asked to come into the big R&D facility of a large international firm to help them create a Quadrant II culture. The assumption was that I would do some analysis, and then work with the director of the division to create a series of custom training workshops that would accomplish this objective.

In the process, I visited in the offices of several of the management and staff. As I was escorted from one office to another, I became increasingly intrigued to see the identical scene over and over again. In each office, a somewhat frazzled man or woman—one hand on the phone, another on the computer, desk literally piled with papers—would look up and say, "Just a minute! I'll be right with you!"

After hurriedly completing some task or phone conversation, the person would sigh, take a quick look at the clock, and push papers aside long enough to tell me how incredibly busy they were and how there was literally more to do than could possibly be done. Between offices, people rushed down the halls. There was a sense of gushing energy and panic everywhere.

Finally, I went back to the director of the division and said, "These people don't want a Quadrant II environment. I suggest we not do it."

She said, "What do you mean?"

I said, "These people love urgency. They're out there trying to convince each other and themselves that they have more to do than anybody else. This is where they're getting their security. Urgency dominates the culture. I suspect that the real problem is that nobody really knows what the priorities are."

She sighed. "That's right. There's a big power struggle between the vice-presidents in terms of what R&D is supposed to do. Each one has a following. Frankly, we're at odds with each other. There's not a clear set of signals. We don't know how long it's going to last, but one of these days things are going to come unglued."

These people were trying to keep some sense of security and identity in the organization by being frantically busy. The underlying paradigm was: "When the showdown comes and heads start to roll, I'm the last person they'll get rid of because I'm the busiest, most hardworking person around here and everybody knows it."

Soon after that experience, there was a big shake-up in the organization and quite a few people lost their jobs. Before their reorganization, we could have taught traditional time management till we were blue in the face and it wouldn't have created the Quadrant II culture they desired. The core problem was a lack of shared vision.

Recently, we shared this story at one of our programs where there were people from a number of large corporations. Afterward, several of them came up and said, "You must have been talking about my organization!" "Were you talking about mine? That's exactly the way we are!" Interestingly, it wasn't any of them. But it's such a typical experience.

This problem is exacerbated in our culture as so many companies are into "right-sizing." People scurry around being incredibly busy, wanting to create the feeling that they're indispensable. Busyness on the job becomes their primary source of justification and security—regardless of the fact that what they're doing is essentially in Quadrant III.

Just think of the cost in terms of time and effort wasted in organizations because people don't have a clear sense of shared importance! One of the large companies we've worked with did a study a few years ago, and compiled information from companies that had won the Deming Award for quality in Japan. They looked at the percentage of management time spent in Quadrant II. Based on that information and our time logs of other organizations, we found that companies that are unusually productive, such as the Deming Award–winning companies, have a significantly different time profile than typical organizations. On the chart on the following page, the typical pattern is shown in regular type; the pattern of high-performing organizations is shown in bold.

It's easy to see that the figures showed great polarization—there's not much middle ground—and that the big differences are in Quadrants II and III. The high-performance companies spend significantly

	Urgent	**Not Urgent**
Important	**I** **20–25%** 25–30%	**II** **65–80%** 15%
Not Important	**III** **15%** 50–60%	**IV** **less than 1%** 2-3%

[bold type represents high-performance organizations
normal type represents typical organizations]

© 1994 Covey Leadership Center, Inc.

more time doing things that are important, but not urgent—and significantly less time doing things that are urgent but not important. The principal reason behind these differences, in most cases, is in the degree of clarity about what is important.

As we've shared these figures over the years in our seminars, we've found that the majority of people feel the figures representing the non-high-performance companies represent their companies as well, and generally for the same reason. This means that in a large number of companies (big and small), people feel that 50 to 60 percent of management time does not contribute to the company's objectives!

The degree to which urgency drives the organization is the degree to which importance does not. This is not to suggest that there is no urgency. Quadrant I is very real, and a good percentage of time should be spent doing things that are both urgent and important. But so much time is wasted in Quadrant III because importance isn't clear!

THE PASSION OF SHARED VISION

The passion created by shared vision creates synergistic empowerment. It unleashes and combines the energy, talent, and capacities of all involved. Creating shared vision produces its own order; trying to control produces the opposite effect—dysfunctional disorder or chaos.

We've all heard stories of groups, athletic teams, companies, or other organizations that have marshaled their efforts to accomplish great purposes. They perform beyond their resources.

The same is true in a family.

Stephen: I wish I had the language to describe the conscious and subconscious unifying, energizing, harmonizing, and life-directing effect our mission statement has had on our family. We did it several years ago. Most every Sunday for eight months we met for a half hour to an hour in the afternoon or evening to deal with the deeper questions. "What is it we are about? What is truly important? What kind of home do we want? What makes you proud to bring your friends here?"

Eventually, we evolved this statement:

"The mission of our family is to create a nurturing place of faith, order, truth, love, happiness, and relaxation, and to provide opportunity for each person to become responsibly independent, and effectively interdependent in order to serve worthy purposes in society."

My mother occasionally participated in developing that statement, as well as my children, and now my children have children, so we have an intergenerational mission statement that has helped build continuity between generations. We have it hanging on our wall and we constantly examine ourselves by it. We still find areas of misalignment and weakness, but we keep coming back to it. It keeps us focused on what we are potentially.

Shared vision becomes the constitution, the criterion for decision making in the group. It bonds people together. It gives them a sense of unity and purpose that provides great strength in times of challenge.

One man shared this story:

Shortly after I wrote my personal mission statement, I was thinking about my role as a father and envisioning how I wanted to be remem-

bered by my kids. So when we planned our vacation that summer, I decided to apply that principle of vision to the family. We came up with a sort of family mission statement for the event. We called it "the Smith Team." It described for us the perspective we wanted to take when we went off together on our trip.

We each took particular roles that would help contribute to building the Smith Team. My six-year-old daughter chose the role of family cheerleader. Her goal was to be an influence to dispel any contention in the family, particularly while we were traveling together in the car. She made up several cheers, and whenever there was a problem, she would break into one of them—"Smiths! Smiths! Driving down the street! When we stick together, we can't be beat!" Whether or not we felt like it, we'd all have to join in, and it was very helpful in dispelling the bad feeling that might have been there.

We also all had matching T-shirts. At one point, we went into a service station and the attendant wasn't paying much attention. But when he looked up and we were all standing there with our matching shirts, he did a double take and said, "Hey, you guys look like a team!" That just kind of cemented it. We all looked at each other and felt an incredible high. We got back in the car and took off, windows down, radio cranked up, ice cream melting in the back seat. We were a family!

About three months after we got back from our vacation, our three-year-old son was diagnosed with leukemia. This threw our family into months of challenge. The interesting thing to us was that whenever we took our son to the hospital for his chemotherapy treatments, he would always ask if he could wear his shirt. Maybe it was his way of connecting back to the team and feeling the support and the memories he had around the experiences of being together on that family vacation.

After his sixth treatment, he caught a serious infection that put him in intensive care for two weeks. We came very close to losing him, but he pulled through. He wore that T-shirt almost nonstop through those days and it was covered with stains of vomit, blood, and tears.

When he finally did pull through and we brought him home, we all wore our family T-shirts in his honor. We all wanted to connect to that family mission feeling we had created on the vacation.

That vision of the Smith Team helped us through what was the greatest challenge our family had ever faced.

A powerful shared vision has a profound effect on quality of life—in the family, in the organization, in any situation where we work with others. We become contributing parts of a greater whole. We can live, love, learn, and leave powerful legacies together.

CREATING EMPOWERING SHARED MISSION STATEMENTS

So how do we create an empowering statement of shared vision?

Think win-win. Seek first to understand. Synergize.

Organizations, families, or groups of any kind can use this win-win process to create shared vision. As we've seen people do this world-wide, we've seen the reality of true north validated every time four conditions are present:

1. There are enough people
2. who are fully informed
3. and are interacting freely and synergistically
4. in an environment of high trust.

This kind of interaction taps into the collective conscience. We see it in Russia, Singapore, England, Australia, South Africa, South America, Canada, the United States—everywhere we do mission statement work. As people get together and go through the process, they come to a common awareness of many of the basic Laws of Life. They use their creative synergy to envision ways their combined talents and energies can make a difference.

The most empowering organizational mission statements are in harmony with what we've come to call the *universal mission*—"to improve the economic well-being and quality of life of all stakeholders." This statement deals with all four needs. It recognizes that people are not just stomach or heart or mind or spirit, but all four together in a synergistic whole. "All stakeholders" includes *everyone* who has a stake in the success of the effort. In an organization, it's not just management and labor; it's customers, suppliers, families of employees, society, the environment, and future generations. In the family, it includes extended family, past family, future family, and the human family as a whole.

Empowering mission statements focus on contribution, on worthwhile purposes that create a collective deep burning "Yes!" They come from the hearts and minds of everyone involved—not as an executive decree from "Mount Olympus."

If you plan to create an organizational mission statement or want to review one you've already created, you might find the following list of characteristics helpful:

An empowering organizational mission statement:

- focuses on contribution, on worthwhile purposes that create a collective deep burning "Yes!"
- comes from the bowels of the organization, not from Mount Olympus
- is based on timeless principles
- contains both vision and principle-based values
- addresses the needs of all stakeholders
- addresses all four needs and capacities

It takes up-front Quadrant II time to create a statement of shared vision, but it results in tremendous savings of time and effort down the road. The end result is more than just shared vision. The process changes us. It changes our relationships with others who are part of it. It transforms the quality of our lives in fundamental ways.

THE IMPORTANCE OF SYNERGISTIC ROLES AND GOALS

As we seek to effectively carry out shared vision, we begin to see the value of synergistic roles and goals.

In our personal lives, when we see our roles as segmented parts of life, they conflict and compete with each other. But when we see them as parts of a highly interrelated whole, the parts work together to create abundance living.

The same thing is true in the interdependent reality with regard to roles of individuals. When we see how each role contributes to the whole, instead of thinking in terms of scarcity and competition, we can use the win-win process to create abundance and synergy. The key is in the creation of synergistic stewardship agreements.*

As people work together to accomplish any task, sooner or later they have to deal with five elements:

- desired results—What is it we're trying to do? What outcomes do we want—both quantitative and qualitative—and by when?
- guidelines—What are the parameters within which we're trying to do it? What are the essential values, policies,

* For complimentary examples of stewardship agreements, please call 1-800-680-6839.

legalities, ethics, limits, and levels of initiative to be aware of
in going after the desired results?

- resources—What do we have to work with? What budgetary,
systemic, and human help is available and how do we access it?
- accountability—How do we measure what we're doing? What
criteria will indicate the accomplishment of the desired
results? Will they be measurable, observable, or discernible, or
some combination of the three? To whom are we accountable?
When will the accountability process take place?
- consequences—Why are we trying to do it? What are the
natural and logical consequences of accomplishing or not
accomplishing the desired results?

From a time management perspective, how much time is spent trying to repair, redefine, or resolve problems in our interactions with
others because we're not clear on these five issues?

People aren't clear on desired results:

"I thought you wanted me to do that."

"No, that's not what you were supposed to do."

"Well, that was my understanding. I thought this was the priority."

"No, that was the priority."

They aren't clear on guidelines:

"I thought I had the initiative."

"We never gave you the initiative."

"I didn't know there was a company policy."

"Well, there is."

They don't know what resources are available.

They evaluate their job on certain criteria; their boss evaluates on
others.

They get negative consequences they didn't even associate with
their job performance, or they don't know how rewards are connected
to performance.

When we ask people in seminars how much time is spent in their
organizations dealing with the effects of unclear expectations around
these issues, they typically say a minimum of 60 percent. When we're
talking about time management issues, here's one at the heart of effectiveness. We're talking about significant time and energy that's diffused through the organization in Quadrant III or in negative
ways—time and energy that could be spent doing first things.

As we mentioned in Chapter 6, each role is a stewardship. The key
to effective interdependent effort is what we call "win-win stewardship agreements." These agreements represent the critical juncture of

people and possibilities. This is where personal and organizational missions are married and the fire within spreads throughout the organization.

CREATING WIN-WIN STEWARDSHIP AGREEMENTS

The stewardship agreement is a marked departure from traditional delegation, which often degenerates into "dumping" tasks on others. The stewardship agreement creates a synergistic partnership to accomplish first things first together. Delegation becomes stewardship delegation. Instead of feeling "dumped on," people are involved. They're motivated. Both parties are accomplishing things of shared importance.

So how do we create these agreements?

Think win-win. Seek first to understand. Synergize.

As you sit down with a boss, a direct report, a co-worker, a child, go through the process and come to agreement on each of the five elements of win-win stewardship agreement.

1. Specify Desired Results

Desired results are the "shared vision" of the stewardship agreement. This is the statement of what's "important," and is the key factor in putting first things first in every interdependent relationship. This is the test of the abundance mentality, the process of constantly going for third-alternative solutions and synergy.

Many of the same elements that create empowering organizational mission statements are helpful in creating effective statements of desired results, such as:

• focusing on contribution
• addressing all four needs
• understanding what constitutes a "win" for *all* stakeholders

It's also important to specify what will be done to enhance the ability to produce desired results in the future—to nourish PC or production capability. And it's vital to make sure that the desired results are *results,* not *methods.* Whenever we supervise methods, we become responsible for results.

The statement of desired results is essentially where family, group,

or organizational alignment takes place—where the goals and strategies of each stewardship are aligned with the overall mission and with
the efforts of other people or teams in the organization. This creates a
process of "co-missioning," the co-mingling of the missions of the individual and the organization.

2. Set Guidelines

In addition to policies and procedures that may influence the carrying
out of the agreement, it's important to identify other guidelines such
as:

- true north principles that will be used to produce the results
- organizational principles (operating principles, not necessarily
  natural laws) that underlie policies
- "watch outs" and known failure paths (things not to do)
- levels of initiative

A clear understanding of guidelines avoids many major problems.
Consider levels of initiative, for example. A waiter who's given the initiative to "comp" a meal to a dissatisfied customer at one restaurant
could be fired at another restaurant for the same action. An agreed-
upon level of initiative eliminates the problem.

Adapted from William Oncken's work are the following six levels of
initiative:[4]

1. Wait until told
2. Ask
3. Recommend
4. Act and report immediately
5. Act and report periodically
6. Act on own

An agreement might contain different levels of initiative for different functions. A secretary could be at level three in handling corre-
spondence or responding to staff problems and level five in dealing
with visitors and incoming calls.

Levels of initiative can change as capability and trust increase. A
three-year-old child who waits until he's told to clean his room will
hopefully progress to level five by the time he's ten or twelve.

The important thing is to match the level of initiative with the capacity of the individual.

3. Identify Available Resources

This area deals with the financial, human, technical, and organizational resources (such as training or information systems) available in carrying out the agreement. It's important to identify not only the resources available, but also how to access them, how to work with others who use the same resources, and what the limits are.

One of the most overlooked resources—and one that's unique to win-win stewardship agreements—is the participants themselves, particularly those who have leadership, management, or supervisory roles. Because of the nature of the stewardship agreements, the leader can become a leader/servant to the individual.[5] We'll examine this idea more in depth in Chapter 13.

4. Define Accountability

Accountability deals with how we can tell how we're doing. It creates integrity around the agreement. Here the details of communication are spelled out, as well as how the results will be measured.

Accountability includes both P (production) and PC (production capability) criteria associated with every one of the desired results. The criteria may be measurable, observable, or discernible. Without question, the toughest part of setting up win-win agreements is creating a clear and comprehensive set of desired results—both P and PC—and clear criteria for each of them to be put into the accountability process.

In the process of accountability, the individual evaluates himself or herself against the desired results specified in the agreement. Helpful in the evaluation process is 360 degree feedback, which the individual can request from stakeholders. This feedback would be given directly to the individual. We'll also look at feedback in depth in Chapter 13.

5. Determine the Consequences

There are two kinds of consequences: natural and logical. Natural consequences deal with what naturally happens if we do or do not achieve the desired results. Do we lose market share? Does it impact the bottom line? How are other people affected? What happens when the family chores don't get done? What happens when they do? It's important to identify both negative and positive consequences.

Logical consequences could include such things as compensation, opportunities for advancement, additional opportunities for training and development, enlarged or diminished stewardships, or discipline.

Both logical and natural consequences must be dealt with, and both have their place. Sometimes parents must knowingly choose to put logical consequences ahead of natural consequences for a child. If the child insists on running out into the street, for example, a parent would probably let the child experience the logical consequence of not having permission to go outside rather than the natural consequence that might result.

We address each of these five issues of the win-win stewardship agreement—either in quality Quadrant II leadership time up front or in Quadrant I crisis management time down the road. Our choice significantly impacts the quantity of time we spend on these issues and the resulting quality of all our time.

As one woman said:

I love win-win. I came out of a marriage where I never knew what was expected of me, and constantly felt like I was failing because I was always trying to meet expectations I didn't understand. It's wonderful to be able to talk to somebody and say, "This is what you expect from me; this is what I expect from you. Let's meet in the middle and do it."

Frustration is essentially a function of expectation. Clarifying interdependent expectations up front does a great deal to contribute to quality of life.

BUT WHAT IF WE DON'T AGREE?

Chances are good you'll often see things differently when you begin to create stewardship agreements. That's great! Difference is the beginning of synergy! By going through the process, you talk about it. You get the issues out on the table before they cause problems. You seek for creative third-alternative solutions. You don't tiptoe around the issues and live with the negative consequences of unresolved issues and unexpressed feelings. Instead, you use your human endowments to address and synergistically resolve the difference.

Think Win-Win.

You genuinely want the other person to win. You also want to win. You commit to interact until you can come up with a solution you both feel good about.

Seek First to Understand

As you seek mutual understanding, you may find it helpful to address the following questions:

- *What is the problem from the other point of view?* Really listen with intent to understand, not to reply. Step out of your own autobiography. Work at it until you can express the other person's point of view better than he or she can. Then encourage the other person to do the same.
- *What are the key issues (not viewpoints) involved?* Once the viewpoints are expressed and both parties feel thoroughly understood, look at the problem together and identify the issues that need to be resolved.
- *What results would constitute a fully acceptable solution?* Find out what would constitute a "win" for the other person. Identify what would constitute a "win" for you. Put both criteria on the table as the foundation for synergistic interaction.

Synergize

Open the door to the discovery of creative third-alternative solutions. Brainstorm. Use your MacGyver mentality. Open your mind. Be prepared for surprise. Try to create a list of possible options that would meet the criteria you've set up.

Let's look at two examples of how this process might work:

Example #1:

Suppose you're a sales representative for your company. It's a tough market, and there are several competing vendors in your area. Most of your clients operate on just-in-time delivery, and your ability to meet committed delivery dates is essential to keeping business.

But lately, your manufacturing facility has been shipping things out at the last minute. You've had a couple of late deliveries to some key clients. You understand their situation and know that they'll move to another vendor if your company continues to be unreliable. You don't want to lose any accounts, so you go to the production facilities manager to find out what's going on.

When you get there, you find this manager is buried alive in Quadrant I, feeling beat up by the demands that you and everybody else in marketing are placing on his plant. He says it's a miracle that you get the deliveries at all.

What do you do?

Think Win-Win

You want to win. You want this manager to win. You want your clients to win. You're not thinking "either/or," but "and." You're looking for third-alternative solutions that will meet everyone's needs. You're looking for solutions to chronic problems instead of symptoms.

Seek First to Understand

1. *What is the problem from the other point of view?*

As you listen to this manager, you find that in the past six months demand has increased by 30 percent and no funding has been approved to add capacity. Current shifts have stayed on overtime and maintenance has been ignored, increasing labor costs and downtime, and significantly straining this manager's relationship with headquarters. He feels he's getting pressure from all sides, and that the delivery times you request are unrealistic. You also sense that this manager wants to do a good job. He's not trying to hold things up; he wants to deliver on time just as much as you do. He simply feels that he's up against a wall and there's no end in sight. After thoroughly exploring his situation, you share your client's situation and your own concerns. With all the viewpoints out on the table, you're ready to work together to identify issues and find solutions.

2. *What are the key issues?*

As you communicate openly, you recognize that this problem is a symptom of a much larger series of problems. Key issues might include such things as:

* capacity
* funding
* relationships with headquarters
* relationships with clients

3. *What would define a solution acceptable to both of you?*

You want to work on both short-term and long-term solutions. You realize that he can't simply push other orders aside and put yours first. That only creates more problems for everyone. You also want to minimize costs and future downtime, so additional overtime is not a real win either. Whatever happens, there needs to be consistency and reliability. And the foundations need to be laid for long-term improvement.

Synergize

As you explore third-alternative solutions, you might come up with several viable possibilities:

- You might be able to create greater lead times for the plant by gathering projected product needs from your clients.
- Some of your clients might be just as happy in the short run if the plant delivered partial orders on the scheduled delivery date and completed the order within a few days.
- You may be able to work within the marketing department to help the other sales representatives understand the issues. It may be that, in the attempt to gain business, the reps are overpromising to their clients, creating an artificially inflated demand on the plant.
- Perhaps the plant manager could come and discuss the issues with the marketing department.
- A representative from marketing and the plant manager might look at the trends and write a joint analysis for headquarters around the value of added capacity for the plant.
- Perhaps, by working together, you could improve efficiency in the order-processing system, so that more time is spent producing rather than documenting.

You could pursue these or any number of other possible steps toward a solution. The point is that you're working together on the problem instead of against each other through the problem. By thinking win-win, seeking to understand, and creating synergy, your time and energy are spent generating solutions instead of creating conflict. The final outcome could be captured as part of an overall stewardship agreement.

Example #2:
Suppose your sixteen-year-old daughter wants her own car. She wants to be able to come and go without being dependent on the

availability of the family automobiles. She has some money saved up, but not enough to purchase a car for herself. Additionally, she says, many of her friends have their own cars and she feels that she's responsible and that you should trust her.

Your first inclination is to say no. You know she's generally responsible, but she's been driving for less than a year, and has already gotten a ticket. The fact that she's dependent on the family cars has allowed you to control (to some extent) where she goes and whom she goes with. You feel that at her age she should not be free to go and do whatever she wants. In addition, you have to fork out money not only for the car, but for insurance premiums, gas, and overall maintenance.

Again, this is not a situation with one simple answer. But how often does a situation like this become an open wound in a parent-child relationship? How easy would it be for your daughter to rebel because she feels you don't understand or trust her, or for you to put your foot down and assert your parental authority because you feel you know what's best? How much time and energy could be wasted in negative conflict? How can you come to a satisfactory resolution? Remember: *think win-win, seek first to understand, synergize.*

As you work together to understand viewpoints, identify issues, and create synergistic third-alternative solutions, you might consider creating a win-win stewardship agreement around an additional family car. She could use this car as long as certain criteria were met. You could specify maintenance requirements, and have her pay for the additional insurance and gas. You might come to an agreement about communicating where she's going and with whom. As part of the agreement, you might also specify that she help out with the transportation needs of some of the younger children, freeing up time for you or your spouse.

The point is not that this solution is the ideal, or that third-alternative solutions are easy to come by. The point is that when the problem is before you instead of between you, you avoid generating negative cycles in a critical relationship that could take months or years to resolve, and this powerfully affects time and quality of life for everyone involved.

BUT WHAT IF WE REALLY DISAGREE?

Although most win-win stewardship agreements would not deal with such explosive and divisive issues as those involved in the following experiences, we'd like to share them with you just to give an idea of how powerful this process can be. It can apply to most any divisive issue imaginable.

Stephen: At one time, I was training two hundred MBA students at an eastern university, and many faculty and invited guests were there as well. We took the toughest, most sensitive, most vulnerable issue they could come up with—abortion. We had a pro-life person and a pro-choice person who both felt really deeply about their positions come to the front of the classroom. And they had to interact with each other in front of these two hundred students. I was there to insist that they practice the habits of effective interdependence—think win-win, seek first to understand, and synergize.

"Are you two willing to communicate until we can come up with a win-win solution?"

"I don't know what it would be! I don't feel they—"

"Wait a minute. You won't lose. You will both win."

"But how could that possibly be? One of us wins, the other loses."

"Are you willing to try to go for it? Remember not to capitulate. Don't give in. Don't compromise."

"I guess."

"Okay. Seek first to understand. You can't make your point until you restate his point to his satisfaction."

As they began to dialogue, they kept interrupting each other.

"Yeah. But don't you realize that—"

I said, "Wait a minute! I don't know if the other person feels understood. Do you feel understood?"

"Absolutely not."

"Okay. You can't make your point."

You cannot believe the sweat those people were in. They couldn't listen. They had each other judged right off the bat because they took different positions.

Finally, after about forty-five minutes, they started to really listen. And you cannot imagine the effect upon them—personally, emotionally—and the effect upon the entire audience watching this process go on.

When they listened openly and empathically to the underlying needs and the fears and the feelings of people on such a tender

*issue, it was a very powerful thing. The two people in front had tears
in their eyes. Half the audience had tears in their eyes. They were cat-
egorically ashamed of how they had judged each other, labeled each
other, and condemned all who thought differently. They were totally
overwhelmed by the synergistic ideas that came out about what
could be done. They came up with a number of alternatives, including
new insights into prevention, adoption, and education. After two
hours, each said of the other, "We had no idea that's what it meant
to listen! Now we understand why they feel the way they do."*

This spirit of true empathy is foundational to effective synergy. It
transcends negative energy around positioning. It creates openness
and understanding and unites people in problem solving. The *key*
issue becomes the quality of the relationship between the people involved and their ability to communicate and synergize with each other
in seeking third-alternative solutions.

We've seen this spirit of empathy transform situations time and
time again. It happened as the head of a hospital system and the director of medicine grappled with a tender issue around the hiring of
primary care physicians for two hours in front of an audience of about
one hundred and fifty hospital trustees, administrators, physicians,
and others involved in a very large hospital system.

It happened with an organization that had overreacted to a regulatory environment that was suppressing the initiative, creativity, and
ingenuity of the design engineers to the point that they wanted to
leave the culture and go somewhere else. The top executives were still
gun-shy and reeling from the regulatory people coming down hard on
them. But as the top people representing the two different points of
view went through this process, they came up with a whole new approach that maintained the creativity and ingenuity of the design engineers and also met the criteria of the regulatory agency.

It happened in a large corporation where there was a long-term fight
going on between one of the major divisions and the top executives
about how assets should be devalued. The division felt it was totally
demoralizing their culture. The top executives were defending the
practice. But as they began to go through this process, the spirit of
empathy transformed them. People started looking, both in the same
direction, with a sense of shared vision and stewardship toward it instead of fighting each other. They began to be respectful in their communications, creative in their suggestions, and in a period of literally
half an hour, a deeply embedded issue that had divided the company

to the point that no one would even discuss it, was resolved. And people were totally astounded at the power of this interdependency.

When people really think win-win, when they seek to deeply understand each other, and they focus their energy toward solving problems synergistically instead of against each other, the effects are profound. We've seen the power of this process in the most tense, difficult situations imaginable.

Stephen: At one time, as I was traveling to work with a major corporation, I called and they said, "Go home. They just canceled the meeting."

"Why? What happened?"

"The union walked out."

"Why?"

"Because some of the people were not being treated as agreed."

"Does management acknowledge it?"

"Yes, they do."

"Then now's the time. The circumstances are right. Hold the meeting. Don't withdraw. People will just tend to polarize and get into their positions and gather people to attack."

Earlier we had taught the win-win process to people throughout the organization, and it was having a profound effect on personal and family lives. Some of the people in the middle had even put together a video with testimonials of the power of this process. But the top people in a sense felt they were above it, they didn't need it.

We said to management, "Apologize. It's such a small thing. Get that meeting back on. Now is the time."

They apologized. It was the first time something like that had ever happened. But it was a correct principle. The union president was taken back. "Okay," he said, "we'll come. But we'll come in late as a statement so that you don't think we're just selling out."

When I went to the meeting, I said to the president of the company and the president of the union, "I'm going to ask you to do something that will take a lot of courage. Are you willing to try?" After some hesitation, they both agreed.

I asked the two of them to come to the front of the auditorium. I said, "I just want you to listen to what these people are saying.

"You know the ambitious, almost heroic goals that have been established for you, and that apparently you have bought into." I turned to the audience. "How many here honestly believe with the present state of your culture, you could achieve those goals?" This was a big auditorium with seven hundred or eight hundred people there, from

first-level supervisors all the way to the top executives. I didn't see a hand.

"Now how many of you believe that if we literally practice the process we've been talking about—think win-win, seek first to understand, synergize—that we could accomplish those seemingly impossible heroic goals?" Almost to a person, their hands were up.

I turned to the two of them and I said, "Look at the message of this organization. I want to ask you two to commit in front of everybody that you will learn and team-teach this process to your direct reports. And to have them with their counterparts team-teach their direct reports until everyone gets involved in this and you resolve this issue. Now, if you're not prepared to live by that commitment, don't make it. Say, 'I want to think about it. Let's wait.' You don't want to create an expectation you cannot deliver on."

They looked at each other for a long time. You can't imagine the tension in that room. Finally, they put out their hands and shook, then embraced. The place exploded with applause.

Today, they're one of the leading organizations in America, not just because of that experience—there were many variables—but their willingness to apply this process made a quantum difference in the quality of life for all stakeholders.

Is there any time management technique that will save that kind of time? We're not talking about control and "gofer" delegation or even good delegation. We're talking about moving out of transactional and into transformational relationships—into true empowerment. We're talking about tapping into the power of the unique human endowments of everyone involved in a synergistic process by which we can discuss even the undiscussables and resolve tender issues in ways that benefit everyone.

Win-win is not adversarial; it's synergistic. It's not transactional; it's transformational. And everyone who participates in it or witnesses it can see it.

THE DIFFERENCE OF FIRST THINGS FIRST TOGETHER

What if we all lived and worked in cultures with shared vision and stewardship agreements, where win-win was a way of interacting? What difference would it make?

Consider *supervision.* In a low-trust culture, supervision is associated with words like *control, monitor, hover over,* and *check up.* In a high-trust culture, people supervise themselves according to the agreement. The criteria are clear, the consequences are set. There's common understanding of what's expected. A manager, leader, or parent becomes a source of help—a facilitator, helper, cheerleader, advisor, counselor, and coach—someone to remove the oil spills and then get out of the way.

What about *evaluation?* In a low-trust culture, you're into forced ranking, external performance evaluation, judgment. In a high-trust culture, the judgment goes into the performance agreement before the fact instead of after the fact. People judge themselves. Their evaluation is not just a function of measurement, but also of discernment. "The numbers are looking good, but I feel a concern about this particular area . . ." People are much more aware of the issues that affect their performance and success.

What about *span of control?* In a low-trust culture, the span of control is small. It takes time and energy to hover over, check up. You can only control so many people. In a high-trust culture, you don't need to hover over and check up. You aren't trying to control but to release. Instead of one to eight or ten, you have one to fifty, one to a hundred, one to two hundred.

What about *motivation?* In a low-trust culture, you're into "the great jackass theory of motivation"—the carrot out in front, the stick behind. In a high-trust culture, people are internally motivated. They're fueled by the fire within. They're driven by a sense of passion about fulfilling a shared vision that's also a co-mission, a synergy between their own mission and the mission of the family or organization.

What about *structure and systems?* A low-trust culture is filled with bureaucracy, excessive rules and regulations, restrictive, closed systems. In the fear of some "loose cannon," people set up procedures that everyone has to accommodate. The level of initiative is low—basically "do what you're told." Structures are pyramidal, hierarchical. Information systems are short-term. The quarterly bottom line tends to drive the mentality in the culture. In a high-trust culture, structures and systems are aligned to create empowerment, to liberate people's energy and creativity toward agreed-upon purposes within the guidelines of shared values. There's less bureaucracy, fewer rules and regulations, more involvement.

Now what kind of impact does this difference have on our time?

How much time is spent in low-trust cultures controlling, monitoring, hovering over, checking up, "snoopervising"?

How much time is spent on competitive evaluation systems, evaluation game-playing, and "motivational" programs?

How much time is spent dealing with bureaucratic systems, rules, and regulations?

How much time is spent sorting out the myriad of communication problems that grow out of low trust?

And what about the time and opportunity cost when people are so busy micromanaging and taking care of immediate crises that they don't invest in high-leverage Quadrant II planning, prevention, and empowerment activities that make the significant difference?

We spend an incredibly inordinate amount of time dealing with symptoms of low trust, and *learning how to deal with the symptoms faster is not going to make a qualitative difference.*

"First things first together" is a function of empowerment. It's the ultimate way of moving the fulcrum over from the "one to one" ratio to a "one unit of effort to one thousand units of results" ratio. There's no time management technique that can even begin to approach the results. And that's why empowerment is at the heart of Quadrant II.

13: *Empowerment from the Inside Out*

*Anytime we think the problem is "out there"
that thought is the problem.*

IT would be wonderful if we all lived and worked in empowered, high-trust cultures. Obviously, we don't. The organizations we work in are often inundated by rules, regulations, and red tape. We have mixed directions, competitive systems. Levels of initiative are low. People essentially get their satisfaction *off* the job. They spend much of their on-the-job time in Quadrant III—politicking, backbiting, blaming, accusing, and confessing each other's sins. Then they stand around in the halls massaging each other's hearts:

> *"Can you believe what this manager did?"*
> *"Really! Let me tell you about my experience!"*
> *"No wonder we can't get anything done around here."*
> *"Well, what do you expect?"*

So what can we do?

Anytime we think the problem is "out there," that thought *is* the problem. We disempower ourselves. In other words, we give away our space—the space that allows us to choose a constructive response. We empower circumstances and the weaknesses of other people to control us. We put our energy into our Circle of Concern, into things over which we have no control.

Principle-centered leadership is the personal empowerment that creates empowerment in the organization. It's focusing our energy in our Circle of Influence. It's not blaming or accusing; it's acting with integrity to create the environment in which we and others can develop character and competence and synergy.

We may not be *the* leader, but we're *a* leader. And as we exercise principle-centered leadership, our Circle of Influence grows.

Stephen: Several years ago, a man who was in lower-level management in an organization wanted to come to one of our seminars. The program was for top executives, but he wanted to come so badly he literally begged them to let him come. Finally, the sheer pressure of persistence broke them down and they agreed.

This man was so proactive, he just took the ball and started running. He began to focus on personal and professional growth and enlarging his skill base. He got one promotion after another, and within two years he was the number three man in the organization.

Then he decided to go out into the community and help solve some of the larger social issues. He was so dynamic, he became an executive secretary in a service organization and was even asked to join them full-time, but he didn't want to leave his organization.

I'm convinced you could drop that man naked and penniless anywhere and within a short period of time, he would rise to the top of an organization because he is so proactive, sensitive, and aware. I'll never forget the light in his eyes when he started to sense the power of working in his Circle of Influence.

In this chapter, we'd like to look at three specific things we can do in any Circle of Influence to work in Quadrant II to empower ourselves and help transform our environment:

1. cultivate the conditions of empowerment
2. feast on the lunch of champions
3. become a leader/servant

1. CULTIVATE THE CONDITIONS OF EMPOWERMENT

Empowerment can't be installed; it has to be grown. It's a matter of nurturing the conditions that create it. The more these conditions are present, the more empowered the culture will be.

We don't really "empower" other people, but by nurturing these conditions, we create the environment in which they can empower themselves through the use of their four endowments. This is high-leverage Quadrant II investment that brings great returns.

To one degree or another, each of these conditions is in our Circle of Influence. Let's consider these conditions to see where and how we can focus our efforts to create empowering change.

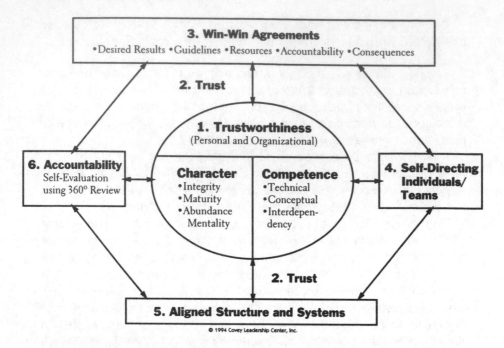

3. Win-Win Agreements
•Desired Results •Guidelines •Resources •Accountability •Consequences

2. Trust

1. Trustworthiness
(Personal and Organizational)

6. Accountability
Self-Evaluation
using 360° Review

Character
•Integrity
•Maturity
•Abundance
  Mentality

Competence
•Technical
•Conceptual
•Interdepen-
  dency

**4. Self-Directing
Individuals/
Teams**

2. Trust

5. Aligned Structure and Systems

© 1994 Covey Leadership Center, Inc.

Condition 1: Trustworthiness

At the heart of empowerment is trustworthiness—which is a function of character and competence. Character is what we are; competence is what we can do. And both are necessary to create trustworthiness.

> *Stephen: A man I know well has a slight limp because of a loose left knee. He went to a doctor who was a very fine person, but incompetent—he wasn't skillful in performing a three-dimensional activity while looking at a two-dimensional monitor. He did a little cleaning up of the cartilage, but he didn't diagnose the extenuated anterior cruciate ligament. As a result, this man never got into therapy. He never paid the real price. Later, when his daughter and son had their knees injured in athletics, he didn't send them to this doctor. He didn't trust him.*

One CEO, hearing that story, said, "Now I understand for the first time why I don't trust some people. I think, 'You're a good person. You're honest. So why don't I trust you?'

"I realize now it's because they're not competent. They haven't stayed current in their profession. They're obsolete. They've been carried by the organization. They don't have the spirit of continuous improvement."

But competence without character doesn't inspire trust either. You wouldn't want to go to a doctor who had the competence but was dishonest. Perhaps you only need therapy, but there's money in an operation, so he may convince you to submit to surgery you don't even need.

Both character and competence are necessary to inspire trust. And both are completely within our Circle of Influence. Character includes:

- *integrity*—the ability to walk your talk, a thorough integratedness of public, private, and deep inner life around a balanced set of principles
- *maturity*—the balance of courage and consideration that enables you to say what needs to be said, to give honest feedback, to address issues in a straightforward way, but with consideration and respect for the feelings, thoughts, and opinions of others
- *abundance mentality*—the paradigm that life is ever expanding, that there are an infinite number of third alternatives (in contrast to the paradigm that life is a zero sum game, that the pie is only so large and if anyone else gets a piece, that means less for me)

Competence includes:

- *technical competence*—the knowledge and skill to achieve the agreed-upon results; the ability to think through problems and look for new alternatives
- *conceptual competence*—the ability to see the big picture, to examine assumptions and shift perspectives
- *interdependent competence*—the ability to interact effectively with others, including the ability to listen, communicate, get to third alternatives, create win-win agreements, and work toward synergistic solutions; the ability to see and operate effectively and cooperatively in complete organizations and systems

Character and competence are high-leverage areas of focus that make each of the other conditions possible.

A division of a large international firm was able to see how this connection was impacting their unsuccessful attempt to implement a total quality program. They essentially said:

242   FIRST THINGS FIRST

*Our problem is scarcity. We have scarcity in the way we admit peo-
ple into our ranks, scarcity in the way we promote them, scarcity
in the way we compensate them, scarcity in the way they're made
partners, scarcity in the way the rewards of partnership are distributed. No wonder we have such a messed-up culture! No wonder
there's so much jealousy. There's so much feigned, pretended, cos-
metic unity, but down deep inside there are forces that are splitting
this culture apart—hidden agendas operating everywhere, relationship problems, departments at the throats of other departments.
We have to have heavy structures and systems, rules and regulations just to bring sufficient order to the organization to enable it to
survive the changing environment. There are benchmarking evi-
dences that we are not with it anymore. We realize we're not going to
get with it with a quick-fix, compartmentalized paradigm that isn't
based on an ecological understanding of what creates this synergistic culture.*

We see it happening time and time again. People scripted in competition create competitive rather than cooperative systems. People
with a fundamental urgency paradigm create systems that grow out of
it. Even when someone else comes in and tries to install win-win or
importance-based systems and structures, if the fundamental paradigm remains unchanged, people will revert to their paradigms when
push comes to shove.

The reality is that character and competence drive everything else
in the organization. To nurture character and competence is the most
high-leverage thing we can do to create empowerment.

One powerful way we can nurture character and competence is to
ask ourselves questions as we prepare to set our weekly goals:

- What knowledge or skills do I need to do the job better and to
  interact more effectively with other people?
- Am I exercising courage to move things ahead and deal with
  the issues?
- Am I being considerate and sensitive to the needs of others?
- Am I constantly looking for third-alternative solutions?
- Am I listening to my conscience and acting in a way that's in
  alignment with my mission and true north?

These questions invite conscience to pinpoint areas for focused
effort. Based on the answers, we can set "sharpen the saw" or role-
related goals for improvement.

In addition to individual trustworthiness, collective character and competence are necessary conditions of empowerment for the organization.

- Can I trust the company to back up their commitments?
- Can I trust the team to perform when needed?
- Can and do family members support each other?

Remember, there is no such thing as organizational behavior; there is only behavior of individuals within the organization. An organization becomes trustworthy only as the individuals in the organization become trustworthy.

Condition 2: Trust

Trust is the glue that holds everything together. It creates the environment in which all of the other elements—win-win stewardship agreements, self-directing individuals and teams, aligned structures and systems, and accountability—can flourish. Then, as each of these other conditions is fulfilled—as people create win-win stewardship agreements, as individuals and teams become self-governing, as structures and systems are aligned and accountability is an ongoing process—trust increases even more. The process is recursive.

Again, trust is the natural outgrowth of trustworthiness. So the highest-leverage thing we can do to create trust is to be trustworthy.

Condition 3: Win-Win Stewardship Agreements

We may not be in a formal leadership position in our group or organization, but that doesn't mean we can't initiate stewardship agreements concerning our area of responsibility. We can do it in our family. We can do it in our work team. We can do it in our community service group.

- What are the results we want to accomplish?
- What guidelines should we follow?
- What resources do we have?
- To whom are we accountable in this effort?
- What are the consequences?

Whatever your Circle of Influence, whatever the culture, you can work toward creating shared expectations and understanding. Questions we might ask during weekly organizing to help us set goals to nurture stewardship agreements might include:

- Do I have meaningful stewardship agreements in each of my roles?
- Are there any agreements that need to be strengthened, modified, or taken to a higher level?
- Am I acting with integrity to carry out the agreements I've made?

Anytime we help create shared vision and strategy—with a boss, a peer, a direct report, a spouse, a child, an associate—we empower ourselves and others.

Condition 4: Self-Directing Individuals and Teams

In a high-trust culture, who supervises? The agreement.

Self-direction based on the agreement is in our Circle of Influence. We can accept the responsibility to govern ourselves as individuals and as part of groups or teams in harmony with true north and according to the agreements we've made. We can do what we've agreed to do—including plan, act, and evaluate—without someone having to direct, control, check up, and hover over. And we can build this capacity in others not by supervising methods but by holding people accountable for results and being a source of help to them in achieving those results.

Questions we could ask during Quadrant II organizing might include:

- Do I typically wait until I'm told to do things I already know ought to be done?
- Do I allow others the freedom to use those methods that work best for them, regardless of my personal preference, as long as they accomplish agreed-upon results?
- Do I give others space while they work, or am I constantly hovering over and checking up?

Condition 5: Aligned Structures and Systems

When structures and systems are aligned, they facilitate empowerment; when they aren't, they work against it. If you're trying to use importance as a governing paradigm and your planning system is set up on a daily to-do basis, your system is not aligned. If you're trying to build responsibility in your children and you're constantly giving them detailed "gofer" delegation—what to do, how to do it, and when to do it—your system is not aligned. If you're trying to encourage cooperation in your organization, but you're rewarding competition, your system is not aligned. In each of these cases, you're working against the very things you're trying to accomplish.

When structure and systems are aligned, they create integrity or integratedness. They facilitate rather than roadblock what you're trying to do.

Some structures will be in our Circle of Influence; others will not. If we're in a position of formal leadership, we may have responsibility for systems such as compensation, information, or training that will impact the time and quality of life of many people. Investing in Quadrant II time to create abundance-based, principle-based systems develops powerful alignment in the culture.

But even if we're not in a position to create structures and systems for the organization, we can still take appropriate opportunity to influence their creation or re-creation. We can take Quadrant II time to create aligned systems and structures in our personal life—our organizer, our personal information systems, our personal development program. We can create them in our family and nurture an environment where stewardship agreements become the way of interacting. We can help create them in our work team, or in community service or special interest groups. In any sphere where we interact with others, we can raise the issues and help create structures and systems that are based on true north.

This reiterates another important difference between management and leadership. While management works *in* the system, leadership works *on* the system. As we do our weekly organizing, we can nurture aligned structure and systems as we ask:

- Are there any systems or structures that are getting in the way of the desired results?
- Are there any systems or structures that could be created to better facilitate the accomplishment of the desired results?
- What is the best method I could use, within my Circle of Influence, to create or change these systems?
- How can I work synergistically with others to create change?
- What personal systems and structures do I have that I could improve?

Condition 6: Accountability

When we're in an environment of growing trust, where win-win stewardship agreements are being developed and structures and systems are aligned, how does accountability take place? Largely through self-accountability against the criteria of the agreement.

Specific things we can do to nurture accountability include:

- building specific criteria into the agreement
- exercising discernment
- requesting and receiving feedback

As we build criteria into the agreement, we create a standard against which we can measure our own performance.

As we develop discernment, we depend less on external factors—such as promotions, awards, formal recognition, or social acknowledgment—for the feeling that we've done a good job. We accept the responsibility for our own excellence. We don't blame shoddy performance on someone else; we're not lifted up by praise we don't deserve. Criticism or praise from others is secondary to our own connection with conscience.

But we also have the humility to seek feedback from others as a vital part of our evaluation, planning, and decision-making process. We'll discuss feedback in depth as we look at feasting on "the lunch of champions."

Identifying and understanding these six conditions of empowerment enable us to focus our efforts on the highest-leverage Quadrant II activities. When we don't recognize or know how to solve the chronic problems in families, groups, and organizations, we spend an inordinate amount of time dealing with crises in Quadrants I and III, and even our Quadrant II work is on the symptom level—we hack at the leaves instead of working at the root.

But understanding these conditions enables us to focus our efforts on the deeper, underlying issues. It helps us know how we can act within our Circle of Influence—whatever it may be—to make a powerful difference.

2. FEAST ON THE LUNCH OF CHAMPIONS

Building character and competency is a process, and one of the highest-leverage things we can do in this process is to regularly seek 360 degree feedback. It takes humility to ask for and receive it. You may have to take oxygen to get through it. But understanding it and acting wisely with regard to it can powerfully impact your time and quality of life.

Because of its value, some people have called feedback "the breakfast of champions." But it isn't the breakfast; it's the lunch. Vision is the breakfast. Self-correction is the dinner. Without vision, we have no context for feedback. We're just responding to what someone else values or wants. We're living out of the social mirror. We fall into the trap of trying to become all things to all people, meeting everybody's expectations, and we end up essentially meeting nobody's, including our own.

But with a clear sense of vision and mission, we can use feedback to help us achieve a greater integrity. We have the humility to recognize that we have blind spots, that getting other perspectives will help us improve the quality of our own. We also have the wisdom to realize that feedback tells us as much about the people from whom we receive it as it does about ourselves. The responses of others reflect not only how they see us, but also how well they feel we do those things that are important to them. Because people are important to us, and because part of our leadership is creating shared importance, this dimension of feedback is vitally important as well. But we aren't governed by feedback; we're governed by the principles and purposes we have built into our mission statement.

We can get feedback as employees—from bosses, subordinates, associates, peers. We can get feedback as parents—from our children, our spouse, other parents, our own parents. We can get feedback in our community role, our extended family role, or in any role where additional perspective would be helpful.

Rebecca: I remember the first time Roger asked for feedback from our children. I just about fell through the floor! I thought, "Great! Now we're going to hear about it—piano practice, spinach, bedtime, household jobs . . ." My mind almost cringed as I thought about all the things they'd be sure to bring up.

Roger asked each of the children to write three words on a piece of paper: continue, stop, and start. Then he said, "What are the things I'm now doing you'd like to see me continue to do? What would you like to see me stop doing? What would you like to see me start doing that I'm not doing now?" I had to admit I admired his courage.

But what I admired even more was the depth of the children's replies. They somehow sensed this was the time for a different kind of response. Their replies were thoughtful, helpful, and supportive. They reflected awareness and appreciation. The suggestions they had made us both aware of things that were important to them, changes we could make that would really make a difference. Some time later, I got up the courage to do it myself and was once again astonished at the maturity of the replies.

Through the years, we've come to value our children's feedback deeply, especially as some of our older ones have left home and gained greater perspective of their experience with us. It's not only been personally helpful; it's also given the children a sense of participation and investment in creating the kind of family we want to be.

As soon as you receive feedback, it's good to carefully analyze it and then go back to those who gave it and say, "Thank you. I appreciate this feedback. Let me share it with you. This is what you're saying to me." Feed it back to them and then involve them in creating an action plan based on that feedback. As you do this, you become a change catalyst. You model change, and when people around you see that happen, they become open to your change and to their own as well.

There are a variety of simple and effective methods to get feedback; the "continue/stop/start" method is just one example. There are formal and informal methods. Feedback can be anonymous or face-to-face. Feedback tools that have objective criteria, such as our *Seven Habits Profile*, are generally more powerful because the criteria tie into the collective conscience—into principles people can identify with—instead of reflecting more of the values of the person giving the feedback.

It's extremely important that people don't judge each other's character. Feedback should be given against performance and effectiveness criteria—not character criteria. When desired results deal with performance criteria, people will go inside and work on their character if that's what it takes to achieve those results.

A CEO of one organization asked people to give feedback based on two questions. These questions were designed around the idea that we spend our time in three different roles:

- *producer* (doing things necessary to produce desired results)
- *manager* (setting up and working with people in systems)
- *leader* (providing vision and direction and building a complementary team based on mutual respect)

He asked people to indicate by the size of the letters P, M, and L where they felt he spent most of his time. He then asked them to represent how they felt he *should* be spending his time. When he got his feedback he found that his profile was **P M** L, but that the desired profile was overwhelmingly **P** M **L**. His people wanted him to spend more time leading the organization. They felt that he needed to be looking ahead, reading the trends, and establishing direction for their company in an industry that was rapidly changing. They felt management and production were things they could do by themselves, and that his energies would be best spent in providing leadership.

Based on this feedback, this CEO made significant changes in his activities. He focused his attention on the business environment. Those who gave him feedback encouraged and supported his change. A short time later, the benefits of this move became obvious. He was able to spot and respond to some emerging trends in a way that catapulted his company forward dramatically and created a significant increase in market share.

The point here is not that leadership is more important than production or management; all three were critical to this company's success. The point is that leadership was being neglected. By seeking and acting on feedback, this CEO became aware of the need and was able to move his company forward in powerful ways.

Most executives neglect Quadrant II leadership and focus on management. But this management focus actually generates the need for *more* management to deal with all the problems that result from neglecting leadership. This points out another advantage of the Quadrant II process. Weekly organizing encourages leadership with vision and perspective. Daily planning, on the other hand, increases the need for management because so much time is spent prioritizing crises.

Good feedback given early in a project can make a significant positive difference down the road. One associate shared this experience:

The first week I had a new assignment, I had this great vision of what I wanted to do and I thought, "I'm the king," so to speak. I felt like I was in control.

Then a junior in the organization who'd only been with us a couple of years walked up to me and said, "I really think this plan you've got going stinks." He didn't say it in quite those words, but that was the message. "This thing is never going to work. I don't think we should do it at all."

I felt like saying, "That's the dumbest thing I've ever heard!" But I just gritted my teeth and said, "I value the differences. Why don't you come in and we'll talk about it?"

In fifteen minutes, that individual outlined all of the major potholes in my plan and created a whole new paradigm for me. It was such a powerful learning experience, I started a process of polling, talking to, listening to all of the stakeholders I could find. I asked them, "What's your paradigm of this division?" I still have stacks of notes I draw out of from time to time to allow me to get around the potholes.

Many organizations do not get 360 degree feedback. They're focused on the numbers, the bottom line. It's short-term, hard-line data. But this is an incomplete information system because it doesn't deal with people. It doesn't even claim to. It might record their activities and their costs. But it says nothing about their hearts and minds, their power, their capacities. It creates a bottom-line mentality that drives the organization in such a way that they neglect many of those key factors that can't be measured, such as people development, quality improvements, work on the system, long-term investment, team spirit, trust in the culture, and second-mile service.

The more we work with organizations, the more convinced we become that this 360 degree feedback from all stakeholders—customers, suppliers, employees, affiliates, vendors, investors, community, self— has a powerful impact on quality. We sometimes call this 360 degree review process "Stakeholder Information Systems," or SIS.

Stephen: At one time I did a training program for the commanding generals of the Air Force in a country with a history of challenge and conflict. I was talking about the importance of SIS and I noticed that the generals were nodding their heads in agreement. I turned to the general in charge and said, "Does this mean you're using Stakeholder Information Systems?"

He said, "That's the way we train these people. They're top pilots, not trained managers. Everyone gets an annual printout of the perceptions of all those they interface with, and the strength of those perceptions. They use it as the basis for their personal and professional development, and no one gets promoted unless they have high marks, including from their subordinates."

I said, "You have no idea how hard it is to get that concept bought into by many organizations in my country. What keeps it from becoming a popularity contest?"

He replied, "Stephen, the very survival of our country depends on these people and they know it. Sometimes the most unpopular people are given the highest marks because they perform."

It takes humility to seek feedback. It takes wisdom to understand it, analyze it, and appropriately act on it. But it truly is the lunch of champions.

3. BECOME A LEADER/SERVANT

When we're in a formal leadership role, if we're not into micromanaging, hovering over, checking up, and managing crises, what do we spend our time doing?

We create shared vision. We strengthen, coach, and mentor to help develop the capacities of individuals and teams. We build relationships of trust. We do long-range planning, scan horizons, look at stakeholders' needs, study the trends of the market, work on systems, create alignment. In other words, we spend time doing the important, non-urgent Quadrant II activities that make the significant difference. We're not just into managing our time to do what's in front of us; we literally do different things. We become a "leader/servant."

The idea of "servant leadership" has been around for a long time, but it's never really taken hold because the conditions of empowerment have not been in place. It becomes just another nice phrase, another way of exercising a benevolent authoritarian kind of control. Eventually it creates cynicism.

But when the conditions of empowerment are in place, servant leadership creates powerful results.

Stephen: I remember my first experience working with a truly empowering leader. Up to that point in my life, my experience with leadership was basically with a "kind control" approach—sort of a benevolent autocracy. Then I came into a situation where I had a new boss. He didn't see the world through that paradigm at all. He saw the world through an empowerment paradigm. And my first experience with him utterly disarmed me.

I had been put in charge of a large operation and had many managers reporting to me. My first contact with this man was one day when he called me on the phone. As I look back now, I see that all the elements of win-win—the desired results, guidelines, resources, accountability, and consequences—were in place through the organization, though they weren't written down or labeled in that way at the time.

This man said, "Stephen, I see my role as one of being a source of help to you, so I would like you to think of me in this way and let me know what I can do to help you." I thought to myself, "Well that's one of the nicest, most considerate approaches I've ever heard, but basically he's just trying to build the relationship so he can come in and make sure things are going right and correct whatever's wrong." We judge others by ourselves, and that was the way I thought. So when I heard his words, I projected my own motive on his behavior, unaware of the paradigm out of which he was operating.

He said to me, "I really mean it, Stephen. I'd like to come and visit with you, but perhaps this is not an appropriate time. You may have a number of things going on there, and now wouldn't be the best time to try to give you help. You decide."

And I thought, "I think he does mean it. It looks like I can call the shots here. He's not just a hovering supervisor checking up on me. He really wants to be a source of help."

Then he said, "Maybe I could tell you a little about myself and what my experience has been, and that might give you an idea of how I could be a resource to you." Well, he had had something like twenty-five years' more experience than I had. He had a rich resource base and was extremely wise. But I did have a lot of things going on at the time, so I said to him, "Perhaps another time would be better." So we put it off.

When I did ask him to visit a few weeks later, he took the same attitude. I met him at the airport and asked what he wanted to look into. But he said, "I'm here to help. We'll do whatever you would like." So I took him to a meeting, and I said, "It would help if you were to reinforce this point that I'm trying to get across." So, he did it. Then I made another request and he fulfilled it. Each time, he would turn to me and say, "Is there anything else?"

Well, I started feeling, "I'm the one that's responsible. He's here to help me." And I started being very open to him. As I would leave a meeting after handling some problems in the way I'd traditionally handled them, I would turn to him and say, "What do you think about the way I handled that? Was it congruent with your experience?"

And he would answer, "Well, Stephen, you might consider what they're doing in another division. Or you might consider this other option." He didn't tell me to do one thing. He basically affirmed my responsibility and my power to make the decisions, but he gave illustrations of examples of things I might consider.

So what happened was that my conscience, not this man, became the dominant force. He had other areas of responsibility. He would leave me and go on to do other things, but my conscience never would. It was always with me.

Boy, did I feel responsible! So I started to plumb him for his wisdom and his experience, and he came forth in abundance. But he *never told me what to do. He always said, "You might consider this option" or "Had you thought about this possibility?"*

Well, that enthroned my conscience in a way I had never experienced before.

Shortly after that I went to work with another supervisor who was a very fine person as well, but very controlling. And I eventually found how easy it was to just do what he told me to do. But there was no creative opportunity, no learning opportunity. I felt totally disempowered. So I found most of my satisfactions off the job, not on the job. And all the people around this person did this same thing. They accommodated his style.

It's these kinds of experiences that help me contrast empowerment and control.

As we've interviewed a number of Malcolm Baldrige National Quality Award winners, we've asked them, "What's been the most difficult challenge?" "Giving up control!" has been the almost unanimous reply. It's hard. It goes against our scripting. Most of us have not had empowered and empowering mentors to teach us how to do it. But as former President George Bush said at a Malcolm Baldrige Award presentation ceremony, "These winning companies . . . realize that they are only as strong as the intelligence, judgment, and character of their employees."[1]

The job of the leader/servant is to help build that intelligence, judgment, and character. It may require significant breaks with traditional ways of seeing and doing. For example, you might:

• Take your son to your next parent-teacher meeting and let him help conduct the interview. Let him describe his work, talk about his desires and hopes, and respond, if he chooses, to his teacher's feedback. You and the teacher become leader/servants. Say, in effect, "Your education is your stewardship. What can we do to help?"

• The next time the bureaucracy requires you to do a performance review, give the review form to the employee *before* the period of time to which it pertains. Be sure to discuss the elements of the form because they become part of the desired results, guidelines, resources, accountability, and consequences of the performance agreement. Then be a source of help to the employee. As you "run along beside" the person, ask the questions:

> How's it going?
> What are you learning?
> What are your goals?
> What can I do to help?

When the time comes for the performance review to be turned in, have the employee fill it out and then review it together. Discuss your performance as well. Have you provided appropriate resources and support?

• When someone comes to you with a problem, ask him or her, "What do you recommend?" Don't be quick to solve problems that people can and should solve for themselves. Encourage them to use their creativity to find newer, better ways to do things. Hold people accountable for results, not methods.

Rebecca: Some time ago, I was asked to work with a group of young people in creating and producing a musical play. I was just learning about the leader/servant concept at the time, and I decided that, more than producing a play, I wanted to help these young people grow and develop their talents and leadership skills.

In cooperation with those who had asked me to help with this production, I set up certain guiding principles I felt would best accomplish that purpose:

- *Fix responsibility and teach the young people how to carry it.*
- *Don't tolerate incompetence; help them become competent.*
- *Teach them correct principles and let them govern themselves.*

The leaders—Becky and Brent—were both seventeen. They were talented and enthusiastic about the project, but they'd had no experience in doing what they were trying to do. As I met with them, I said, "I'm thrilled to be working with you on this. I know it's going to be a wonderful production. I'd like to meet with you regularly, and I'm willing to do anything I can to help you succeed. My job is to be a resource to you. What would you like me to do?"

At first, they were somewhat taken aback. They didn't really have any idea of what needed to be done and assumed I was going to tell them. But I didn't. As I explained the leader/servant role to them, we established a psychological contract and I assured them that I would be there at any time to provide information, help, and support. Once they had a clear sense of their own roles, they started thinking. "Well, we're going to need a script."

"Great!" I said. "Where are you going to get it?"

As they talked it over, the first idea they came up with was to an-

nounce the theme and ask other young people for submission of scripts. Frankly, I didn't know whether or not that approach would work. We only had six months until performance. I wanted them to learn, but I also wanted them to succeed. I expressed my concerns, but I also expressed my faith in their leadership and made it clear that the decision was in their hands. They decided to set a deadline for submission that would still give them time to work out another option if no suitable scripts came in.

None did. So at our next meeting, I said, "Okay, what can we learn from this? And what's your next plan of action?" They talked over various possibilities and decided to write it themselves—Becky would write the script and Brent the music. Although Becky enjoyed writing and Brent loved music, neither of them had ever done anything like this before. They felt overwhelmed and a little scared. But I expressed confidence in their ability to make it happen. They went to work.

Within a few weeks, they were able to produce what I felt was a great script and a number of beautiful original songs. In subsequent meetings, they decided to involve other young people as leaders in every aspect of the production. The director, the choreographer, the set designer, the accompanist were all young people between the ages of twelve and seventeen. I met with Becky and Brent before each of their meetings with the other youth leaders to help them plan and prepare for the meeting. I met with them after each of those meetings to help them evaluate and implement what they learned. I suggested that one way I could help would be to provide an adult advisor for each of the youth leaders to counsel, coach, and help—but not to do their job. Becky and Brent liked the idea, so I enlisted the aid of adult specialists in each area and met with them to explain the approach we wanted to take to help the young people grow.

It was thrilling to watch things progress. As the three of us met regularly, I'd ask, "How's it going?" They would share their experience and talk about their frustrations and concerns. When they asked for advice, sometimes I'd make a suggestion—"Have you considered this possibility?" or "Maybe you could approach it this way." But more often I'd say, "That's a real concern. What do you recommend?" On some occasions, I gently brought up things they hadn't considered. I was absolutely amazed at the creative ideas they came up with as they realized that it really was their responsibility and that nobody was going to do it for them, but that they had plenty of people willing to work under their direction and help turn their dream into reality.

Staying to the guidelines was not always easy. At one of the rehearsals, one of the adult leaders—who was very technically competent and was used to a more controlling style of leadership—began to take over the job of the youth leader he was supposed to advise. My immediate impulse was to walk over and say, "What are you doing? You know we're trying to help these kids learn how to do this themselves!" But I decided that it was more in harmony with what we were trying to do to wait and see what the youth leaders would do. They finally came to me and described the problem. I said, "That is a problem. What are you going to do?" They talked it over and decided that the youth leader whose stewardship it was would approach this adult advisor with the concern. She handled it with courage and consideration, and the problem was resolved.

In the end, they involved ninety young people in the production. The youth leaders and everyone who participated in it worked and sweated and learned far more than they would have if the adults had run the show. And the quality of the production was incredible. People who saw it were moved to tears. After performing the play locally, the young people were asked to give two additional performances for hundreds of people in a convention hall in a large neighboring city. It received standing ovations both nights.

I discovered that being a leader/servant was a lot tougher—at least the first time—than being a controlling leader. But the rewards were so much greater! The production was exciting—but even more exciting to me was the thought that, wherever these young people went in the future, they would carry with them the increased capacity to make a qualitative difference in whatever they did.

"Accomplishing tasks through people" is a different paradigm than "building people through the accomplishment of tasks." With one, you get things done. With the other, you get them done with far greater creativity, synergy, and effectiveness . . . and in the process, you build the capacity to do more in the future as well.

ALL THIS SOUNDS GREAT, BUT . . .

Most people can see the powerful impact principle-centered leadership can have in creating an empowering environment. But there are challenges. Where the rubber meets the road, we sometimes run into situations that test us deeply, that call on us to access our endowments and capacities in new and powerful ways. As a conclusion to this chapter, we'd like to address some of the most commonly faced challenges in creating empowerment from the inside out.

What if My Boss Has Never Heard of Win-Win?

Even if your boss has never heard of win-win, he or she has at least heard of "win," so start there. You don't even have to use the words "stewardship agreement." Just say to your boss, "I've been going over my roles and I just want to make sure that we have a clear agreement of what I'm supposed to be working on. Here's the list as I see it in priority. Would you mind looking at it and letting me know if you see it differently?" Seek to understand. Talk it over. Agree on desired results.

At another time, you can go back and say, "Now here are the key policies and guidelines I'm aware of. Is there anything I don't know about that I should?" In the same way, you can go through each of the five elements of win-win.

This may take weeks, even months. But then you can perform based on that. And if a request comes down the line that's not in harmony with the agreement, you can go back to it and say, "Now here are the priorities I understood you wanted me to follow. What would you like me to change?" It may be that the request is a genuine change of direction. Or it may be that it was just another "to do" that was about to be passed on to you (and will now get passed on to some urgency-driven person instead). The agreement will give you—and your boss—a standard to measure against.

What if My Boss Doesn't Want Me to Be Empowered?

One woman shared this experience:

I work in a culture that's really a "good old boys" club. Their top management are all sixty-year-old men who've been in the business for years, and their attitude is "Go get me a cup of coffee, girl." It's really difficult to be taken seriously and to move up in the ranks. They've been doing things the same way for thirty years and they don't want to change. And when some bright-eyed secretary comes up and says, "I really want to do this win-win," they don't have time for her.

Realistically, there are some situations where the culture is so deeply ingrained and people have been into this for so long that it's very difficult to change it, particularly if your Circle of Influence is small. If the situation is not a win for you, your best option may be to look for a better one.

However, there are many, many examples where people in such situations have been able to effect great change.

Roger: Some years ago, I was put in charge of developing a training program for a large organization. When I arrived, I inherited a secretary who had been there for a while. My attitude certainly wasn't "Go get a cup of coffee, girl," but in the midst of my challenges, I just took one look, checked her off on my list—"competent secretary, check"—and hurriedly moved on to "more important" things.

She did everything I expected a secretary to do very well. But gradually, she began to do more. After a few sessions of dictation, she brought the letters in for me one day, opened and sorted, and she said, "If there are any of these letters you'd like answered in a way similar to the ones we did yesterday, I'd be happy to draft them for you to save you time. You could look them over and see what you think." I was feeling a time crunch, so I said, "Why not?" The drafts she gave me were well written and sensitive—better than I could have done myself. Within a short period of time, she was doing 95 percent of the letters and bringing them to me for my approval.

Because I was impressed with her writing, I asked if she'd like to be involved in creating a training manual. She agreed, so I gave her a particular section and asked her to jot down a few ideas. She not only put down her ideas; she produced an excellent draft of the proposed material.

Eventually, she ended up as a trainer and assistant manager in the department. I finally discovered that she had a master's degree in communication and accepted the secretarial position at the time because that was what was available. She became a major reason why that training program was so successful.

This woman raised my vision of how effective someone could be in fulfilling a role. Since that experience, my view of secretaries and their potential has forever been changed, and it's affected the way I've interacted with every secretary since. Some of my greatest work associates have been people who have started out as secretaries and increased their capacities and moved on, or have continued to be incredible secretaries because that's what they wanted to be.

In almost every situation, if you build your skills and capacities and work within your Circle of Influence, you can change people's paradigms of you and your job over time. If you don't have a clear vision of what you want to do in your job and a willingness to pay the price to create change, it's easy to disempower yourself, to get into blaming and accusing. The key is to stay empowered, to realize that you can make the choice to try to change the paradigm or to change the situation.

What if the People I Lead Don't Want to Be Empowered?

Some people have been so beaten up by "management by objective" experiences where they exercised some freedom and got shot out of the saddle that they have deep scar tissue. Their attitude is, "Just tell me what to do. Let me make as much money as I can in the least time possible and let me get out of here." Others think what happens at work doesn't have any impact on quality of life. They get their satisfaction off the job. They've reached a sort of equilibrium, and they just don't want to be bothered.

Win-win takes people where they are, not where you want them to be. So you can meet them where they are. You can set up a stewardship agreement based on whatever level of initiative they feel comfortable with. But be totally open. Keep your agenda on the table.

"I sense you'd prefer to just meet expectations like you've been doing. You feel if you do that well, that should be enough. As long as we can agree on performance and levels of accountability that are good for both of us, if that's your win for now, that's fine.

"But I want you to know that I really value you and want your contribution. As opportunities come up, I'll keep you informed. I'm convinced that over time, if we can find areas of greater interest for you and work toward higher levels of initiative, it will be better for both of us."

Other things you could do to help build empowerment might include the following:

- Involve them in the creation of a mission statement for the group or organization.
- When they come to you with problems, ask, "What do you recommend?"
- Be patient and let the example of others in the group with high-level initiative agreements speak for themselves.

What if the System I Work in Is Win-Lose?

Suppose you're a manager of a small department, and you really believe in a team management approach. You've worked with your team to create a mission statement, and that mission statement has really worked well. All the team members buy into it. They like it. They're excited about it. It's empowered them. They have a sense of stewardship.

But you're in an organizational arrangement that forces you to rank your four people. It's a misaligned system—you hire winners and then spend your time sorting them out. So what can you do?

Involve them in the problem; work out the solution together.

You can get them together, explain how the system operates, and ask them if they have any creative ideas of how you can work together within the system to meet their needs. "Here is our problem. What do you suggest?"

If your trust level is high, you can generate genuine third-alternative solutions together.

Depending on your Circle of Influence and the trust you have with others, your efforts to change the system may spread to affect the entire organization. If you're patient and persistent, and you operate in harmony with correct principles, the positive change you create may benefit everyone.

What if There's a Scarcity Reality?

In a large oil organization one time, someone said, "What happens in bad times? What happens when you're into significant downsizing?"

Another person stood up and said, "I'll tell you what happens. We not only downsized, we closed an entire plant." He proceeded to tell us how their senior executives involved everyone in the problem from the beginning. They were seeking to understand, going for synergy and win-win. Together, they looked at the economic and financial data, their industry, their company situation. Everyone could see the economic realities that were spelling doom for the plant. It was obsolete. The market was drying up. They could all see that this was not a salvageable operation. So together, they focused their attention on outplacement work.

The day the plant closed, the media came in expecting to see picket lines, protests, anger, and hostility. Instead, they were amazed to see a huge Kentucky Fried Chicken farewell party. There was such a high sense of trust in the culture because of the openness of the senior executives in involving people in the problem and working out the solution together.

What if the Situation Changes?

What happens when you get a new boss, when the department you're in is reorganized, when you find out that the desired results are no longer desirable?

And what about changes outside the organization? How do you account for the changing environment? What happens when the supplier changes, or the stock market crashes, or market trends take a sudden turn? How do you compensate for all these things within the framework of the agreement?

The assumption in creating a stewardship agreement is that the situation *will* change. It's not a legal agreement. People aren't running scared of it. It's built on trust. It's not designed to tie people down, but to free them up. It's a better form of communication and clarification around expectations. It's designed to change with changing situations. It can be opened by either party at any time. It's a living document.

What if I'm Afraid to Rock the Boat?

A participant in one of our programs—a manager in a major corporation—shared this experience:

One day, I was sitting in a company meeting where people were discussing important policies that could have a significant negative impact on the environment. As I sat there, I came to the realization that, while I felt very strongly about these issues, I was essentially silent.

"Why?" I asked myself. "Why am I afraid to open my mouth? When I was hired into this company from the outside years ago, I had no fear. I openly expressed my feelings and concerns. I was confident. I felt I could act with integrity. What's made the difference?"

As I thought about it, I realized that since that time, I had acquired substantial retirement benefits. I'd bought a new home. I was making payments on a new boat. Essentially, I didn't want to do anything that might jeopardize my economic security. I realized the "golden handcuffs" held me bound.

At that point, I made two resolutions: to get my financial affairs in order and build up some reserves, and to continually improve my marketability. I never again wanted to be in a position where my integrity was compromised by my dependence on a job.

This manager reported that he later walked into a staff meeting, handed each person a newspaper, and told them to turn to the want ads. "Look them over," he said. "See if any of the jobs that are advertised look better than the one you presently have." They did, and many of them found jobs that looked really good. "All right," he said. "Go check them out. See if you can qualify for those jobs. Come back and share your experience."

When they returned the following day, most of them had been

shocked to discover that they couldn't qualify. The jobs required new skills, new knowledge and information they didn't have. This manager shared his personal experience with them and encouraged his staff to build their security on their capacity instead of their job.

If you find yourself afraid to act authentically, to speak courageously, to challenge the assumptions, you're doing a disservice to yourself and your organization. Examine your fears, and free yourself so that you can be—and give—your best.

What If the People I Work with Aren't Trustworthy?

What if you have serious doubts about the people you work with? What if you question their competency or even their character? How do you establish a stewardship agreement built on trust?

Here are some key principles:

1. *Look into your own heart first.* Success is always inside out. Start with yourself. How do you see this person? Could your paradigm be part of the problem? Do you genuinely want this person to succeed? Do you believe that this person has the capacity to grow and develop?

It's our experience that most people are not intentionally incompetent. Neither are they purposefully mean, duplicitous, or manipulative. They just don't have their act together . . . yet. Often negative judgments about character grow out of misunderstandings. Assume good intentions. Your deeply held beliefs about someone will create the tone for any interactions you have. Character and competence are always on a continuum. Make sure your paradigms are true to principle.

2. *Nurture self-accountability and self-government.* It's important to realize that we are not ultimately responsible for the development of anyone else. We can never really change someone; people must change themselves. But we can help. We can be a resource. We can nurture, encourage, and support. We can be a leader/servant.

Use the stewardship agreement as a vehicle for growth. It's flexible enough to deal with a broad range of character and competence. Adjust the agreement to meet the situation.

Be realistic and clear about the desired results. Talk them through. You don't do anyone a favor by artificially creating a soft set of expectations. Make sure you represent the interests of all involved—the company, the family, or the work group as well as the individual. In some cases employees may even self-select out of their current job and move to another position more suited to their skills.

Discuss the guidelines. Should more guidelines be established? Maybe you'd like to have more frequent communication. Discuss the level of initiative. Perhaps level two is as high as you want to go at this point. As performance improves, it can be adjusted upward.

Look at the resources. What might be particularly helpful? Give the person every chance to succeed. Perhaps the agreement could include support for attending evening classes or a company training course, or goals for a personal reading program. In a family, it might include certain skills for family members to work on, identifying parents as a resource in their development.

Talk specifically about accountability and consequences. Use shorter-term accountability. Help people develop the ability to evaluate their own performance against the criteria. Again, you gain nothing by being artificially soft—or artificially hard. Deal with the realities. Help people see the results of their behavior.

Sometimes it's best to offer direct feedback. Don't set yourself up as the judge and jury. Be a source of help. Focus your feedback around the elements of the stewardship agreement. Let the agreement govern. As you look at the agreement together in a non-threatening environment, defenses are down and principles do the teaching. Encourage people to access their inner compasses. Ask questions such as, "How do you feel about your performance as it relates to this agreement?" "How do you think your co-workers feel about your involvement?" Create self-awareness. Help them see the logical outcomes of their current level of performance. With clear communication and trustworthiness on your part, people will be open to learning and growth. Their own conscience can instruct.

You may want to suggest that a person gather feedback from others as well. It may be that this person is unaware of how his or her behavior affects others. This feedback must be given in a dignified way—directly to the individual and not to you. If a person is highly dependent on others' opinions, he or she will likely have serious "blindspots"—weaknesses that are too sensitive to be admitted to consciousness. If people are too vulnerable and sensitive, you can involve them in professional development dealing with weaknesses they're aware of. Gradually they'll gain security and be open to blindspot feedback.

Generally speaking, once relatively secure people get this 360 degree feedback on their blindspots, it brings them down to earth. It tends to puncture egotistical tendencies. It humbles them. Even though they may not acknowledge it or express appreciation, it will have its effect.

It's very important at those times to give extra support and attention so that they know you care about them. They must know that you have no secret delight in telling them what they really need to hear.

If the person you don't trust is your boss, open communication is just as valuable. Give honest feedback based on the criteria in the agreement. It may take a long time to build the trust you want. If you feel you can't express your concerns, or find that the person is unwilling to change, you may want to explore other positions or employment opportunities. Working in an environment of mistrust is a drain on you and on the organization.

The fact that people aren't perfect shouldn't hold back your efforts to create a high-trust environment. Don't take the easy way out by reverting to a hard-line, domineering style of interaction. Establishing excessive controls to protect against the problems of a few people will affect the performance of the entire organization.

As the insightful leadership of one company observed in their annual report:

> Trusting people to be creative and constructive when given more freedom does not imply an overly optimistic belief in the perfectability of human nature, it is rather a belief that the inevitable errors and sins of the human condition are far better overcome by individuals working together in an environment of trust, freedom, and mutual respect than by individuals working under a multitude of rules, regulations, and restraints imposed upon them by another group of imperfect people.[2]

What Happens When Someone Makes a Mistake?

In a high-trust culture, honest mistakes are taken for what they are—an opportunity to learn. If at first you don't succeed, *find out why.* Communicate. Open a dialogue. Discover what can be gained from the experience. And then move ahead. It's not a win for the organization if people are afraid to take risks, if they're constantly scared of getting shot out of the saddle. People are not truly self-governing unless they are free to fail.

One manager said:

Things come up all the time where independent decisions need to be made. As a manager, I want these people to be fully functioning, empowered human beings, using their best judgment to create their job as they go along. I know that's the way to get their hearts and not just their hands. The agreement we have is that if they make a mistake, it's my fault. But if they make it again, it's their fault. They're covered to make an empowered decision.

If the same mistake is consistently repeated, this is an indicator that the agreement may be out of sync with reality. There may be a need for more frequent communication and accountability. Perhaps the situation has changed. Perhaps the expectations are not as clear as you thought. Perhaps new knowledge or a new skill is needed.

There are so many reasons why errors may occur that you rarely gain anything by coming unglued when people make a mistake. That one act will send a clear signal throughout the culture of your group or organization—a signal that may snuff out the creativity and initiative you need to be competitive. Rather than pulling out your six-shooter, pull out the agreement. Look at it carefully. Discuss it together. Be open and honest. Give clear feedback. Make what changes need to be made and then move on.

THE MIRACLE OF THE CHINESE BAMBOO TREE

The Chinese bamboo tree is planted after the earth is prepared, and for the first four years, all of the growth is underground. The only thing visible above the ground is a little bulb and a small shoot coming out of it.

Then, in the fifth year, the bamboo tree grows up to eighty feet.

Principle-centered leaders understand the metaphor of the bamboo tree. They understand the value of working in Quadrant II. They know what it means to pay the price to prepare the ground, to plant the seed, and to fertilize and cultivate and water and weed, even when they can't see immediate results, because they have faith that ultimately they will reap the fruits in the harvest.

And what wonderful fruits they are!

Your organization's culture is the one competitive advantage that cannot be duplicated. Technology can be copied. Information can be acquired. Capital can be bought. But the ability of your organization to collaborate effectively, to work in Quadrant II, to put first things first, cannot be bought, transferred, or installed. A high-trust, empowered culture is *always* home-grown.

The same is true for a family, or any other group of people. A quality culture must be nourished over time. Only by acting in harmony with correct principles, exercising patience, humility, and courage, and working within your Circle of Influence can you transform yourself and positively influence your organization. You can only create empowerment from the inside out.

Section Four

THE POWER AND PEACE OF PRINCIPLE-CENTERED LIVING

What are the results of a Quadrant II lifestyle? When first things are first—when we see things in terms of principles, when we pause in the space between stimulus and response, when we act on the basis of importance—what difference does it make in our lives?

In this last section of the book, we'll show how the Quadrant II paradigm plays out in common situations—in the office, in the family, and with teams. We'll show how the fourth generation literally changes the things you do and the reasons why you do them. You'll see how the clock and the compass combine with new maps to create a life of happiness, fulfillment, and tremendous results. We'll identify the keystones as well as the chief obstacles to a principle-centered life. We'll talk about courage and confidence in life's turning points.

Principle-centered living is not an end in itself. It's the means *and* the end. It's the quality of our travel along life's road. It's the power and peace we experience each day as we accomplish what matters most.

In a principle-centered life, the journey and the destination are one.

14: *From Time Management to Personal Leadership*

Management works in the system;
Leadership works on the system.

AT the beginning of this book, we said the fourth generation is different in kind. More than time management, it's personal leadership. It's not just a new process in an old paradigm; it's a new process in a new paradigm.

We'd like to take a look now at the difference personal leadership makes where the rubber meets the road in daily living—at the office, in the family, in a work team or group. As we go through these examples, we realize they probably will not represent your circumstances exactly. But don't get caught in the example; look for the principle in practice. Look for the difference in thinking. Then apply the principle in your own situation. Think of the impact the fourth generation has on time and quality of life.

MONDAY MORNING AT THE OFFICE

Suppose it's a typical Monday morning. You're an account manager in the marketing division of your company. You belong to a team of account managers, each of whom manages thirty to forty accounts. You have your own office and you share a secretary with two other account managers.

You did your weekly planning last night, and you've just sat down to review your day. You create the following list of items and estimate the time it will take to do each of them. The items with an asterisk represent high-leverage Quadrant II activities you wanted to do today.

- Prepare for tomorrow's meeting with the McKinley account representative who is coming to town tomorrow to review pricing and negotiate a bulk purchase (3 hours).*
- Develop and fax proposal to Jameson Industries by end of day (2 hours).
- Call ten people on the account development list (15 minutes to 1 hour).
- Have lunch with Bill to discuss Woffinden account strategies (1 hour 30 minutes).*
- Go through memos and mail stack (1 hour).
- Retrieve internal e-mail messages . . . 17 messages (15 minutes).
- Retrieve phone voice-mail messages (10 minutes).
- Complete refiling (1 hour).

In addition to what you had planned, several things have come up that require your attention.

- Two messages have been placed on your desk: "Shipment did not arrive at key Anderson account" (this is the second time this month). "Quality Council meeting scheduled for Wednesday has been moved to today at 3:00 P.M." (2 hours).
- You're informed that the secretary has been assigned to one of the other account managers for a big project and is unavailable for you today.
- Your boss dropped by while you were reviewing this list and asked if you could prepare a quick three-month projection—by product—for your largest accounts. He needs to take this to report to the division manager by 2:00 P.M. (1 hour).

How would you approach this day? To get the most out of this example, you might want to get out a piece of paper and rough out a schedule. What would you do first? What would you do next? How would you handle the challenges to your plans? How long would you be at the office? What would you be like at the end of the day?

One approach would be to ask yourself:

- Which of these activities is most important?
- What can I safely postpone?
- What can I delegate?

- What can I get out of?
- What can I do more quickly?
- How can I arrange my schedule to accomplish what is most critical?

If you were to follow that approach, you might be able to reschedule a few things—maybe your lunch with Bill, the refiling, and the account development calls. You could delegate the task of tracking down the Anderson shipment. You could arrange your schedule to accomplish what you felt was most important—perhaps the Jameson proposal, the McKinley preparation, the memos, the e-mail and voice mail messages, the account projections. You might even make it to the Quality Council meeting.

You may schedule the day differently, but let's say you took this basic approach. How would you feel about your day? Would you feel that you had managed to put first things first in a difficult situation?

Now, consider this question: What will your next Monday be like? Or the Monday after that? What about all the Mondays for the rest of your life? Will you essentially be facing the same challenges? Although the specifics may differ, will the basic nature of the challenges be the same?

This is the fruit of the third generation. If nothing changes, you will essentially be delegating, postponing, and getting out of things for the rest of your life. Is that really putting first things first?

How is the fourth-generation approach different?

Rather than activities and appointments, you see your day in terms of people and relationships. You see processes in progress as new possibilities for contribution to the mission of the organization. It's not only a matter of when to do things, but whether or not to do them at all. It's asking questions of *why* and *how* as well as *when*. It's consulting your compass as well as your clock.

In making your decisions, you'd want to pause and connect with conscience. You'd want to:

- Ask with intent
- Listen without excuse, and
- Act with courage

As you decide what's most important for you to do, you'd want to think about the conditions of empowerment and consider where you could focus your effort with the greatest positive long-term result.

You might want to begin by questioning the very nature of each activity:

- How did this activity come about?
- Why am I doing it now?
- What are the underlying reasons for the activity?
- What are the ultimate objectives?
- Does this activity contribute to the purpose of the organization?
- Is this the highest and best use of my capacities and our combined resources?

The answers to questions such as these would determine the action you decide to take. In almost all cases, you would want to improve the underlying system. You would see tasks, not as things to do, but as indicators of a larger process that you want to improve.

Let's look at a few items on the list to see how this would play out. As we examine these items, we'll suggest some possible Quadrant II decisions. You might choose something different. That's fine. The point is to get a feel for the basic process.

1. The Jameson Proposal

Let's think about this activity. Why is it being done at the last minute? When did you know about it? What is your system for making proposals? What is your basic paradigm around proposals? Do other account managers have a better way to do it?

Suppose you realize that it's due today because that's when you said you would do it. You were anxious to get the business, to let them know you were eager. So you made a bold promise: "I'll have it to you by Monday afternoon!"

But does that really meet their needs? Was it an unrealistic expectation? Was it an unnecessary expectation? When will they actually review the proposal? Is there a format they like best?

It may turn out that they would like to have it today. In that case you would simply need to get it done. But it may work out better to clarify expectations with them today and work on the proposal tomorrow with a better understanding of what they really need. In any case, what about future proposals? Is there something you could do today that would create greater leverage in the future? Could you create effective synergy with others on your team around proposals? Could you establish some standard formats that would be helpful?

As you consider this question, you may begin to realize that the account managers spend very little time communicating with each other. Part of it is because of the competitive feeling you have between you. You're paid on commission, and that tends to pit you against each other. You realize that people hold their best ideas and methods close to the chest. And yet, the people who can benefit from the business are the very ones you're competing against. Why is this happening? What can you do to change things? Is compensation within your Circle of Influence? What can you do to make a difference?

Perhaps today you could send out a memo to your co-workers and set up a meeting around proposals. Perhaps you could suggest that a standard proposal format be established. Later, you may find an opportunity to split commissions on joint projects. A secretary for the department could be put in charge of generating proposals, and all you would need to do is supply the nonstandard information. This could be set up with a stewardship agreement.

By taking this type of action, you're transforming the system. Instead of just getting the job done, you're saving future time for yourself and for everyone else. You're building relationships of trust and meeting the needs of clients and customers in a more effective way.

2. The Shipment Problem

Why has this problem occurred twice? Is there a root cause? Has this happened to other people? Who else needs to be involved?

Suppose that today you talk to the shipping people—not with an attitude of blaming, but in an effort to understand and be helpful. How was the order given to them? Is there a way to improve the system? If the problem occurs regularly, perhaps you could be involved with the shipping department in creating a solution. Is there a forum where the problem can be analyzed? Could you get this on the agenda for the Quality Council? Perhaps you could prepare a presentation for the council with the shipping people on what needs to be done. Involve people in the problem; work out the solution together. As you solve the problem, build relationships that will empower you to effectively solve problems in the future as well.

3. Your Shared Secretary

Why weren't you notified earlier that the secretary would be unavailable today? Is that person fully empowered? Would he or she like to do more to contribute? Based on your secretary's input, perhaps today you could set up an appointment to include your two co-workers later in the week and start the process of creating a stewardship agreement around shared resources. Ask questions. Listen. Look at the desired results. What would constitute a win for everyone?

It may be helpful for the secretary to sort the mail, memos, e-mail, and phone messages for all three of you. Those items that needed your immediate attention could be prioritized and placed on your desks; the rest could be put in a file for later review. If the secretary isn't yet able to make decisions about the prioritization of this information, work with him or her. Communicate your criteria. Help that person become more capable. Nurture self-government and self-accountability. Build capacity.

4. The Revenue Projection

You'll probably decide to prepare the revenue projection for the boss today, but perhaps you could ask yourself some questions:

- Why does my boss need this today?
- What information am I not supplying regularly that creates this urgent need now?
- Is there a system I could set up so that the information would be readily available?
- Is there a chance that other account managers need to communicate the same information?
- Can we set up something together and share the information whenever we need it?

Today you could get yourself on the agenda for the next account managers meeting. You could draft a proposal around what can be done on this system to help everyone.

5. The Quality Council

Why has the Quality Council meeting been moved up? It's a strange meeting. You never know what's on the agenda. People are never effectively prepared. You aren't either. This has been going on for quite a while. You suspect that when you talk to the shipping manager about preparing a presentation for the Quality Council, he may say that's the last group he wants to be involved with. It's seen as a waste of time. The credibility is low. So, what can you do to make a difference?

Maybe the thing to do is call the chair of the Quality Council. Explain that you have a major proposal and report to generate today and you won't be able to switch times, but you would like to get on the agenda for the next meeting. You have a ten-minute presentation on applying principles of quality to the meetings. You may also suggest that you're going to be working with shipping on an opportunity for quality improvement and will get in touch in a few days to see when that can be put on the agenda.

We've only touched on a few of the items on the list, but consider the difference. Instead of simply managing problems, you're working on solutions. You're building people and synergistic relationships. You're nurturing a Quadrant II mind-set in yourself and others. You're looking at a schedule and seeing opportunities for improvement. Where others see isolated events, you see systems.

Of course you're still going to have a busy day and a lot to do. And it's not realistic to believe that everything will totally change in one day. But you're taking some steps to build margin. You're making Quadrant II opportunities out of Quadrant I and Quadrant III items. You're working on the roots. You're making sure that next Monday won't be essentially the same thing all over again. You're setting the stage for significant improvements downstream. You're putting your ladder against a different wall.

SUNDAY MORNING WITH THE FAMILY

When we start to look through a leadership instead of a management paradigm, we begin to see opportunities in places we never really thought of before.

One of our associates demonstrates this well. Like some who have families, he and his wife used to take a few minutes once a week to sit down with their children and try to coordinate the rides, the lessons, and the many other activities of normal family life. They had been doing this regularly for some time, but at one point they decided this could be an opportunity for leadership as well as management.

They changed the format of their time together so that now, instead of diving right into the schedule, they begin by reviewing their family mission statement. They talk about what it means to be a family. They discuss what everyone can do to make the family successful. They review their progress. They revisit their principles and values. Then they discuss each of their roles as they pertain to the family—son, daughter, sister, brother, student, friend. They take a few minutes during the planning time to help the children set a principle-based goal to improve in each role, such as working together on chores or asking about each other's day. These goals are simple, and geared to the capacity of each child—the older ones do a little more, the younger ones do a little less. They all learn by example and talk about it.

Every week they put the calendar on the refrigerator where everyone can see it. They block out time to work on some of the goals and joint activities, to be together as a family, to go to school plays, for Mom and Dad to go out on a date. They put the big rocks in first. It's taken some time, but members of the family are beginning to learn about relationships and how they can make a difference together. This man reports: "My seven-year-old recently told us she realized that it makes sense to help her sister with her chores because her sister, in turn, will help her. She said that she doesn't hate doing her chores anymore."

Different families may do it differently, but to involve every member of the family in understanding what they want to accomplish and in deciding how to work together to accomplish it, is empowering. Instead of a hassle, planning becomes a time of positive interaction and sharing. Our associate shares this thought:

One of the most significant insights in the value of this process came when, as part of a family game, our four-year-old was asked to identify something hanging on her bedroom wall. Of all the things hanging on the wall—a Beauty and the Beast *picture, an* Aladdin *poster, and assorted drawings she's done herself—she chose her copy of the family mission statement. I was deeply touched by her answer. I became more strongly aware of the influence for good we can have over our children, as well as the importance of understanding and recognizing the good that's already in them.*

We sometimes fail to think of our role in the family as a leadership role, but what an opportunity for impact! One of the greatest legacies we can leave our children is a sense of purpose and responsibility to correct principles.

ANY MORNING WITH YOUR TEAM OR WORK GROUP

What about a team at work? A department? A whole organization? How can we look at the tasks we do, the challenges we approach day to day, in ways that make a significant positive difference in the way we plan and organize?

Most teams typically do some sort of planning. They look at budget requirements or sales figures and determine what has to be done to meet their production obligations. They look at goals. They talk about the pressures and politics they have to face. Then they go down the list, make specific assignments, set up dates, create follow-up systems, and move ahead.

Suppose you're part of such a team. How could you transform the planning process into a leadership activity?

What if you were to begin the planning meeting by reviewing your group's mission and vision? What if you evaluated the last cycle's performance against the mission and learned from it? You might ask questions such as:

- What led us toward our mission?
- What led us away?
- What processes got in the way of accomplishing our mission?
- Were we true to correct principles?
- How can we create better alignment?

What if you were to look at the various roles and functions and evaluate them against the mission, asking questions such as these:

- Are we streamlined?
- Are there processes that could be improved?
- Who are the people involved?
- Who would like to be involved?
- Who needs to be involved?
- What principles apply?
- What can we do to help release the capacities of individuals?
- Can we create effective synergy among the tasks and/or goals?
- Are there things the team should start doing?
- Are there things the team should stop doing?
- How empowering are the stewardship agreements?
- Do we share common expectations?

There are literally an infinite number of questions you could ask. It doesn't matter whether you're a formal team or organizational leader. Work within your Circle of Influence. Ask questions. Listen. Create a pause for the team or group. Help people reflect. How can we transform the nature of our effectiveness to a new level? How can we move forward dramatically? These are not management questions; these are leadership questions. These are Quadrant II questions. They represent the difference of the fourth generation.

WHAT A DIFFERENCE A DAY MAKES

As we exercise self-awareness and examine our paradigms, we discover that they are deeply ingrained. The change is not easy. Often we look at the to-do lists, the tasks in front of us, and we retreat to independence.

I feel like a time warrior. I'm constantly asking myself, what can I do to survive, to move more quickly, to cut to the chase? I've got to fix things. I've got to replace things. I know it's a mechanical approach, but I feel like I need to go faster—to get home a little earlier once in a while, to have a few less problems. The clock ticking on my wall keeps increasing the pressure of the day. I've got to get this done by then, this by then, this before that, and what will happen if . . . I've got to control more. I've got to be able to pin things down. I've got to keep these unexpected things from popping up and throwing my day off.

These paradigms carry their own weight. They are a downward spiral. The harder we work, the deeper we get.

In a Quadrant II day, what changes first is our thoughts—the way we see the day. Tasks provide an opportunity for growth, for improvement. We can work on our competence—to learn, to expand our skills, to broaden our ability to perform—or on our character—to be more honest, more understanding, to see the other point of view, to pause frequently and listen to conscience. We can apply ourselves to change the systems and make them more effective. The creativity that comes when we stop to pause and listen is amazing.

I stand back. I look at the big picture. I see challenges, but I see them as opportunities to build relationships and create synergy. What a difference it can make! I look forward to personal orienteering, to pausing to check my compass and maps. I ask myself, how does it fit? I look at the strength that comes as the parts of my life fit together. I'm amazed at what I can learn when I stop and look at the processes of my life—what happens when I'm in harmony with principles. I see a pattern, a beauty, an order. The more I align with principles, the more opportunities I see. I'm accomplishing something. I feel growth. I feel contribution. I'm making a difference. Slowly but

surely, my vision and mission are coming to pass. I feel my trustwor-
thiness growing. I'm gaining strength of character and competence.
My trust in others is increasing. It's exciting!

Sometimes it's tough. We make mistakes. We fall back into old habits of urgency addiction, old paradigms of getting more done in less time—even if what we're doing is in Quadrant II.

But the more we exercise personal leadership and move into Quadrant II, the more we can feel growth, feel life. It gets better. It's an upward spiral. Each part of life starts to add to the others. There's more of every good thing.

15: *The Peace of the Results*

We know not of the future, and cannot plan for it much. But we can hold our spirits and our bodies so pure and high, we may cherish such thoughts and such ideals, and dream such dreams of lofty purpose, that we can determine and know what manner of men we will be whenever and wherever the hour strikes that calls to noble action. . . . No man becomes suddenly different from his habit and cherished thought.
—*Joshua L. Chamberlain, General Commander, 20th Maine, Union Forces, Battle of Gettysburg*[1]

Roger: As I drive up into the canyon to Sundance where we do many of our programs, I often become aware of a change that comes over me. The hustle and bustle of the office with its demands and concerns evaporates as I begin to feel a part of the majesty of the mountains, the flow of the river, and the blend of colors and shapes.

I find myself listening more. There's a stillness where I can hear more clearly. I become increasingly more peaceful as I allow the inner voice to speak.

These times are some of the most precious to me because I touch something that is often set aside, but is richer than many of the things I embrace daily. I find myself reviewing, re-thinking, and re-committing.

Many of us feel a sense of peace when we're out in nature. We feel a sense of timelessness. We become aware of the reality and absolute operation of natural law. We become aware of our own almost insignificance in relation to it. We can't change it; we can't control it. But the thought is somehow reassuring. We feel content to be a part of something so awe-inspiring and unarguably "there."

There's a sense of balance and harmony in nature. Seasons come and go with regularity. There are cycles of life, giving and receiving in a beautiful harmonious whole. Even cataclysmic events—storms, earthquakes, floods—are part of a larger harmony, a natural cycle of growth and change. Nature is always becoming. The beauty of nature constantly unfolds in accordance with its laws.

Nature teaches us much about peace. It reminds us that there are laws and that they are in control. With that reminder is a sense of comfort that there is order in the universe. We might as well attempt to reorder the seasons or annul the effects of gravity as to change the consequences of violating natural law in the human dimension. We simply cannot be a law unto ourselves without consequence. Peace and quality of life come only as we discover and align with the fundamental Laws of Life.

WHAT IS PEACE?

The peace we're talking about is obviously more than the absence of war. It's not a retreat into the wilderness to avoid the complexities and conundrums of daily living. The peace we're talking about is a function of our deep inner life. It's joyful living. It's found in the midst of life, not in retreat from it.

The independent achievement approach generally seems to say that peace and happiness come from such things as:

- money in the bank
- control
- recognition and fame
- a new house, a fancy car, or other material possessions
- superior social status

The focus is essentially on becoming faster and better at getting more of these things. But what's the result? Is it peace? Is it built on things that will last?

Take a moment and think about your own life. What does "peace" mean to you? Where does it come from? Are you satisfied with the amount and quality of peace in your life?

The principles and processes we've described in this book create different paradigms based on true north principles, purposes, and perspectives that help create happiness and peace. In nurturing these paradigms and principles of the fourth generation, we can see how all the true strengths of the first three generations of time management are retained and enhanced—and the weaknesses eliminated. The chart on pages 282 and 283 summarizes and illustrates.

In identifying the strengths and weaknesses of these generations, we acknowledge that many individuals in these generations use their tools in ways that reflect fourth-generation paradigms. In fact, we're convinced that people in each of the generations have been tapping into the principles of the fourth generation all along—because the principles live in their hearts. We know that many people are in the first generation because they are fundamentally committed to simply living by conscience and serving where they're needed. We know that as people in the third generation identify their values and live by them, many of them are solidly founded in the principles and laws of life that govern peace and happiness. But we also know that systems and processes that are aligned with these fundamental paradigms and desires of the heart empower us to more fully translate them into the fabric of our daily lives.

Peace is essentially a function of putting first things first. Foundational to "first things" are the four needs and capacities—to live, to love, to learn, to leave a legacy. Putting first things first is a function of using our four endowments—self-awareness, conscience, independent will, and creative imagination—to fulfill our needs and capacities in a principle-centered way.

As we integrate fourth-generation paradigms and processes in our lives, we find a different kind of peace:

- peace in our ability to live, love, learn, and leave a legacy with balance and joy
- peace in the development of our human endowments that empower us with character and competence in the moment of choice
- peace as our roles cooperate rather than compete, as they become parts of a synergistic, living whole
- the transcendent peace of learning to listen to and live by conscience

There are principles. We do have conscience. And those two things make all the difference. They impact our thoughts and how we see everything around us. We see how vital it is to pause in that space between stimulus and response so that we can listen to our conscience and exercise the attributes of the heart to make the "best" choices. We see that there are purposes higher than self toward which we can focus our energies and efforts with passion and confidence that we can create quality-of-life results. We see the world as a place of infinite third-alternative solutions. We see the importance of creating aligned systems so that the very way we go about organizing and planning our lives reinforces the habits of the heart that create peace.

	Summary	Tool
First Generation	Reminders	Simple notes, checklists
Second Generation	Planning and preparation	Calendars, appointment books
Third Generation	Planning, prioritizing, controlling	Planners that unify values with goals and daily schedules

Fourth Generation	**Strengths Retained**	**Weaknesses Eliminated**
The Four Needs and Capacities: To Live, to Love, to Learn, to Leave a Legacy	• Some needs fulfilled through goals and prioritization (3rd generation)	• "First things"—those things right in front of you (1st generation) • More of what you *want*—not necessarily what you *need* or what is fulfilling (2nd, 3rd generations)
"True North" Principles *Four Endowments: Self-Awareness, Conscience, Creative Imagination, Independent Will*	• Assumes responsibility for results (3rd generation)	• Skills alone don't produce effectiveness and leadership—need character (2nd and 3rd generations) • Can lead you to believe *you* are in control, rather than natural laws or principles—"Law unto oneself" pride (3rd generation) • Values clarification not necessarily aligned with principles that govern regardless (3rd generation) • "First things" set by urgency and values (3rd generation)
The Passion of Vision	• More effective meetings and presentations through preparation (2nd generation) • Connects with values (3rd generation)	• Power of vision untapped (1st, 2nd, and 3rd generations)
The Balance of Roles	• Less stress (1st generation)	• Commitments to others ignored or forgotten; relationships suffer (1st generation) • Can lead to guilt, over-programming, and imbalance between roles (3rd generation)

	Strengths Retained	**Weaknesses Eliminated**
The Power of Goals	• Much more accomplished through goals and planning (2nd generation) • Taps into power of long-, medium-, and short-term goals (3rd generation) • Translates values into goals and actions (3rd generation)	• Things fall through the cracks (1st generation) • Relatively little accomplished (1st generation)
The Perspective of the Week	• Not overscheduled and over-structured (1st generation) • Tracks "to-do's" (1st generation) • Tracks commitments and appointments (2nd generation) • Increases personal productivity through planning and prioritization (3rd generation) • Increases efficiency (3rd generation) • Gives structure/order to life (3rd generation) • Strengthens skill of managing time and self (3rd generation)	• No real structure (1st generation) • Move from crisis to crisis as consequence of ignoring schedules and structure (1st generation) • Daily planning rarely gets past prioritizing the urgent, the pressing, and crises management (3rd generation)
Integrity in the Moment of Choice	• Ability to adapt when something more important arises—Go-with-the-flow flexibility (1st generation)	• "First things"—those things on the schedule (2nd generation) • Leads to putting schedule over people (2nd, 3rd generations) • Less flexibility/spontaneity (3rd generation)
The Synergy of Interdependence	• More responsive to people (1st generation)	• Independent thinking and action—sees people as means or barriers to goals (2nd, 3rd generations) • May see people as "things" (3rd generation)

FIRST THINGS FIRST NURTURES PEACE

The principles and processes we've described in this book nurture peace in all four dimensions of life—peace of conscience, peace of mind, peace in our relationships . . . even peace of body. Vision gives purpose and meaning. Roles become synergistic avenues of contribution. Goals become conscience-driven, purposeful, integrated accomplishment. The week bridges the mission and the moment in a cycle of growth. Sharpening the saw is daily and weekly renewal. Each moment of choice becomes a space in which we can exercise our human endowments to act with integrity.

Shared vision and stewardship agreements empower us to see people in terms of opportunities instead of problems. We realize that people are not things. Neither are they simply "delegatees." They're living, breathing human beings with their own space between stimulus and response, their own unique endowments, and the capacity to synergize with us to create first things together in a way that far surpasses what we could ever do on our own.

These principles and processes change the expectations many of us have about time and the quality of our lives. This is critical to peace because frustration is essentially a function of unmet expectations— we expect something to be a certain way or to produce certain results, and it doesn't. As a result, we feel frustrated.

At the root, the problem is that many of our expectations come from scripting, the personality ethic, or the social mirror instead of true north. They're flawed paradigms. They're not based on the fundamental Laws of Life.

Many of *us expect*—consciously or subconsciously—to be able to go through a day and accomplish what we planned. As a result, when some unexpected challenge comes up, we're frustrated. When someone has a need we didn't anticipate, we're frustrated. We see people essentially as interruptions. We view change as the enemy. Our peace and happiness are a function of whether or not we're able to make it through that day and check off everything on the list.

But what happens when the expectation changes—when we see each day as an exciting new adventure for which we have a roadmap, but also a compass that empowers us to navigate through uncharted terrain . . . when we see problems as opportunities to help others . . . when we look forward to meeting situations that challenge our priorities, confident that our compass will help us keep moving toward the "best"? What happens when our peace and happiness are a function of going to bed at night knowing we made the choices to put first things first throughout the day? Does that expectation make a difference in the way we interact with the realities of the day?

Let's consider another expectation. Consciously or subconsciously, many of us *expect* life to be without challenge. As a result, any challenge or problem creates frustration. It doesn't match the expectation.

But that expectation is not based on reality. Opposition is a natural part of life. Just as we develop our physical muscles through overcoming opposition, such as lifting weights, we develop our character muscles by overcoming challenges and adversity. As M. Scott Peck observed in *The Road Less Traveled*:

> *Life is difficult. This is a great truth, one of the greatest truths. It is a great truth because once we truly see this truth, we transcend it. Once we know that life is difficult—then life is no longer difficult. Because once it is accepted, the fact that life is difficult no longer matters.[2]*

If our expectation is that there will be challenge, then challenge does not create frustration.

For another example, many of us *expect* other people to agree with us, to carry out what we feel should be done. When others disagree with us, when they have questions or concerns, when they don't enthusiastically support our decisions, or when they come up with alternative ideas, we feel frustrated.

What difference does it make when we expect people to see things differently, when we value that difference, when we anticipate the synergistic use of human endowments to create third-alternative solutions?

Unmet expectations create frustration, but our expectations are within our control. We're not talking about lowering our expectations, but about basing them on the realities of true north. One of the richest areas for eliminating much of the frustration we experience in our lives is to examine our expectations. Whenever we feel frustrated, we can go back to the root of the problem.

- What expectation did I have that's been violated?
- Was that expectation based on true north?
- What should I do to change the expectation?
- What can I learn from this that will affect my expectations in the future?

When our expectations aren't based on true north realities, we set ourselves up for frustration and lack of peace.

THE TWO KEYSTONES: CONTRIBUTION AND CONSCIENCE

Of all the principles and processes we've discussed, the two most essential keystones to peace are *contribution* (to leave a legacy) and *conscience*. While each of the four needs is vitally important, contribution gives meaning to and energizes the rest. While each of the four endowments is vitally important, conscience gives meaning to and energizes the rest. Together, contribution and conscience help us know where we want to go and how to get there.

Contribution

Recently, the Covey Leadership Center participated with our local PBS station in making available to the Public Broadcasting System a video dramatization we developed and filmed in England. The central figure in this remarkable story is an Englishman who transcended a childhood spent as a street urchin to become a reasonably successful writer with a nice home and a loving family. At the time of the story, however, he had reached a point where he was experiencing "writer's block." For some time, he had been unable to feel inspired in his writing. It seemed his creativity had turned off. His debts were mounting. He was under tremendous pressure from the publisher. He was becoming more and more depressed with a growing fear that his own children would end up on the streets like so many he saw around . . . like he, himself, had as a youth.

He was discouraged. He couldn't sleep. He began to spend his nights walking the streets of London. He saw the poverty, the inhumane conditions of children working nights in the factories, the terrible struggle of parents trying to eke out a living for their families. Gradually, the full reality of what he was seeing began to hit him—the impact of selfishness and greed and those who would take advantage of others. An idea touched his heart and began to grow in his mind. There was something he could do that would make a difference!

He returned to his writing with an energy and enthusiasm he had never known. The vision of contribution impassioned him, consumed him. He no longer felt doubt or discouragement. He didn't worry about his own financial concerns. He wanted to get this story out, to make it as inexpensive as possible, to make it available to as many people as possible. His whole life had changed.

As a result, the world was changed. Charles Dickens's masterpiece "A Christmas Carol" has brightened the lives of millions of people around the world. For one hundred and fifty years his vision has left a wonderful legacy of hope, warmth, and caring.

Most of the ends of the independent achievement paradigm, in and of themselves, are empty. Without a context of meaningful purpose, they're illusory. They create cotton-candy satisfaction.

Only as we focus more on contributing than consuming can we create the context that makes peace in all aspects of life possible. It's in leaving a legacy that we find meaning in living, loving, and learning.

Conscience

Much of the third generation includes some combination of self-awareness, independent will, and creative imagination. But without conscience, there is no peace.

Stephen: At one time when I was working at a university, I had the privilege of hosting a prominent psychologist and former president of a national psychological association. This man was considered the father of "integrity therapy," a method of psychological treatment based on the idea that peace of mind, true happiness, and balance are a function of living a life of integrity to conscience. He believed that conscience tapped into the universal sense of right and wrong common to all enduring cultures, religions, and societies throughout time.

One afternoon between lectures, I drove him into the mountains to see the breathtaking views. I took the opportunity to ask him how he came to believe in integrity therapy.

He said, "It was very personal. I was a manic-depressive and most of my whole life had been a series of highs and lows. Over time, as I counseled people, I would begin to feel stressed and very vulnerable. I would start slipping into depression—almost to the point where I wanted to take my life. I had enough awareness of what was happening because of my professional education and my professional activity, that I knew I was dangerous. At this point, I would institutionalize myself to preclude taking my life. After a month or two, I could come out and go back into my work. Then, after a year or so, I would slip back into it, hospitalize myself, and gradually come back to go on with my research and writing."

He continued, "At one point when I was president of the association, I became so ill, so depressed, that I was unable to go to the meetings and take up the gavel of my office. At that point, I asked myself, 'Is it possible I'm working out of the wrong framework in my life and profession?' I knew deep inside that I had been living a lie for many years. There was a dark part of my life that I had not owned up to."

As we were driving along and he began to share these things, I became very sobered and humbled. I was also a little scared of what he might say. He continued, "I decided to make a major break. I gave up my mistress. I came clean with my wife. And for the first time in many years, I had peace—a kind of peace that was different from what I had experienced when I came out of my depressions and went back into productive work. It was an inner peace of mind, a kind of self-honesty, a kind of self-unity, an integrity.

"That's when I began to explore the theory that perhaps many of the problems I saw were the result of the natural conscience being ignored, denied, violated, creating a loss of personal integrity. So I began to work with this idea. I researched it. I involved other clinicians who began working from this paradigm with their patients. I became convinced from the data that this was the case. And that's what got me into integrity therapy."

This man's openness and the depth of his conviction powerfully impressed me, as it did hundreds of students the following day in a university forum.

This psychologist's personal experience and research clearly show the essential role of conscience in achieving peace. And it was, according to his account, "a different kind of peace." Obviously, he had developed some of his endowments to a great degree. To see his own situation clearly enough to institutionalize himself shows remarkable self-awareness and independent will. Recognition for his work in the field bore witness of his highly developed creative imagination. But it was not until he connected with conscience that he was able to find the peace he sought.

The results of decades of experience in psychotherapy, positive mental attitude, and creativity development validate the futility of trying to achieve peace and long-term quality of life without the crucial element of conscience.³ Conscience is our connection to true north, to the principles that make peace and quality of life possible.

THE TWO STUMBLING BLOCKS: DISCOURAGEMENT AND PRIDE

Two of the most deadly roadblocks to peace are discouragement and pride.

Discouragement

Discouragement is literally dis-courage-ment—a lack of courage. Discouragement is the antithesis of everything we've talked about. It comes as a result of building our lives on illusion instead of principle, of facing the consequences of climbing ladders against wrong walls. It comes when we're tired, out of shape, or in debt, when we have broken relationships, when we're not growing, when we have no sense of meaning or purpose in life. It comes when we have no vision, when we live with imbalance, when we fail to achieve our goals. It comes when we get lost in the urgent, limited perspective of the day, when we fail to act with integrity in the moment of choice. It comes when our thinking is competitive and scarce, when win-lose interactions fill our lives and our environment with backbiting, politicking, and comparative thinking.

Discouragement is being lost in the woods without a compass or an accurate map. It's discovering that many of the maps people hand us lead us farther away from where we really want to go.

Courage, on the other hand, comes as a result of knowing there are principles, of fulfilling our needs and capacities in a balanced way, of having clear vision, balance between roles, the ability to set and achieve meaningful goals, the perspective to transcend the urgency of the moment, the character and competence to act with integrity in the moment of choice, the abundance mentality to function effectively and synergistically in the interdependent reality. Courage comes from the heart, and being in touch with the heart creates hope.

Wherever we are, the best way to develop courage is to set a goal and achieve it, make a promise and keep it. No matter how small the goal or promise, this one act will begin to build our confidence that we can act with integrity in the moment of choice. It may be a matter of just getting up in the morning—putting "mind over mattress"—or of subordinating taste to nutrition, even for a day. But as we begin to make and keep promises to ourselves and others, we take the first steps on a path that leads to confidence, growth, and peace.

Pride

An even greater stumbling block, and the biggest danger to our effort to become principle-centered, is pride. Although we often use the word to describe deep pleasure or high satisfaction toward something or someone—we may take *pride* in excellent work or be *proud* of a son or daughter who does something well—pride also describes one of the most destructive paradigms in life.

We can more easily understand this negative dimension when we think of the word "prideful." A prideful person is essentially competitive in nature, constantly seeking to elevate himself or herself above others. In the words of C. S. Lewis:

> *Pride gets no pleasure out of having something, only out of having more of it than the next man. . . . It is the comparison that makes you proud; the pleasure of being above the rest.*[4]

Consider the impact of pride in fulfilling our fundamental needs and capacities.

- Pride in *living* means people are not so much concerned with whether their income meets their needs, as they are that their income is more than someone else's. They're always comparing their appearance—their hair, their clothing, their physique—to that of others.
- Pride in *loving* comes when people measure their worth by the number and prestige of the friends they think they have, or the amount of praise they receive from others.
- Pride in *learning* is not so much in what people know, but in whether they have the best degrees, the highest status.
- Pride in *leaving a legacy* is not finding meaning in giving, but in giving more than others, in receiving recognition for giving.

Pride is the ultimate emotional parasite. There is no deep joy, no satisfaction, no peace in it because there's always the possiblity that someone else is better-looking or has more money, more friends, a bigger house, or a newer car.

Pride is insidious because it pollutes meaning and purpose. It dulls, ignores, and even dethrones conscience. As C. S. Lewis observed, "Pride is a spiritual cancer: it eats up the very possibility of love, or contentment, or even common sense."[5] It eventually leads to hate, envy, and war.

Prideful people get their security from how far up the ladder they are compared to others, rather than whether or not their ladder is leaning against the right wall. They feel worthwhile when they see people beneath them. The reward, the focus, is being ahead . . . even if it means being ahead in the wrong things.

And as well as from the top looking down, there's a pride that comes from the bottom looking up. In the words of former U.S. Secretary of Agriculture and religious leader Ezra Taft Benson:

Most of us consider pride to be a sin of those on the top, such as the rich and the learned, looking down at the rest of us. There is, however, a far more common ailment among us—and that is pride from the bottom looking up. It is manifest in so many ways, such as fault-finding, gossiping, backbiting, murmuring, living beyond our means, envying, coveting, withholding gratitude and praise that might lift another, and being unforgiving and jealous.[6]

Pride is the essence of the scarcity mentality. It's devastating to peace. It creates a false integrity of alignment with extrinsic things. And consider the cost! How much time and energy is spent worrying over who has the most, does the most, looks the best, lives in the best part of town, has the largest office, makes more money, does more work, is of the most value? When the cry of competition is louder than the whisper of conscience, what's the impact in terms of really putting first things first in our lives?

The antidote for the poison of pride is humility—the humility to realize that we're not an island, that the quality of our lives is inseparably connected to the quality of the lives of others, that meaning is not in consuming and competing, but in contributing. We are not laws unto ourselves, and the more we begin to value principles and people, the greater will be our peace.

CHARACTERISTICS OF PRINCIPLE-CENTERED PEOPLE

Becoming principle-centered is just that: *becoming*. It's not arriving; it's a lifetime quest. But the more people align their lives with true north, the more they begin to develop certain characteristics common to principle-centered people.

They're more flexible and spontaneous. They're not chained to plans and schedules. Schedules are important, but not all-important. Principle-centered people see life as an adventure. They're like courageous explorers going on an expedition into uncharted territory—they're really not sure what's going to happen, but they're confident it will be exciting and growth producing, and that they will discover new territory and make new contributions. Their security is not in their comfort zone, but in their compass—their unique human endowments that empower them to navigate confidently in uncharted terrain.

They have richer, more rewarding relationships with other people. They put people ahead of schedules. They clarify expectations. They're not into comparing, competing, or criticizing. Others begin to feel they can depend on them to be honest, direct, and nonmanipulative, to make and keep commitments, to walk their talk. Principle-centered people don't overreact to negative behaviors, criticism, or human weaknesses. They're quick to forgive. They don't carry grudges. They refuse to label, stereotype, categorize, or prejudge. They're genuinely happy for and help facilitate the successes of others. They believe in the unseen potential of all people. They help create a climate for growth and opportunity.

They're more synergistic. Instead of doing "their thing" *to* others, they find far greater rewards in working *with* others to achieve shared vision. They value the difference. They believe in the synergy of third-alternative solutions. In team endeavors, they learn to build on their strengths and work to complement their weaknesses with the strengths of others. When they negotiate and communicate with others in seemingly adversarial situations, they're better able to separate the people from the problem. They can focus on the other person's interests and concerns instead of arguing over positions.

They're continually learning. Because they know there's a true north, they're constantly seeking to discover, understand, and align their lives with it. They become more humble and teachable. They read widely, feast on the wisdom of the ages, and listen to others. They're continually educated by their experience.

They become more contribution-focused. They channel their time and energy toward contributing more than consuming, toward giving rather than getting. They're more service-oriented. They seek to improve quality of life for others as well as themselves.

They produce extraordinary results. Because they balance "producing" with increasing their capacity to produce, they develop the ability to produce significantly more, long-term. They don't burn the candle at both ends. They're continually acquiring new skills. They grow in their ability to work with others and facilitate high-quality interdependent production. In whatever they do, they apply principles that create quality results.

They develop a healthy psychological immune system. They can handle problems. They're not inflicted with psychological AIDS. They can be sideswiped or blindsided by disease, financial setback, or disappointment and they have the resources to come back. They nurture healthy immune systems in their marriages and their families, so that they can discuss jugular issues and handle problems such as finances, in-laws, or child discipline with principles rather than scripting. They work to create healthy immune systems in their work teams, groups, or organizations.

They create their own limits. They don't work until they drop from exhaustion, spend until there's no credit left, or keep going on projects until they run out of time. They become less dependent on extrinsic factors to tell them when to quit. They learn to apply principles and use wisdom in creating their own limits to maximize their effectiveness. They focus effort during times of peak energy and creativity. They take time for re-creation. They spend wisely and save and invest for future needs.

They lead more balanced lives. They don't become workaholics, religious zealots, political fanatics, crash dieters, food bingers, pleasure addicts, or fasting martyrs. They're active physically, socially, mentally, and spiritually. They live more abundant, synergistic lives.

They become more confident and secure. They grow in their confidence that living in harmony with true north will bring quality of life, and they become more patient and peaceful in the process. Their security doesn't come from work, associations, recognition, possessions, status, or any other extrinsic factor. It comes from within—from centering their lives on principles, from living by their conscience.

They're better able to walk their talk. There's no conscious duplicity, double-mindedness, or hypocrisy. They increase their ability to make and keep commitments to themselves and others. They build a high balance in their Personal Integrity Account.

They focus on their Circle of Influence. They don't waste time or energy in their Circle of Concern. They focus on the things they can do something about and work to improve almost any situation they're in.

They cultivate a rich inner life. They draw strength from regular spiritual renewal. They feast on wisdom literature, think, meditate, or in other ways nurture context, meaning, and purpose in their lives.

They radiate positive energy. They become more cheerful, pleasant, optimistic, positive, upbeat. They see possibilities. They neutralize or sidestep strong negative energy forces; they charge weaker forces that surround them.

They enjoy life more. They don't condemn themselves for every foolish mistake or social blunder. They forgive themselves and others. They don't brood about yesterday or daydream about tomorrow. They live sensibly and joyfully in the present, carefully plan for the future, and flexibly adapt to changing circumstances. They develop a rich sense of humor, laughing often at themselves, but never at the expense of others.

The more people develop these characteristics, the more peaceful and happy their lives become. They begin to significantly impact quality of life for themselves and for everyone around them.

Becoming principle-centered is not always easy, but it does create quality-of-life results. The important thing is to keep trying, to keep working to create more and more alignment with true north.

LETTING GO

The movie *The Mission* tells the story of a man involved in capturing natives and selling them into slavery. Upon his return to the village one day, he kills his brother in a fit of jealous rage. Deeply affected by what he has done, he sits for weeks in a hopeless stupor until a priest finally convinces him that there is something he can do to make amends.

Following the priest's instructions, he attempts to do penance by making his way into the jungle with a group of missionaries, carrying a large, heavy fishnet bundle filled with all his weapons and armor on his back. The path is incredibly difficult. He struggles with his load up the mountains, across narrow ravines, and up waterfalls. One member of the group, concerned for his welfare, asks the priest if it's not time for this man to let go of his bundle. The priest replies, "He will know when it is time."

At one point, after Herculean effort, this man crawls over the top of a ridge, scraped, torn, utterly exhausted. As he lifts his eyes, he comes face-to-face with one of the natives. There's a moment of silence, then the native raises his knife . . . and cuts the ropes. In that moment is a tremendous feeling of release, of *letting go* of all the things that were holding him back. From that point on, this man devotes his life to helping the natives improve their quality of life.

As we said earlier, every breakthrough is a break-with, a letting go. As we work to put first things first in our lives it may be time for us to let go of things that are holding us back, keeping us from making the contribution we could make.

Let go of paradigms that are popular and pleasing, but based on illusion. It may seem nice in the short run to think we can set goals and accomplish anything we want and create quality-of-life results. But the reality is that true north principles govern quality of life. When we pursue values that are out of harmony with true north, we end up trying to control consequences and other people. It doesn't work. When we pick up one end of the stick, we pick up the other. There are principles; there are consequences. Only as we let go of illusory paradigms are we free to act in harmony with the laws that create peace and quality of life.

Let go of things that aren't "first things." At one of our conferences in Singapore, we had European, Asian, and Western executives meeting together. When we introduced the Circle of Influence and Circle of Concern, the Western executives began talking about how the Circle of Influence would help them focus on what they needed to do. The Asian executives said, "That's very interesting. When we looked at these circles, our immediate response was, 'This is wonderful! This Circle of Concern will help us know what to let go of!' " We can only free ourselves to work on first things first as we let go of other things and focus our time and effort on the most important.

Let go of rational-lies-ing. As long as we burden ourselves with self-justification and rationalization, we aren't free to respond to the voice of conscience. One of the most liberating experiences in life is to make the commitment to simply respond to conscience. People who try it, even for a week, are literally amazed at the release and at how much time and energy they discover has been spent justifying action contrary to conscience.

Let go of unnecessary guilt. Guilt that comes from conscience is a great teacher. It helps us know when we're out of alignment with true north. But much of the guilt many of us carry with us is from the social conscience. It doesn't teach; it impedes our progress. We free ourselves when we examine our guilt. If it comes out of the social mirror, we can let go of it. If it comes from conscience, we can face it, align our lives, do whatever is necessary to make restitution, and move on. Whatever that requires, it is not as hard and debilitating as living with the guilt. Life is learning—from our mistakes as well as our successes. "The only real mistake in life," said one, "is the mistake not learned from."

Let go of extrinsic sources of security. As long as we get our sense of security from being incredibly busy, from our profession, from recognition for talent, from relationships, or from anything other than our own basic integrity to conscience and principle, we've fundamentally sold out as far as putting first things first in our lives is concerned. These things will be more important to us than doing what we deeply feel we should do. Only as we let go of these things, and draw our security from our deep inner life, will we be free to do what really matters most.

TURNING POINTS

Each decision we make is an important decision. Some may seem small at the time, but the reality is that they add upon one another to become habits of the heart that move us with increasing force toward some destiny.

Some of our choices, often unknown to us at the time, become real turning points in our lives—times when putting first things first makes all the difference. Sometimes these decisions are hard. They require us to take a stand that may be unpopular, even illogical to others. But as we listen to our conscience and subordinate the "good" to the "best," we find incredible quality-of-life impact down the road.

As we conclude this book, we'd each like to share an experience that was a real turning point in our own lives and helped convince us of the power of putting first things first.

Rebecca: Several years ago, I reached the point where my children were in school, and I decided it was time to go back to school myself. Years earlier, I had gone to the university on a four-year academic scholarship, but partway through had felt confident that, although this was "good," what was "best" for me was to marry and raise a family. I never regretted that decision—it led to more happiness, joy, challenge, and learning than I could ever have imagined. But as a result, I hadn't completed my degree, and I thought that perhaps now was the time.

I hadn't expected the feelings I would have as I went back on campus to investigate the possibilities. It was exhilarating! I loved the sense of adventure, the excitement of learning, even the smell of the books! I was in my element. I was on a tremendous high as I went to the administration building where I was able to review my credits and see that there really was a reasonable path to accomplish my goal. As I left the building, I was more than ready to see if I could hire somebody else to take over all my home and family responsibilities and thrust myself full-time into the academic arena.

I went home on a cloud. I was thrilled with the possibilities. I had taken a few classes through the years and had done a lot of personal study on my own. But the thought of being able to devote full time and energy to something that had been such a source of enjoyment and security for me in the past was almost overwhelming.

I say "almost" because it nearly did drown out a little voice inside me that said, "Rebecca, your family needs you."

I didn't want to hear that. I came up with scores of reasons why I ought to go back to school. But that inner voice created a small discomfort inside me that all my enthusiasm and rationale couldn't extinguish. When I finally stopped fighting and really listened to it, I came to the deep realization that I had far more important things to do at that point in my life than go back to school.

That was one of the hardest decisions I'd ever made. It was almost like I could taste it—then, suddenly, it was gone. But I knew deep inside that my decision was right. I knew I needed to refocus my efforts and recommit myself to contribute in a way that only I could at that point in the lives of my children. They were going to face incredible pressure in their moments of choice, and the ability to be there, to build the relationship to be a strong positive influence in those moments, would make a powerful difference in the quality of their lives.

I redoubled my efforts to create a nurturing home for my family. I did manage to fit in one evening class a semester and, in the process, learned a lot about physiology, microbiology, and the humanities. It was fun. It was enriching. But it couldn't begin to take the place of the wonderful experiences with my children, or of the two additional children that joined our family in the next few years. I look at them all now and think, "What if I had chosen another path?"

That inner voice has led me to make choices that completely defy rationale and social pressure. It led me to make a decision to put my family first at a time of great enticement to do otherwise. It led me later to accept a surprising opportunity to work with Stephen on the 7 Habits book and contribute in ways I had never imagined. It's been the source of every truly good decision I've ever made. I feel compelled to acknowledge that there is a wisdom far greater than my own, and that living in harmony with it is the key to contribution and joy.

Roger: Several years ago, as our business was going through intense growth pains, Rebecca and I made the decision to go into a period of conscious imbalance for a year or two. We agreed that I would spend more time traveling during this time of growth and challenge. We knew this would result in my being away from the family an inordinate amount of time according to our standards, but we felt it was an important contribution to the business and would help us accomplish our shared long-term goals.

This imbalance accomplished the desired results, but when the period of time was over, it became very difficult to back off. There were so many good things to do that would benefit other people and the business, and so many pressures to do them. The weeks ran into months, and it seemed that imbalance was becoming a way of life.

One of those turning points came as I paused long enough to ask myself, "Am I allowing good things to take the place of best things?" It was a moment of truth, and as I thought through the situation and listened to my heart, I began to feel that I needed to take a stand and set some limits on the number of nights I would be gone each month.

That decision was sorely tested during the next several weeks. But gradually, other people at work began to acknowledge that this really was a conviction and a commitment, and many developed a supportive approach to help honor it and create third-alternative solutions to maximize my contribution to our shared vision.

I am absolutely convinced that my ability to contribute to this mission has increased since that limit was set and meaningful alternatives sought. It was, in fact, one of the primary decisions that made it possible for us to work on First Things First.

From personal experiences such as this, and from closely observing many others during this process of trying to live a life of first things first, I am absolutely convinced that there are key turning points—times when we must take a stand and make deep personal commitments in order for change to take place. There's a peace that comes with a commitment to do what you really know is best, even though it's not easy or unopposed. But if we fail to take a stand, we get numbed into imbalance and disharmony, and by abdication, we become convinced that it's easier to live with the imbalance than to pay the price for balance.

Stephen: Several years ago, I decided to leave the university and set up an organization in order to make a wider contribution. I had been with the university for over twenty years, and was very comfortably situated. I served in several different roles, including top administrative positions. I participated in setting up a new department of organizational behavior and had a very satisfying, pleasant lifestyle with a great deal of flexibility and freedom and an excellent salary— particularly when augmented by consulting and speaking opportunities.

Furthermore, I absolutely loved what I was doing! I had some small graduate classes and some large undergraduate classes of over five hundred students. I felt I was having considerable influence for good in the lives of a large part of the student body over the four- to five-year period most studied there.

But I felt impelled to develop new approaches to training executives that would necessitate a full-time commitment. I really struggled with the issue of the good and the best. I finally concluded to go for it, and bring the Seven Habits and Principle-Centered Leadership to as many segments of society as possible. I felt confident it would work financially so that it could adequately provide for my family, but there were still many unknowns and withdrawal pains.

Within a year or two, the level of contribution, the sense of satisfaction, and the intrinsic excitement of the challenges were so real that I only regretted that I had not made the move earlier. It hit me again: don't be seduced by the good; go for the best. Go for that which represents your unique contribution. Make it comfortable to leave the comfort zone and uncomfortable to stay in it—contradictory as all that sounds.

With each stage of a growing business there has been the same challenge—stay with the good and known, or go for the best and the unknown. And with each stage has come a lot of pain. I remember once being in a cab in some city, driving to a hotel and breaking out in a cold sweat with the realization that I had lost an enormous amount of money and put at risk in new loans all the assets I had accumulated over the years, including my home and cabin and all my other financial safety nets. I had also put at risk those for whom I was responsible, and there was a good possibility of losing everything, including the business.

Then I remember thinking that all these losses were really investments in developing markets, developing people, developing products, and that the foolish parts of the losses were investments in learning and insights that we could use for the future. Those thoughts were all intellectual, but the emotional reality was that I was totally vulnerable and at risk. My family was at risk. My future was at risk. It was the first time I had felt truly vulnerable and exposed, and at deep risk in every way.

At each of the critical historical moments of profound change in the structure and the strategy of the business, we experienced the same anxieties and fears of leaving the comfort of the way we'd done things in the past. There always seemed to be so much at risk. We simply had to exercise more faith in the principles of synergistic interdependence—the mother lode of true growth, excitement, and contribution—and more faith in the basic character and competency of the other people who also were engaged in synergistic interchange.

With each occasion, I had to move out of a comfort zone. I had to fall backward off the cliff, and even though I felt there were safety ropes and nets, still there was the emotional period of vulnerability. But in every case, the fears were unfounded, and the risks were infinitely worth it. The mutual excitement, the spontaneous enthusiasm, the genuine new insights and learnings, the new sense of contribution, of meaning, of adding value, of significant work, of blessing lives, of influencing entire organizations, cultures, societies—has been a world I had never known so profoundly before.

The key phase came when we decided to take the material into the public world as well as the private—to influence education, hospitals, churches, foundations, nonprofit organizations, every profession, small entrepreneural start-ups, middle-sized businesses, large businesses, Fortune 500 companies, Fortune 100 companies, federal government, state governments, local governments, local communities, health care systems, alternative medicine organizations—and then to go internationally in an effort to bring principle-centered leadership to the entire world.

This has all taken place in a matter of a few years. And we now have a team of empowered, committed people with complementary skills who share a common vision with lifetime commitment to our mission statement:

> To serve the worldwide community by empowering individuals and organizations to significantly increase their performance capability in order to accomplish worthwhile purposes through understanding and living principle-centered leadership.
>
> In carrying out this mission we continually strive to practice what we teach.

We explicitly declare that we continually strive to practice what we teach because we have learned that you can never accomplish a worthy end with unworthy means, and that the true power of an enduring contribution comes from integrity, example, mentoring, empowering, and aligning.

By far, the most significant challenge, for me at least, is to put my family ahead of my profession, of my work, of my company, of friends, of possessions. I deeply believe that if we attend to all other duties and responsibilites in life and neglect the family it would be analogous to straightening deck chairs on the Titanic. As another put it, "no institution can take its place." The family is the key institution that shapes the emotional, intellectual, spiritual, moral, social, and economic future of individuals and of our entire society.

In all of this, I've come to see the necessity of receiving counsel from many people, and of setting up strong independent boards and advisors with professional competence and deep character strength. I've seen the importance of setting up check-and-balance systems that are not adversarial, but are truly synergistic, inside businesses and organizations. I've seen the importance of council government, of always having advisors or counselors. I've seen the importance of consulting the wisdom of my wife and sensing her intuition, and really being open to it—even though it may run counter to my own desires and plans. All this has forcibly taught me again and again that humility is truly the mother of all virtues, and that all other good things are available to us, if we will be an agent and not a law unto ourselves— if we will be a vessel through which correct principles can operate.

I've learned to turn over the management of the business to other good, competent people and to participate in the strategic issues with them synergistically. I've learned the importance of not borrow-

ing strength from position, power, authority, or ownership—even though I occasionally am tempted to, and perhaps fall back.

Nevertheless, I know what is right. I know what the principles are. And I know I must bow to them and let them have their way with me. When I do, things usually work out well. And if they don't, I nevertheless feel peace.

Together, we affirm that the choices people make in that space between stimulus and response are vital choices. And we are absolutely convinced that the best way to create quality of life is to listen to and live by conscience. We've each had times when we've chosen otherwise, and we've experienced those results. And together we say, there's simply nothing that has greater impact on our time, on the quality of every moment of our lives, than learning to listen to and live by conscience.

There may be several turning points in our lives, but the most critical of all is the point at which we make the decision: "I will live by my conscience. From this time forward, I will not allow any voice—social mirror, scripting, even my own rational-lies-ing—to speak more clearly to me than the voice of conscience. And, whatever the consequence, I will follow it."

In making that decision, we create a lifestyle in which we begin to love consequences instead of fear them. Time is no longer the enemy; it is our friend. Because we're working with true north principles, time is what will bring to pass the delicious fruit we have the patience and confidence to cultivate in our lives.

Our two greatest gifts are time and the freedom to choose—the power to direct our efforts in the use of that time. The key is in not "spending" time, but in "investing" it—in people, in empowerment, in meaningful projects and causes. Like any capital resource, if we spend time, it's gone. We dwindle away our inheritance. If we invest it, we increase our inheritance, and it will redound to the blessing of generations that follow.

WE MUST BECOME THE CHANGE WE SEEK IN THE WORLD

We realize that what we're suggesting is not an easy message. It may not be popular in a quick-fix, short-term, consumption-based world. But we have several assumptions about you, the reader, that have encouraged us to share it.

Because you've chosen to read this book, we believe you probably have a lot in common with many of the people we work with in our organization and in seminars throughout the world. You're incredibly busy. You have a desire to be responsible and productive and do good things. But because you're so busy, like many of us, you may not be contributing in some of the ways you would like to or could.

Our experience has given us tremendous faith in people like you and in our ability together to solve many of the problems we all face. It's our firm conviction that by developing the capacity to listen to conscience and plan and organize effectively to do first things first, we can all make many individual and combined contributions that are currently falling by the wayside.

We would ask you to connect deeply with your conscience for a moment and ask yourself this final question:

Is there something I feel I could do to make a difference?

Think about it. It may require letting go—of illusory paradigms, rationalizing, wants, urgency addiction . . . even your comfort zone. But, deep inside, in all honesty of heart, do you feel there's something you could do, some contribution you could make, some legacy you could leave that would impact your family, your work team, your organization, your community, your society in a positive way?

If there is, we encourage you to act on it. As Gandhi said, "We must become the change we seek in the world." Wherever you are in terms of becoming principle-centered, we encourage you to start exercising the attributes of your heart. Make a promise and keep it. Set a goal and achieve it. There is peace in it. As Emerson said:

Nothing can bring you peace but yourself. Nothing can bring you peace but the triumph of principles.[8]

EPILOGUE

AS we conclude *First Things First,* the spirit that fills our minds and hearts is one of reverence.

We feel a deep sense of reverence for people. As many have shared parts of their deep inner lives with us in the form of mission statements, goals, and personal experiences in working with the principles in this book, we've had the deep feeling that we've stood on holy ground. Our minds have been drawn to cultures in the world where people greet others with palms pressed together and a slight bow in acknowledgment of that reverence for the nobility of the human soul, for that spark of divinity within us all.

We feel a sense of reverence for principles. Our own experience in living in harmony with them—and in violating them—has given each of us a deep and abiding respect for their reality and a conviction that quality of life does depend on the degree to which we align our lives with "true north."

We feel a sense of reverence for the stewardship of life and time—for the moments, days, weeks, years, and seasons we have to live, love, learn, and leave a legacy. We feel a sense of reverence and gratitude for the freedom we have to make choices concerning the way we spend our time.

Above all, we feel a sense of reverence for God, whom we believe to be the source of both principles and conscience. It's our own conviction that it is that spark of divinity within each of us that draws us toward principle-centered lives of service and contribution. But we also recognize—and reverence—the diversity of belief manifest in our own organization and throughout the world by people of conscience and contribution.

As one of the early pioneers of the American West, Bryant S. Hinckley, said:

Service is the virtue that distinguished the great of all times and which they will be remembered by. It places a mark of nobility upon its disciples. It is the dividing line which separates the two great groups of the world—those who help and those who hinder, those who lift and those who lean, those who contribute and those who only consume. How much better it is to give than to receive. Service in any form is comely and beautiful. To give encouragement, to impart sympathy, to show interest, to banish fear, to build self confidence and awaken hope in the hearts of others, in short—to love them and to show it—is to render the most precious service.[1]

There is so much we can do to render service, to make a difference in the world—no matter how large or small our Circle of Influence. It's our hope that each of us will connect more deeply with conscience and give light and warmth to the world from our fire within.

APPENDIX A
MISSION STATEMENT WORKSHOP

One of the most effective ways to go about creating a personal mission statement is to plan time when you can be totally alone—away from phones, friends, neighbors, and even family. Although it isn't necessary, nature provides an ideal setting because it gets you out of the artificial, mechanical, segmented world and puts you in touch with natural harmony and balance. It creates the conditions where you can clear your mind and try to really open up to your innermost feelings.

We suggest you try one or more of the perspective-expanding experiences below. These are seven exercises we've found to be most effective in helping people prepare to write their personal mission statement. There's a wide range of approach. Some of the exercises take only a few minutes; others take hours or even days. You'll probably find some more valuable to you than others. You may even find that something else works better for you than the exercises we suggest.

The important thing is to really get into your deep inner life. Get in touch with what matters most to you.

Exercise #1: Try the visualization experience in Chapter 5 where you mentally transport yourself to your eightieth birthday or fiftieth wedding anniversary (see pp. 107–9).

Exercise #2: Use your unique human endowments to explore each of the needs and capacities in your life. You may find it helpful to use a chart such as the one on the following page.

Exercise #3: Go on a personal retreat and take time to deeply consider questions such as these:

What do I feel are my greatest strengths?

_____

_____

_____

What strengths have others who know me well noticed in me?

_____

_____

_____

	To Live	To Love	To Learn	To Leave a Legacy

Self-awareness

What is my current situation?

What is my paradigm of quality of life?

Conscience

What is within me to fulfill?

What are the principles that will produce quality-of-life results?

Independent Will

What choices do I need to make to fulfill my needs and capacities?

What scripts do I need to rewrite?

Creative Imagination

What are the quality-of-life results I desire?

What can I do to create them?

What do I deeply enjoy doing?

_____

_____

_____

What qualities of character do I most admire in others?

_____

_____

_____

Who is the one person that has made the greatest positive impact on my life?

_____

_____

_____

Why was that person able to have such significant impact?

_____

_____

_____

What have been my happiest moments in life?

_____

_____

_____

Why were they happy?

_____

_____

_____

If I had unlimited time and resources, what would I choose to do?

_____

_____

_____

When I daydream, what do I see myself doing?

_____
_____
_____

What are the three or four most important things to me?

_____
_____
_____

When I look at my work life, what activities do I consider of greatest worth?

_____
_____
_____

When I look at my personal life, what activities do I consider of greatest worth?

_____
_____
_____

What can I do best that would be of worth to others?

_____
_____
_____

What talents do I have that no one else really knows about?

_____
_____
_____

Though I may have dismissed such thoughts many times before for various reasons, are there things I feel I really should do? What are they?

_____
_____
_____

What are my physical needs and capacities?

_____

_____

_____

How satisfied am I with my current level of fulfillment in the physical area?

_____

_____

_____

What quality-of-life results do I desire that are different from what I now have in this area?

_____

_____

_____

What principles will create those results?

_____

_____

_____

What are my social needs and capacities?

_____

_____

_____

How satisfied am I with my current level of fulfillment in the social area?

_____

_____

_____

What quality-of-life results do I desire that are different from what I now have in this area?

_____

_____

_____

What principles will create those results?

_____

_____

_____

What are my mental needs and capacities?

_____

_____

_____

How satisfied am I with my current level of fulfillment in the mental area?

_____

_____

_____

What quality-of-life results do I desire that are different from what I now have in this area?

_____

_____

_____

What principles will create those results?

_____

_____

_____

What are my spiritual needs and capacities?

_____

_____

_____

How satisfied am I with my current level of fulfillment in the spiritual area?

_____

_____

_____

What quality-of-life results do I desire that are different from what I now have in this area?

_____

_____

_____

What principles will create those results?

_____

_____

_____

Where do I see my physical, social, mental, and spiritual needs and capacities overlapping?

_____

_____

_____

What are my important roles in life?

_____

_____

_____

_____

_____

What are the most important lifetime goals I want to fulfill in each role?

_____

_____

_____

_____

_____

_____

What results am I currently getting in my life that I like?

_____

_____

_____

What paradigms are producing those results?

_____

_____

_____

What results am I currently getting in my life that I don't like?

_____

_____

_____

What are the paradigms that are producing those results?

_____

_____

_____

What paradigms would produce better results?

_____

_____

_____

What would I really like to be and to do in my life?

_____

_____

_____

What are the important principles upon which my being and doing are based?

_____

_____

_____

Your answers to these questions should give you some excellent input for your mission statement.

Exercise #4: Use your watch to go through the following timed exercise.

    a) Take one minute and answer the following question:

      If I had unlimited time and resources, what would I do?

      Don't be afraid to dream. Unlock possibilities. Write down everything that comes into your mind.

    b) Take one minute and write down your values. Below is a partial list that might help stimulate your thinking.

- peace of mind
- security
- wealth
- good health
- close relationship with . . .
- recognition or fame
- free time
- happiness
- spiritual fulfillment
- friendships
- family
- longevity
- contributing time, knowledge, or money to . . .
- travel
- sense of accomplishment
- respect of others

    c) Take one minute and go through your list of values, identifying the top five.

    d) Take a few minutes and compare your list of five values to your dreams. You may find you're living with subconscious dreams that are not in harmony with your values. You may dream of living the life of Indiana Jones, but you don't really value the idea of crawling through cobwebs and sleeping with scorpions. If you don't get your dreams out in the open and look at them in the cool light of day, you may spend years living with illusions and the subconscious feeling that you're somehow settling for second best. Work on the two lists until you feel your dreams reflect your values.

    e) Now take one minute and look at your values as they relate to the four fundamental areas of human fulfillment. Do they reflect your physical, social, mental, and spiritual needs and capacities? Work on your list until you feel they do.

    f) Finally, take one last minute to answer this question:

      What principles will produce the values on my final list?

Exercise #5: If you keep a journal, review what you've written over the years. Look for "mountain top" insights you may have had. Look for repeating patterns that may not have been obvious from day to day. Try to identify and write down values and directions.

Exercise #6: Use Lewin's Force Field Analysis model to identify where you want to be, where you are now, and the factors that are working for and against your effort to change.

Desired Results -

RESTRAINING FORCES

↓ ↓ ↓ ↓ ↓ ↓ ↓ ↓ ↓ ↓

Current Results ─────────────────────────────

↑ ↑ ↑ ↑ ↑ ↑ ↑ ↑ ↑ ↑ ↑

DRIVING FORCES

Consider the following questions:
- What is the ideal situation? How would I spend my time? What would be the results?
- What is my current situation? How do I spend my time now?
- What are the specific factors that keep me from the ideal? What can I do to weaken or remove them?
- What are the specific factors that move me toward the ideal? What can I do to strengthen or add to them?

Exercise #7: Use the following chart to look at your life over a period of time. In a day of increasing life expectancy, there can be several seasons to life. Retirement now brings with it a realistic expectation of twenty years or more, opening the door to the possibility of a second career that can add great meaning to life. Often the second career is more of a choice than the first. Experience, resources, and opportunity open many doors that were previously closed.

This exercise is an excellent one to go through with your spouse if you're married. You may be thinking of a second career as a patron of the arts living in a downtown condominium, while your spouse may be planning to purchase a horse ranch in Montana.

Having a sense of purpose often will improve the quality of life now as well as in the future. The vision of later years can revive enthusiasm for your purposes now as you realize these are not the only purposes you may accomplish. In the first column on the following chart, list the things you would really like to do or contributions you would like to make at some time in your life. Then shade in the boxes, indicating when you might do each of these things. Five- to ten-year increments are exact enough for the purpose of this exercise.

Future contributions and accomplishments	When (approximate age)								
	20	30	40	50	60	70	80	90	100

For added perspective, go back now and note the year you will be at each age. For example, if you're now thirty, figure out what year you'll be forty, fifty, sixty, and so on, and write the date above the corresponding age.

Hopefully, these exercises will expand your thinking and help prepare you to create your mission statement. When you get ready to do the actual writing, keep in mind that you're not writing it for anybody but yourself. Write it in your own language. For some people, the right words are flowing and smooth. For others, they're blunt and direct. There are powerful mission statements from a few words to several pages—statements written in poetry, prose, music, and art. Write in whatever way captures and fuels your own inner fire. Be sure to review the characteristics of empowering mission statements listed in Chapter 5, *The Passion of Vision* (pp. 103–17).

Some people like to read statements written by others. Some feel it inhibits their own expression. We've included several here and leave it to you to decide whether or not you feel reading them would be helpful to you in your effort to create your own. Although we have access to a number of statements from "famous" people throughout history, the ones we've chosen to include here come from extraordinary ordinary people living today, worldwide, in all walks of life. Based on the criteria in Chapter 5, some are more empowering than others. But each statement is a statement of the soul. If you read them, try to capture something of the creator as well as the creation. Imagine the impact of that person living what you read.

MISSION STATEMENTS

Climb the Mountain:
I will live each day with courage and a belief in myself and others. I will live by the values of integrity, freedom of choice, and a love of all God's people. I will strive to keep commitments not only to others but to myself as well. I will remember that to truly live, I must climb the mountain today, for tomorrow may be too late. I know that my mountain may seem no more than a hill to others and I will accept that. I will be renewed by my own personal victories and triumphs no matter how small. I will continue to make my own choices and to live with them as I have always done. I will not make excuses or blame others. I will, for as long as possible, keep my mind and body healthy and strong so that I am able to make the choice to climb the mountain. I will help others as best I can and I will thank those who help me along the way.

To live the days gifted to me gratefully with discipline, purpose and as an adventure.
To discover and accept what is really me using and stretching my strengths with confidence and joy.
To treasure my family.
To enrich my life and the lives of all who cross my path or share my hearth, by caring, by affirming their unique worth in love, by giving what I have to give and accepting what they have to give me,
and if they so wish,
by teaching them what I know and learning what I can from them, and by helping them to discover and pursue their way.
To protect and promote the ethos of South Africa and the community in which I live and also the environment upon which I depend.

To recognize and accept that I am not an owner of anything, but a steward in trust, and that rights are much less important than obligations.

To seek my God constantly and understand my way to Him.

While keeping an eye single to the glory of God, to make the world a better place in which to live by empowering people to live more meaningful lives.

Starting first with my family and then expanding my circle of influence:

To live true to the principles I hold dear (charity, fidelity, self-sufficiency, honesty, integrity, proactivity, giving, trust . . .).

To make the burden a little lighter and the way a little brighter for everyone I have regular contact with.

To not take myself too seriously and to keep everything within its proper context.

To live and let live, to learn and teach, to give and receive, to love and be loved, to understand and be understood.

I will embrace and see each day as not just another day, but one filled with opportunity and excitement. I alone will choose for myself those endeavors I wish to pursue.

I desire to live a life of moral fulfillment and simplicity. Concern for my well-being will be my first priority. I believe that if I remain true to my values, I will have a positive influence on those I touch.

I will try with a firm conviction to share more of my innermost thoughts with the ones I love.

I realize that I am both interdependent and respondable to others. With this in mind, I will consciously seek to understand and obtain a closeness with my family and colleagues.

I will continue to grow by stimulating my mind with new learning.

While I value the freedom and financial security my profession provides, I realize that freedom and security alone cannot provide the happiness I seek.

I alone will choose for myself.

My mission is to be a force for positive change and to inspire others to greatness through being a catalyst for action and through developing a shared vision of that which is possible.

I will strive to continually invent the future out of my imagination rather than being a victim of the past. I will strive to choose my way honoring courage, justice, humility, kindness, understanding, and personal integrity.

Finally, I will frequently remind myself that, without risk, there is neither success nor failure. As Thomas Aquinas observed: If the primary mission of a captain were to preserve his ship, he would never leave port.

I pledge myself to being a caring and honest friend to those around me and to always attempt to link that which I know with that which I do.

For myself, I want to develop self-knowledge, self love, and self-allowing. I want to use my healing talents to keep hope alive and express my vision courageously in word and action.

In my family, I want to build healthy, loving relationships in which we let each other become our best selves.

At work, I want to establish a fault-free, self-perpetuating, learning environment.

In the world, I want to nurture the development of all life forms, in harmony with the laws of nature.

To act in a manner that brings out the best in me and those important to me—especially when it might be most justifiable to act otherwise.

To be humble.

To say thanks to God in some way, every day.

To never react to abuse by passing it on.

To find the self within that does and can look at all sides without loss.

I believe in treating all people with kindness and respect.

I believe by knowing what I value, I truly know what I want.

To be driven by my values and beliefs.

I want to experience life's passions with the newness of a child's love, the sweetness and joy of young love, and the respect and reverence of mature love.

My goals are to achieve a position of respect and knowledge, to utilize that position to help others, to play an active role in a public service organization.

Finally, to go through life with a smile on my face and a twinkle in my eye.

To be the person my children look to with pride when they say, "This is my dad."

To be the one my children come to for love, comfort, and understanding.

To be the friend known as caring and always willing to listen empathically to their concerns.

To be a person not willing to win at the cost of another's spirit.

To be a person who can feel pain and not want to hurt another.

To be the person who speaks for the one that cannot, to listen for the one that cannot hear, see for the one without sight, and have the ability to say, "You did that, not I."

To have my deeds always match my words through the grace of God.

I will maintain a positive attitude and a sense of humor in everything I do. I want to be known by my family as a caring and loving husband and father; by my business associates as a fair and honest person; and my friends as someone they can count on. To the people who work for me and with me, I pledge my respect and will strive every day to earn their respect. Controlling all my actions is a strong sense of integrity which I believe the most important character trait.

I will live each day as though I had all the power and influence necessary to make it a perfect world. Through listening to and serving others, I will learn new ideas and gain different perspectives.

I will strive to gain mastery over life's challenges through increasing my circle of influence and deemphasizing those areas of concern over which I have no control.

I will behave in a manner so as to become a light, not a roadblock, for others who choose to follow or lead me.

I will trust my dreams and be the prisoner of nothing.

I will use my private victories unselfishly by trying to create value for others. The pursuit of excellence will determine the options I decide to exercise and the paths I choose to travel.

I will expect no more of others than I expect of myself. I will seek new sources for learning and growth—nature, family, literature, new acquaintances.

I will show love rather than expect love. I choose to focus upon being effective versus efficient. I choose to make a difference in this world.

APPENDIX B
A REVIEW OF TIME MANAGEMENT
LITERATURE

In making our survey of time management literature and tools, we've read, digested, and boiled down the information to eight basic approaches. We'd like to examine each of these approaches—from the "roots" to the "fruits"— and take a hard look at their strengths and their weaknesses. Bottom-line, what is the impact of what's out there on quality of life?

The roots of these approaches are the underlying assumptions or governing paradigms out of which they grow. Do we really buy the fundamental assumptions? Each approach has value. Each makes an important contribution. But if the basic paradigm of the approach is flawed or incomplete, no amount of effective application or implementation is going to bring optimum results. The fact that we put increased effort into some of these approaches without significantly improving the results indicates a fundamental paradigm problem.

1. THE "GET ORGANIZED" APPROACH (ORDER)

This approach assumes that most time management problems are caused by chaos—the lack of order in our life. We often can't find what we want when we want it. Things are constantly falling through the cracks. In most cases, the answer lies in systems: a filing system, an in-out basket system, a reminder system, a database system. These systems usually focus on organization in three areas.

- *organization of things* (creating order for everything from keys to computer screens, filing systems to closets, office space to kitchen space)
- *organization of tasks* (giving order and sequence to "to do's" using tools from simple lists to complex planning charts and project management software)
- *organization of people* (defining what you can do and what others can do, delegating, creating tracking systems to keep on top of what's happening)

The order approach goes beyond personal application into organizational practice. When a corporation is in trouble, it's time to reorganize, restructure, shake things up, and "get our act together."

Strengths: Organization saves time and leads to greater efficiency. We don't waste time looking for keys, clothes, or lost reports. We economize our efforts. Organization brings mental clarity and order.

Weaknesses: The danger is that organizing often becomes an end rather than a means to greater ends. Tremendous amounts of time can be spent organizing rather than producing. Many people think they're getting things accomplished because they're busy organizing, when in reality they may be procrastinating and not completing important work. Applied in excess, the strength of organization becomes a weakness. We can become overstructured, nitpicking, inflexible, and mechanical. This is true for organizations as well as individuals.

2. THE WARRIOR APPROACH (SURVIVAL AND INDEPENDENT PRODUCTION)

The focus of the *Warrior Approach* is on the protection of personal time to focus and produce. Most of us feel besieged by the demands of an extremely busy environment. We work in places where there's more to do than the staff can handle. If we have a computer network calendar, we open it to find our lives are scheduled for the next sixteen months. There are voice-mail messages to return, people constantly knocking on the door. We know there's no way we can make the contribution we need to make unless we have quiet, uninterrupted time to do high-leverage independent work.

The Time Warrior realizes that if we don't do something to fight back, the system becomes an avalanche that will bury us alive. So the *Warrior Approach* is one of defending yourself, protecting your time so you can focus on high-leverage independent action. It includes such powerful techniques as:

- *insulation* (creating protection through the use of secretaries, closed doors, phone-answering machines, baby-sitters, and no-nonsense communication)
- *isolation* (removing to an environment where aloneness creates uninterrupted time)
- *delegation* (assigning tasks to others to free time for more high-leverage tasks)

Although there are few books written exclusively from this approach, we find it in much of the literature in the form of "smart" techniques and tricks.

Strengths: The strength of this approach is in assuming personal responsibility for what happens with our time. We can produce because we have quiet, uninterrupted time to do high-leverage, independent work. We all need this kind of time occasionally, particularly when we're involved in something highly creative.

Weaknesses: The basic assumption of this approach is that others are the enemy. "Do unto others before they do unto your schedule." It's a survivalist paradigm—insulate, isolate, intimidate. Put up barriers. Manage meetings without getting people mad. Say no. Learn how to get people out of your office. Hang up the phone in the middle of a conversation—just make sure it's in the middle of your sentence and not theirs!

This approach may get people out of the way so we can do what we want to do. But when what we want to do includes them, we often find them far from eager to cooperate. In addition, this defensive, reactive posture often leads to manipulative behavior and creates a self-fulfilling prophecy. People sense they're being put off and, consciously or unconsciously, they fight back. They push for time and attention, or they work around you and without you, creating problems that take even more of your time to rectify. This protective, isolationist approach ignores the interdependent reality of quality of life and, in most cases, only serves to exacerbate the problem.

Personal responsibility is a valid and powerful principle. The problem comes when it's coupled with the idea that others are the enemy. Though we may be "highly productive" in the short run, the fruit of this independent achievement paradigm will catch up with us in the long run. The independent approach is ineffective in an interdependent reality.

3. THE GOAL APPROACH (ACHIEVEMENT)

This approach basically says, "Know what you want and focus your effort to achieve it." It includes techniques such as long-term, mid-range, and short-term planning, goal setting, visualization, self-motivation, and creating a positive mental attitude.

Strengths: This is the approach of the world-class performer, the Olympic athlete. It's the power by which the performance of great talent can be exceeded by that of lesser talent willing to pay the price—to marshal the forces, to focus the energy, to refuse to be distracted, to not let anything get in the way. In the field of personal development, one of the few things that can be empirically validated is that individuals and organizations that set goals accomplish more. The reality is that people who know how to set and achieve goals generally accomplish what they set out to do.

Weaknesses: There are countless people who use the *Goal Approach* to climb the ladder of success—only to discover it's been leaning against the wrong wall. They set goals and focus powerful effort to achieve them. But when they get what they wanted, they find it doesn't bring the results they expected. Life seems empty, anticlimactic. "Is that all there is?" When goals are not based on principles and primary needs, the focused drive and single-mindedness that makes achievement possible can blind people to imbalance in their lives. They may have their six- or seven-figure income, but they're living with the deep pain of multiple divorces and children who won't even talk to them. They may have a glamorous public image, but an empty private life. They have the plaudits of the world, but no rich, satisfying relationships, no deep inner sense of integrity.

And what happens when some extrinsic factor suddenly makes the superordinate goal impossible to achieve—the athlete sustains a serious permanent injury, the painter loses his eyesight, the musician loses his hearing? What happens when there's literally nothing else in their lives?

There's a lot in the *Goal Approach* literature about "paying the price." But there isn't much that gives a realistic picture of what that price—including opportunity cost—might be.

4. THE ABC APPROACH (PRIORITIZATION AND VALUES IDENTIFICATION)

The *ABC Approach says,* "You can do anything you want, but not everything." It builds on the *Goal Approach* and adds the important concept of sequence: "Concentrate your efforts on your most important tasks first." It includes techniques such as values clarification and task ranking. The assumption is that if you know what you want to accomplish and focus on those things first, you'll be happy.

Strengths: This is the traditional "first things first" approach. It gives order and sequence. On a daily basis, from ABC's to simple 123's, this approach provides techniques to differentiate between "to do's" and encouragement to keep focused on top-priority tasks. The more recent literature expands the concept to look at lifetime priorities. It says that "first things" are connected with your values and beliefs, and that identifying your values will give you a framework for doing first things first. This deeper analysis around values is helpful and productive.

Weaknesses: The key flaw is that values clarification does not recognize that there are principles, natural laws that govern quality of life. This lack of recognition often leads people to decide on and pursue values that are at odds with the laws of nature. In this case, the pursuit of values only leads to frustration and failure.

There are plenty of people standing at the top of those ladders against wrong walls who tell us that achieving what they valued did not bring them quality of life. Consciously or unconsciously, these people acted on values that seemed very important at the time. They set goals and focused powerful effort to achieve their priorities. But when they got what they wanted, they found it didn't bring the results they expected.

The fact that we may value something at any particular time in our lives does not necessarily mean that achieving it will bring lasting happiness. History is filled with examples of individuals and societies that got what they valued—and it didn't bring "success" or happiness. Sometimes, in fact, it destroyed them.

In addition to self-awareness—knowing what we value—the other endowments must be exercised as well—conscience, imagination, and independent will. Only in this way can we be sure that our values are in harmony with the reality of true north. Bottom-line, if our goals are not deeply anchored in correct principles, we'll never be able to achieve deep fulfillment and quality of life.

5. THE MAGIC TOOL APPROACH (TECHNOLOGY)

The *Magic Tool Approach* is based on the assumption that the right tool (the right calendar, the right planner, the right computer program, the right hand-held or laptop computer) will give us power to create quality in our lives. These tools typically help us keep track of priorities, organize tasks, and more easily access key information. The basic assumption is that systems and structures can help make us more effective. Classy-looking leather planners have even become something of a status symbol—an indicator that people are on the fast track and really have their act together.

Strengths: There's certainly great value in the effective use of tools. From building a house to building a life, the right tools can make a powerful difference. Why dig with a spoon when you could use a backhoe? Why use a simple calendar when you could have an advanced planner that helps you:

- keep track of priorities
- keep your goals in front of you
- organize tasks
- organize and quickly access frequently used information

The sheer number of both paper-based and electronic tools on the market suggests that this is a highly popular approach. Tools are a symbol of hope. There's a sense of order that comes from having something in hand that suggests order. There's a feeling of satisfaction in writing things down, checking things off, keeping track of things in our lives.

Weaknesses: The fundamental paradigms behind the design of most time management tools go back to the *Goal Approach* and the *ABC Ap-*

proach. As we've already observed, these approaches have some strengths, but they also have some serious flaws—stemming largely from the fact that no consideration is given to the extrinsic realities that govern quality of life.

The basic assumption that technology is the answer is also flawed. Even the best tool is no substitute for vision, judgment, creativity, character, or competence. A great camera doesn't produce a great photographer. A great word processor doesn't make a great poet. Neither will even a great organizer create a great life—although a new planner or organizer often carries such an implied promise. A good tool can enhance our ability to create quality of life, but it can never create it for us.

In reality, most of the current tools encourage "human doing" rather than "human being." The daily focus keeps us checking off "to do's" without really asking whether or not the "to do's" should even be done. For many people, the tools seem rigidly structured and unnatural. Instead of servants, they become demanding masters, focused on what isn't done and distorting natural rhythm and balance to cram what should be rich moments of life into daily segmented predetermined time slots.

And how many people use the time management tools in the way they were designed to be used? As even many suppliers of the tools acknowledge, very few. People buy advanced planners and wind up using them as glorified calendars. Office management consultants report finding organizers being used as fancy appointment books or left virtually unopened in office desk drawers. For many people, tools are the symbols of unfulfilled promise.

6. THE TIME MANAGEMENT 101 APPROACH (SKILLS)

The *Time Management 101 Approach* is based on the paradigm that time management is essentially a skill—like accounting or word processing—and that in order to function effectively in today's world, we have to master certain basics such as:

- using a planner or appointment calendar
- creating "to do" lists
- setting goals
- delegating
- organizing
- prioritizing

The theory is that these basics create a form of social literacy necessary for survival. This is a popular organizational approach. When people lack skill in knowing how to plan, set goals, or delegate, it can create serious impact in the organization. As part of their human resource development programs, many companies make tapes, booklets, and courses designed to teach the basics available to their employees.

Strengths: Some improvements are made, especially in terms of work-related skills valued by the organization.

Weaknesses: The depth and quality of the training is the primary issue. What are the fundamental paradigms being taught? Do they tie into correct principles? Or do they propagate inaccurate assumptions about the nature of life and effectiveness?

It's interesting that many people who aren't quite as organized, or don't use a state-of-the-art planner, seem to have more inner peace, richer relationships, and greater satisfaction in life than many who do. And in the long run, these people often make greater contributions to the organization than others who are more "skilled" in time management techniques.

More than skill or technique, individual and organizational quality is a function of aligning both personal character and personal behavior with principles. Much of current time management training is a mixed bag of techniques and time-saving tricks, with a few principles (such as organization and prioritization) thrown in. But rarely do people come away empowered to apply these principles—or to detect and apply other principles—appropriately. Skills alone do not provide the answer.

7. THE "GO WITH THE FLOW" APPROACH (HARMONY AND NATURAL RHYTHMS)

This approach promotes a different set of assumptions about time and life than does traditional time management. The basic paradigm is that learning to "go with the flow" and getting back to the natural rhythm of living will open our lives to the spontaneity and serendipity that's natural to our being.

Much of this literature draws on the philosophies of Eastern cultures, where emphasis is placed on congruity of the inner self and one's harmony with the flow of nature. This approach is also based on biological research, which suggests that all living things have certain vibrations, and that living in our nano-second, mechanical world of clocks, computers, and cellular phones sets us at odds with our natural body rhythms, creating serious illness and other problems. It represents something of a countermovement to traditional time management—a retreat for those who have felt beat up and guilt-tripped by the systems and paradigms of the other approaches.

Strengths: It's been suggested that archaeologists digging up the remains of our civilization at some future date would undoubtedly come to the conclusion that our society worshipped clocks. We have clocks in our schools, clocks in our churches, clocks in the office, clocks in every room of our homes. We even wear miniature clocks on our wrists!

Whether or not we worship them, clocks tick, phones ring, computers beep, honk, zap (or do whatever else we program them to do), and the mechanical cadence sets a brisk, demanding pace.

But sometimes, in the middle of the seemingly forced quick march, we experience one of those "timeless" moments in time when the cadence simply fades into silence in the joy of the moment. It may be out in nature, away from the clocks, phones, and computers, where we feel aware and in tune with the natural rhythms around and within us. It may be when we're involved in something we love—music, art, literature, or gardening. It may be when we're involved with someone we love—sharing, discovering, communicating. The pace is dramatically different, and we sense a quality to the moment that makes it rich and satisfying. We become aware of the stark difference. We want more timeless moments in our lives.

This approach sensitizes us to the value of these moments and helps us to create more of them in our lives. It moves us away from the dominance of "urgent" things constantly pressing against us. It creates and encourages internal and external harmony.

Weaknesses: Often, this approach is a reaction to urgency addiction— an escape rather than an aid to creating quality of life. Vital elements such as vision, purpose, and balance are frequently missing. In addition, there are many times when accomplishing what's important means exercizing independent will and swimming upstream instead of merely going with the flow.

8. THE RECOVERY APPROACH (SELF-AWARENESS)

Some of the most serious recent material has come out of what's known as the *Recovery Approach.* The basic paradigm is that there are essential flaws in the psyche as a result of environment, heredity, scripting, and other influences that manifest themselves as self-defeating or dysfunctional time management behaviors.

Influenced by an early role model or family culture, an individual may become a "perfectionist"—afraid to delegate, tending to micromanage, spending an inordinate amount of time on projects beyond the effective utilization of resources. A childhood or environmentally scripted "people pleaser" may become overcommitted and overworked out of fear of rejection. The "procrastinator" may fear success as well as failure if past success were seen to hurt someone else or exact a great price in family life. The solution is seen in recovery from the psychological and sociological deficiencies that create the time management problems.

Strengths: This approach is valuable because it focuses on some of the paradigms that create our behavior—the roots of the problem. It leads to greater self-awareness and prepares people to make fundamental changes and improvements.

Weaknesses: Suggested methods of recovery are as varied as those in the general recovery movement itself. While this approach provides valuable insights and helps define part of the problem, its value is more diagnostic than prescriptive. It doesn't even pretend to provide a unified approach to the solution, and several accepted approaches contradict each other even on basic issues. In addition, it cuts a very narrow slice. It doesn't begin to address a wide variety of other time management related concerns.

Additionally, while self-awareness is valuable in and of itself, it's incomplete. Understanding our past scripting is only part of creating meaningful change.

The chart that follows summarizes the primary contributions, strengths, and weaknesses of the eight time management approaches:

Approach	Contribution	Strengths	Weaknesses
Get Organized	order	• saves time • reduces or eliminates waste • enables greater productivity	• becomes an end rather than a means to greater ends • gives illusion of productivity • doesn't necessarily help people achieve what's important
Warrior	high independent production	• assumes personal responsibility for time and results • creates uninterrupted time for high-leverage short-term independent action	• breeds strong and even arrogant independence • often offends people • leads to manipulative behavior • creates collusive behavior where others respond in kind • creates long-term ineffectiveness

Approach	Contribution	Strengths	Weaknesses
Goal	commitment and focus	• clarifies values • creates sequential plan for accomplishment of goals	• creates the false expectation that achievement of goals will necessarily bring quality-of-life results • creates life imbalance through exclusive focus of time and energy • puts "do or die" achievement of goals ahead of spontaneous response to rich moments of living • enthrones independent achievement
ABC	prioritization	• gives order and sequence to achievement	• "priority" is often defined by urgency, circumstance, or other people • does not provide for confident response to spontaneous emergence of genuinely higher priorities • does not recognize extrinsic realities that govern quality of life

Approach	Contribution	Strengths	Weaknesses
Magic Tool	leverage	• offers powerful tools to communicate, track progress and results, and organize • increases productivity • magnifies individual capacity • enables creation of high-quality products and services	• creates the illusion that the power is in the tool • sometimes feels restrictive, unnatural • encourages "human doing" more than "human being" • often turns tools into demanding masters instead of helpful servants • underutilizes tool potential as people often use advanced tools as glorified calendars • often focuses on daily prioritization of the urgent
Time Management 101	skills	• develops skills that enhance accomplishment of objectives • increases performance	• creates the illusion that effectiveness is in the skill • varies in quality and "true north" orientation of instruction • generally creates limited focus on skills considered valuable to the organization

Approach	Contribution	Strengths	Weaknesses
Go with the Flow	harmony	• begins to move away from urgency paradigm • creates a pace of living more in harmony with our natural rhythms	• lacks the strengths of more purposeful approaches • lacks balance of a more integrated approach • is at odds with values represented by keeping commitments to others through appointments, schedules, and certain kinds of sequential productivity
Recovery	self-awareness	• helps identify nature and source of dysfunctional time management habits	• provides no unified solution • is incomplete—self-awareness alone does not create quality of life • addresses a narrow slice of concern • focuses on the past rather than the future

Although there are valuable contributions in each of these approaches, for the most part, they grow out of a paradigm of control, independent effort, efficiency, and *chronos* time. The following chart shows how these approaches relate to the three generations of time management described in Chapter 1.

Approach	1st Generation	2nd Generation	3rd Generation
Get Organized (*order*)		X	X
Warrior (*survival and independent production*)		X	X
Goal (*achievement*)		X	X
ABC (*prioritization and values identification*)			X
Magic Tool (*technology*)		X	X
Time Management 101 (*skills*)		X	X
Go with the Flow (*harmony and natural rhythms*)	X*		
Recovery (*self-awareness*)	X*		

* In some ways, these approaches are in the first generation; in other ways, they begin to move us into the fourth generation, asking questions that transcend the limits of the efficiency chronos paradigm.

Pioneers in each generation of time management have contributed in ways that have made a significant difference. We express our recognition of and appreciation for their efforts, and for the efforts of others who are involved in the labor pains of bringing forth a new generation based on the natural laws that govern quality of life. We are convinced that the insights and synergy of many will bring us all to greater heights of understanding and contribution.

TIME MANAGEMENT BIBLIOGRAPHY

Alexander, Roy. *Common Sense Time Management*. Amacom, 1992.

Allen, Jane Elizabeth. *Beyond Time Management*. Addison-Wesley, 1986.

Applebaum, Steven H., and Walter F. Rohrs. *Time Management for Health Care Professionals*. Aspen Systems, 1981.

Barnes, Emilie. *The Fifteen Minute Organizer*. Harvest House, 1991.

Bennett, Robert F. *Gaining Control: Your Key to Freedom and Success*. Franklin Institute/Pocket Books, 1987.

Best, Fred. *Flexible Life Scheduling*. Praeger, 1980.

Billingsley, Anne Voorhees. *Getting the Twenty-fifth Hour*. Hearth, 1988.

Bond, William J. *199 Time-Waster Situations and How to Avoid Them*. Frederick Fell, 1991.

————. *One Thousand and One Ways to Beat the Time Trap*. Frederick Fell, 1982.

Caddylak Systems. *Easy to Make Time Management Forms*. Caddylak Systems, Westbury, New York, 1983.

Carnahan, George R. *T.I.M.E.* Cincinnati: South Western, 1987.

Cooper, Joseph D. *How to Get More Done in Less Time*. Doubleday, 1962.

Criswell, John W. *Maintenance Time Management*. Englewood Cliffs, NJ: Fairmont Press. Distributed by Prentice Hall, 1991.

Culp, Stephanie. *How to Get Organized When You Don't Have Time*. Writer's Digest Books, 1986.

Davenport, Rita. *Making Time Making Money*. St. Martin's, 1982.

Douglass, Merrill E., and Donna N. Douglass. *Manage Your Time, Manage Your Work, Manage Yourself*. AMACOM, 1980.

————. *Time Management for Teams*. AMACOM, 1992.

Douglass, Merrill, and Phillip H. Goodwin. *Successful Time Management for Hospital Personnel*. AMACOM, 1980.

Eyre, Richard, and Linda Eyre. *Life Balance*. Ballantine, 1988.

Fanning, Tony, and Robbie Fanning. *Get It All Done and Still Be Human*. Menlo Park, CA: Open Chain Publishing, 1990.

Guaspari, John. *It's About Time*. AMACOM, 1992.

Hedrick, Lucy H. *Three Hundred and Sixty-Five Ways to Save Time*. Hearst, 1992.

Helmer, Ray G. *Time Management for Engineers and Constructors*. American Society of Civil Engineers, 1991.

Hobbs, Charles R. *Time Power*. Harper & Row, 1987.

Hopson, Barrie, and Mike Scally. *Time Management*. Mercury, 1989.

Hummel, Charles. *Tyranny of the Urgent*. InterVarsity, 1967.

Hunt, Diana, and Pam Hait. *The Tao of Time*. Simon & Schuster, 1990.

Hutchins, Raymond G. *High School Time Tracker*. Prentice Hall, 1992.

Januz, Lauren Robert. *Time Management for Executives*. Scribner's, 1982.

Josephs, Ray. *How to Gain an Extra Hour Every Day*. Plume, 1992.

Keyes, Ralph. *Timelock*. HarperCollins, 1991.

Kobert, Norman. *Managing Time*. Boardroom Books, 1980.

Kofodimos, Joan R., Ph.D. *Why Executives Lose Their Balance*. Center for Creative Leadership, 1989, Report #137.

LaBoeuf, Michael. *Working Smarter*. McGraw-Hill, 1979.

Lakein, Alan. *How to Get Control of Your Time and Your Life*. Signet, 1973.

Levinson, J. Conrad. *The Ninety Minute Hour*. Penguin, 1990.

Littleton, Mark. *Escaping the Time Crunch*. Moody Press, 1990.

Love, Sydney. *Mastery and Management of Time*. Prentice Hall, 1978.

Mackenzie, R. Alec. *Teamwork through Time Management*. Dartnell Press, 1990.

———. *Time for Success*. McGraw-Hill, 1989.

———. *The Time Trap*. AMACOM, 1990.

Maher, Charles A., editor. *Professional Self-Management Techniques*. P. H. Brookes, 1985.

Marvin, Philip. *Executive Time Management*. AMACOM, 1980.

Mayer, Jeffrey J. *If You Haven't Got the Time to Do It Right, When Will You Find the Time to Do It Over?* Simon & Schuster, 1990.

McCay, James T. *The Management of Time*. Prentice Hall, 1959.

McCullough, Bonnie. *Totally Organized the Bonnie McCullough Way*. St. Martin's, 1986.

McGee-Cooper, Ann. *Time Management for Unmanageable People*. Bowen & Rogers/Self, 1993.

———. *You Don't Have to Go Home from Work Exhausted*. Bantam, 1990.

McRae, Bradley C. *Practical Time Management*. International Self Counsel Press, 1988.

Neal, Richard G. *Managing Time*. Richard Neal Associates, Falls Church, VA, 1983.

Olney, Ross, and Patricia Olney. *Time! How to Have More of It*. Walker, 1983.

Pearson, Barrie. *Common Sense Time Management*. Mercury, 1989.

Posner, Mitchell J. *Executive Essentials*. Avon, 1982.

Randall, John C. *How to Save Time and Worry Less*. Hotline Multi-Enterprises, 1979.

Reader's Digest. *Organize Yourself*. Berkley Reader's Digest Books, 1980.

Reynolds, Helen. *Executive Time Management*. Prentice Hall, 1979.

Saltzman, Amy. *Downshifting*. Harper Perennial, 1992.

Schlenger, Sunny, and Roberta Roesch. *How to Be Organized in Spite of Yourself*. Signet, 1990.

Schofield, Deniece. *Springing the Time Trap*. Shadow Mountain, Salt Lake City, 1987; Signet, 1989.

Scott, Dru. *How to Put More Time in Your Life*. Signet, 1980.

Seiwert, Lothar J. *Time Is Money, Save It*. Dow Jones—Irwin, 1989.

Sherman, Doug, and William Hendricks. *How to Balance Competing Time Demands*. Navpress, 1989.

Shippman, Leo J., and Jeffrey Martin, A. Bruce McKay, Robert A. Amastasi. *Effective Time Management Techniques for School Administrators.* Prentice Hall, 1983.

Silver, Susan. *Organize to Be the Best.* Adams-Hall, 1989.

Smith, Hyrum W. *The Advanced Day Planner Users Guide.* Franklin Institute, 1987.

———. *Ten Natural Laws of Successful Time and Life Management: Proven Strategies for Increased Productivity and Inner Peace.* Warner, 1994.

Smith, Ken. *It's about Time.* Crossway Books, 1992.

Smith, Marian. *In Today, Out Today.* Prentice Hall, 1982.

Stautberg, Susan S., and Marcia L. Worthing. *Balancing Act.* Avon, 1992.

Stokes, Steward L., Jr. *Time Is of the Essence.* QED Information Sciences, 1983.

The Success Group. *How to Get Organized.* Self/Palm Beach Gardens, FL.

Swenson, Richard A. *Margin: How to Create the Emotional, Physical, Financial, and Time Reserves You Need.* Navpress, 1992.

Tassi, Nina. *Urgency Addiction.* Taylor, 1991.

Treuille, Beverly Benz, and Susan Schiffere Stautberg. *Managing It All.* Master Media, 1988.

Turla, Peter, and Kathleen L. Hawkins. *Time Management Made Easy.* Dutton, 1983.

Webber, Ross Arkell. *Breaking Your Time Barriers.* Prentice Hall.

———. *A Guide to Getting Things Done.* Free Press, 1980.

———. *Time and Management.* Van Nostrand Reinhold, 1972.

Whisehunt, Donald W. *Administrative Time Management.* University Press of America, 1987.

White, T. Kenneth. *The Technical Connection.* Wiley, 1981.

Winston, Stephanie. *Getting Organized.* Norton, 1978.

———. *The Organized Executive.* Norton, 1983.

Wright, Howard. *Success and Time Management.* Wright Financial, 1992.

Time Management Related

Alesandrini, Kathryn. *Survive Information Overload.* Business One, Irwin, 1992.

Arnold, William W., and Jeanne M. Plas. *The Human Touch: Today's Most Unusual Program for Productivity and Profit.* Wiley, 1993.

Baker, Kim, and Sunny Baker. *Office on the Go.* Prentice Hall, 1993.

Barker, Joel Arthur. *Paradigms: The Business of Discovering the Future.* HarperCollins, 1992.

Bennett, William J. *The De-Valuing of America: The Fight for Our Culture and Our Children.* Summit, 1992.

Bittel, Lester R. *Right on Time.* McGraw-Hill, 1991.

Black, Joe. *The Attitude Connection.* Life Vision Books, 1991.

———. *Looking Back on the Future.* Life Vision Books, 1993.

Blanchard, Ken, and William Oncken, Jr., and Hal Burrows. *The One Minute Manager Meets the Monkey*. Morrow, 1989.

Block, Peter. *Stewardship*. Berrett-Koehler, 1993.

Boldt, Laurence G. *Zen and the Art of Making a Living: A Practical Guide to Creative Career Design*. Penguin, 1991.

Bolles, Richard N. *The 1994 What Color Is Your Parachute?* Ten Speed Press, 1994.

——. *The Three Boxes of Life*. Ten Speed Press, 1978.

Booher, Diana. *Clean Up Your Act*. Warner, 1992.

Bremer, Sidney Newton. *Spirit of Apollo*. Successful Achievement, 1971.

Burka, Jane B., and Lenora M. Yuen. *Procrastination*. Addison-Wesley, 1983.

Burns, James MacGregor. *Leadership*. Harper & Row, 1978.

Burns, Lee. *Busy Bodies*. Norton, 1993.

Campbell, Andrew, and Laura L. Nash. *A Sense of Mission: Defining Direction for the Large Corporation*. Addison-Wesley, 1992.

Chopra, Deepak. *Ageless Body, Timeless Mind*. Harmony, 1993.

Coleson, Chuck, and Jack Eckerd. *Why America Doesn't Work*. Word, 1991.

Collins, James C., and William C. Lazier. *Beyond Entrepreneurship: Turning Your Business into an Enduring Great Company*. Prentice Hall, 1992.

Cooper, Dr. Kenneth H. *The Aerobics Program for Total Wellbeing*. M. Evans, 1982.

Dardik, Irving, and Dennis Waitley. *Quantum Fitness*. Pocket, 1984.

Dominguez, Joe, and Vicki Robin. *Your Money or Your Life*. Viking, 1992.

Drucker, Peter. *The Effective Executive*. Pan, 1970.

Gleick, James. *Chaos: Making a New Science*. Penguin, 1987.

Goldberg, Philip. *The Intuitive Edge: Understanding Intuition and Applying It in Everyday Life*. Jeremy Tarcher, 1983.

Goldratt, Eliyahu M. *The Goal*. North River Press, 1984.

Hickman, Craig R. *Mind of a Manager, Soul of a Leader*. Wiley, 1990.

Hillman, James, and Michael Ventura. *We've Had a Hundred Years of Psychotherapy and the World's Getting Worse*. HarperCollins, 1992.

Hunnicutt, Benjamin Kline. *Work without End*. Temple University Press, 1988.

Jamison, Kaleel. *The Nibble Theory*. Paulist Press, 1984.

Jones, John W. *High-Speed Management*. Jossey-Bass, 1993.

Kinder, Dr. Melvyn. *Going Nowhere Fast*. Fawcett Columbine, 1990.

Kotter, John P., and James L. Heskett. *Corporate Culture and Performance*. Free Press, 1992.

Kouzes, James M., and Barry Z. Posner. *Credibility: How Leaders Gain It and Lose It, Why People Demand It*. Jossey-Bass, 1993.

Kuhn, Thomas S. *The Structure of Scientific Revolutions*. University of Chicago Press, 1962.

Langer, Ellen J. *Mind-fulness*. Addison-Wesley, 1989.

Materka, Pat Roessle. *Time In, Time Out*. Time Enough, Ann Arbor, 1993.

McCarthy, Kevin W. *The On-Purpose Person*. Pinon Press, 1992.

McWilliams, John-Roger, and Peter McWilliams. *Do It!* Prelude Press, 1991.

Meyer, Christopher. *Fast Cycle Time*. Free Press, 1993.

Mitroff, Ian I., and Harold A. Linstone. *The Unbounded Mind: Breaking the Chains of Traditional Business Thinking*. Oxford University Press, 1993.

Myers, David G. *The Pursuit of Happiness*. Morrow, 1992.

Nave, Jean Russel. *The Quest for Real Success*. Windemere Press, 1987.

Nielsen, Duke. *Partnering with Employees: A Practical System for Building Empowered Relationships*. Jossey-Bass, 1993.

Noble, Valerie. *Guide to Individual Development: An Annotated Bibliography*. Special Libraries Association, Washington, D.C., 1986.

Oakley, Ed, and Doug Krug. *Enlightened Leadership: Getting to the Heart of Change*. Simon & Schuster, 1993.

Orsborn, Carol. *Enough Is Enough*. Putnam, 1986.

————. *Inner Excellence: Spiritual Principles of Life-Driven Business*. New World Library, 1992.

Osterbreg, Rolf. *Corporate Renaissance: Business as an Adventure in Human Development*. Nataraj, 1993.

Parker, Marjorie. *Creating Shared Vision*. Senter for Ledelsesutvikling A/S (The Norwegian Center for Leadership Development), 1990.

Proat, Frieda. *Creative Procrastination*. Harper & Row, 1980.

Quigley, Joseph V. *Vision: How Leaders Develop It, Share It, and Sustain It*. McGraw-Hill, 1993.

Rubin, Theodore Isaac. *Overcoming Indecisiveness*. Avon, 1985.

Russo, J. Edward, and Paul J. H. Schoemaker. *Decision Traps*. Fireside, 1989.

Rutherford, Robert D. *Just in Time*. Wiley, 1981.

Ryan, Kathleen D., and Daniel K. Ostereich. *Driving Fear out of the Workplace*. Jossey-Bass, 1991.

Schaef, Anne Wilson, and Diane Fassel. *The Addictive Organization*. Harper, 1988.

Schofield, Deniece. *Confessions of an Organized Housewife*. Writer's Digest Books, 1982.

Schor, Juliet B. *The Overworked American*. Basic, 1991.

Seligman, Martin E. P. *Learned Optimism*. Pocket, 1990.

Selye, Hans. *Stress without Distress*. Signet, 1975.

Senge, Peter M. *The Fifth Discipline*. Doubleday, 1990.

Shames, Laurence. *The Hunger for More*. Vintage/Random House, 1986.

Sherman, Doug, and William Hendricks. *Your Work Matters to God*. Navpress, 1987.

Skopek, Eric W., and Laree Kiely. *Taking Charge*. Addison-Wesley, 1991.

Tyssen, Theodore G. *The First Time Manager*. International Self-Counsel Press, 1992.

Vetterli, Richard, and Gary Bryner. *In Search of the Republic*. Rowman & Littlefield, 1987.

Waldrop, M. Mitchell. *Complexity*. Simon & Schuster, 1992.

Wheatley, Margaret J. *Leadership and the New Science: Learning About Organization from an Orderly Universe*. Berrett-Kohler, 1992.

Whitney, John O. *The Trust Factor: Liberating Profits and Restoring Corporate Vitality*. Donnelly, 1994.

Wick, Calhoun W., and Lu Stanton Leon. *The Learning Edge: How Smart Managers and Smart Companies Stay Ahead*. McGraw-Hill, 1993.

Time/Philosophical, Sociological, Scientific, Etc.

American Institute of CPAs. *Controls for the Effective Use of Time*. American Institute of Certified Public Accountants, New York, 1958.

Bender, John, and David E. Wellbery, editors. *Chronotypes: The Construction of Time*. Stanford University Press, 1991.

Blackwell, B. *The Nature of Time*. Oxford, 1986.

Carlstein, Tommy. *Time Resources, Society and Ecology*. Allen & Unwin, 1982.

Carlstein, Tommy, Don Parkes and Nigel Thrift. *Human Activity and Time Geography*. E. Arnold, London, 1978.

Carr, David. *Time Narrative in History*. Indiana University Press, 1986.

Das, T. K. *Time Dimensions*. Praeger, 1990. (This impressive work is a huge bibliography of literature covering various dimensions of time. This literature offers insights and perspectives from such areas as anthropology, sociology, biology, geography, history, linguistics, literature, management, physics, physical science. It has a definite academic orientation, but it contains over three hundred pages of references that give a sense of the scope of thought and research focused on the subject of time over the centuries. Its complete study would represent more than a professional lifetime. It is interesting to note that, with rare exception, the time management literature does not reflect any connection with this huge body of knowledge.)

Denbigh, Kenneth. *Three Concepts of Time*. Springer-Verleg, 1981.

Dossey, Larry. *Space, Time and Medicine*. Shambhala Publications, 1985.

Elton, L. R. B., and H. B. Messel. *Time and Man*. Pergamon Press, 1978.

Ewing, A. C. *The Fundamental Questions of Philosophy*. Routledge and Kegan Paul, 1951.

Frazer, J. T. *Time, The Familiar Stranger*. University of Massachusetts Press, 1987.

Hatano, Seiichi, translated by Ichiro Suzuki. *Time and Eternity*. Greenwood Press, 1963.

Herrin, Donald Arthur. *"Use of Time by Married Couples"* (unpublished dissertation), Brigham Young University, 1983.

Holmes, Ivory H. *The Allocation of Time by Women*. University Press of America, 1983.

Juster, F. Thomas, and Frank P. Stafford, editors. *Time, Goods and Well Being*. Survey Research Center, Institute for Social Research, University of Michigan, 1985.

Lee, Mary Dean, and Rabindra N. Kanungo, editors. *Management of Work and Personal Life*. Praeger, 1984.

Norbert, Elias. translated by Edmund Jebhcoth. *Time, An Essay*. 1992.

Pleck, Joseph H. *Working Wives, Working Husbands*. National Council on Family Relations, Sage, 1985.

Rifkin, Jeremy. *Time Wars*. Henry Holt, 1987.

Robinson, John. *The Rhythm of Everyday Life*. Westview Press, Boulder, 1989.

Sharp, Clifford. *The Economics of Time*. Oxford, 1981.

Tivers, Jacqueline. *Women Attached*. St. Martin's, 1985.

Van Vliet, Willem. *Theories, Methods, and Applications of Activity*. Vance Bibliographies, Monticello, IL, 1978.

vonFranz, Marie-Louise. *Time, Rhythm and Repose* (143 illustrations, 16 color). Thames & Hudson, 1978.

Wolf, Fred Alan. *Taking the Quantum Leap*. Harper & Row, 1981.

Zee, A. *Fearful Symmetry*. Macmillan, 1986.

APPENDIX C
THE WISDOM LITERATURE

We define "wisdom literature" as that portion of the classic, philosophical, proverbial, and religious literature that deals specifically with the art of living. Some of the literature available now predates formal science and philosophy and was originally passed from one generation to another through oral tradition, proverbs, and symbolic art, as well as through the written word.

Some of the oldest written literature is "the Wisdom of Ptah-hotep" (Egyptian, 2500 B.C.), which, along with other Egyptian writing, had significant effect on Greek culture. The Greek and Hebrew traditions have had remarkable effect on shaping modern Western thought. Eastern Wisdom literature such as the writings of Confucius (551–479 B.C.) and Mencius (371–289 B.C.) along with Indian works such as the Bhagavad-Gita and the Dhammapada are more widely known and read in the West. Native American literature is also becoming more known and available.

Not all of this literature would be considered wisdom literature—the more practical, almost "how to" flavor is what characterizes this group of writings from its wider religious and philosophical context. From the Hebrew tradition, for example, the books of *Job*, *Proverbs*, *Psalms*, and the apocryphal *Wisdom of Solomon* would characterize the wisdom literature.

MAJOR RECURRING THEMES

We recognize there are cautions in drawing too many conclusions from such a vast array of material with deep differences in philosophy, core paradigms, and language. But even with these differences, we feel there is significant benefit to be gained by looking for the most general themes, as well as learning to appreciate the differences.

From our own study and from our efforts to learn from scholars who have devoted tremendous time and effort to this area, we would suggest that the following are some of the most common themes:

Choice
In our hands is the power to choose. Some choices produce better results than others. There is a "cause and effect" relationship between choices and consequences. This relationship is sometimes referred to as "the Law of the Harvest," or what we have called the Law of the Farm.

Reflectiveness
By taking time to reflect on life instead of spending all our time just living, we can become aware of the consequences of our choices and learn from living.

Value of Choices
The value of one choice over another is not always completely rational or easily defensible, but is discernible. With some form of intuition, people know the "right thing to do," and life is better to the degree to which one learns to follow this "guide."

Truth
There are "truths"—fundamental Laws of Life that operate with unerring consistency—and we are better off to the degree to which we learn and live according to them.

Basic Needs
There are universal human needs, and nothing works well very long in the human experience that ignores them.

Nature
People are part of a bigger ecological whole. Living in harmony with nature is a vital part of quality of life.

Relationships
The law that governs quality in our relationships with others is the Law of Reciprocity, or the Golden Rule. Life is better when we treat others as we would be treated.

Contribution
The great apparent dichotomy is that the more we give, the more we get.

Perspective
There is more to life than "me" and "now." The bigger picture produces better-quality decisions.

What is remarkable about "wisdom literature" is that, to the degree that we find patterns, consistencies, and themes, it represents the most validated database in all human experience. To ignore it—not to try to learn from it—would seem an absurd disregard of resource. Certainly regular immersion in the great database of living is a powerful course in conscience education.

WISDOM LITERATURE BIBLIOGRAPHY

We realize that there are many issues in the study of wisdom literature, including the definition of wisdom literature itself. We recognize and honor those scholars who have devoted years to study and contribution in this area. As they, and others well versed in literature, will immediately recognize, the bibliography that follows is in no way comprehensive. Our purpose in listing these books at this point is to give a feeling for the variety and scope of such literature, to illustrate the commonality of some of the general themes we've suggested, and to provide a useful starting place for those who are interested in using this vast body of human experience as a resource in educating the conscience.

We are currently in the process of compiling a more comprehensive list which we feel will be a valuable resource to many, and we welcome suggestions of works that could be included. If you are interested in helping with this project, please write the Covey Leadership Center, 3507 N. University Avenue, Suite 100, Provo, Utah 84604, or fax 801-342-6236 and we will send you a response form to submit your suggestion, along with why you feel it should be included and ways in which it has impacted your life.

We've divided the list that follows into "basic works" and "collections" and alphabetized them by title. Those who are familiar with some of these works will recognize that some basic works are collections in the technical sense. But for the purpose of this bibliography, "collections" are essentially proverbial quote books.

Basic Works

The Analects of Confucius. Translated by Arthur Waley. Vintage, 1938.
The Art of Virtue. Benjamin Franklin. Acorn, 1986.
As a Man Thinketh. James Allen. Running Press, 1989.
As a Man Thinketh, Volume 2. James Allen. MindArt, 1988.
The Bhagavad Gita. Translated by Eknath Easwaran. Nilgiri Press, 1985.
Book of the Hopi. Frank Waters. Ballantine, 1963.
The Book of Mormon. The Church of Jesus Christ of Latter Day Saints, 1986.
The Collected Dialogues of Plato. Edited by Edith Hamilton and Huntington Cairns. Princeton University Press, 1961.
The Dhammapada. Translated by Eknath Easwaran. Nilgiri Press, 1985.
The Essential Gandhi. Edited by Louis Rischer. Vintage, 1962.
The Holy Bible.
The Instruction of Ptah-Hotep and the Instruction of Ke'Gemni: The Oldest Books in the World. Translated by Battiscombe Gunn. London: John Murray, 1912.
The Lessons of History. Will and Ariel Durant. Simon & Schuster, 1968.
The Meaning of the Glorius Koran: An Explanatory Translation. Translated by Mohamad Marmaduke Pickehall. Mentor Books, n.d.

The Meditations of Marcus Aurelius. Translated by George Long. Avon Books, 1993.

The Nicomachean Ethics. Aristotle. Oxford University Press, 1991.

The Opening of the Wisdom-Eye. H. H. Gyatso, the Dalai Lama Tenzin. Quest Books, 1966.

Ramayana. R. K. Narayan. Penguin, 1972.

The Sayings of Confucius. Translated by Lionel Giles. London: Charles E. Tuttle, 1993.

The Sayings of Mencius. James R. Ware. Mentor Books, 1960.

Siddhartha. Hermann Hesse. New Directions, 1951.

Sufism, The Alchemy of the Heart. Labyrinth Publishing, 1993.

Tao, to Know and Not Be Knowing. Labyrinth Publishing, 1993.

Tao Te Ching. Lao Tzu. Penguin, 1963.

The Torah. Translated by W. Gunther Plaute. Central Conference of American Rabbis, 1981.

The Upanishads. Translated by Eknath Easwaran. Nilgiri Press, 1987.

Walden, Or, Life in the Woods. Henry David Thoreau. Shambhala, 1992.

The Way of Chuang Tzu. Thomas Merton. Shambhala, 1965.

The Wisdom of Confucius. Peter Pauper Press, 1963.

Wisdomkeepers: Meetings with Native American Spiritual Elders. Steve Wall and Harvey Arden. Beyond Words Publishing, 1990.

The Wisdom of the Vedas. J. C. Chatterji. Quest Books, 1992.

World Scripture: A Comparative Anthology of Sacred Texts. International Religious Foundation. Paragon House, 1991.

Zen, The Reason of Unreason. Labyrinth Publishing, 1993.

Collections

The Art of Peace. Morihei Ueshiba. Translated By John Stevens. Shambhala, 1992.

The Art of Worldly Wisdom. Balthasar Gracian. Translated by Joseph Jacobs. Shambhala, 1993.

The Book of Virtues. William J. Bennett. Simon & Schuster, 1993.

Words of Wisdom. Ariel Books, 1992.

The Enlightened Heart: An Anthology of Sacred Poetry. Edited by Stephen Mitchell. HarperCollins, 1989.

The Enlightened Mind: An Anthology of Sacred Prose. Edited by Stephen Mitchell. HarperCollins, 1991.

Light from Many Lamps. Edited by Lillian Eichler Watson. Fireside, 1979.

Native American Wisdom. Running Press, 1993.

Oneness. Jeffrey Moses. Fawcett Columbine, 1989.

The Pocket Aquinas. Edited by Vernon J. Bourke. Pocket, 1960.

Prayer of the Heart, Writings from the Philokalia. Translated by G. E. H. Palmer, Philip Sherrard, and Kallistos Ware. Shambhala, 1993.

The Sayings of Muhammad. Allama Sir Abdullah Al-Mamun Al-Suhrawardy. Charles E. Tuttle, 1992.

Spiritual Illuminations. Edited by Peg Streep. Viking Studio Books, 1992.

Thoughts in Solitude. Thomas Merton. Shambhala, 1993.

Wisdom: Conversations with the Elder Wise Men of Our Day. James Nelson. Norton, 1958.

Wisdom Is One. B. W. Huntsman. Charles E. Tuttle, 1985.

Words of Wisdom. Thomas C. Jones. Chicago: J. G. Ferguson, 1966.

A *World Treasury of Folk Wisdom*. Reynold Feldman and Cynthia A. Voelke. HarperCollins, 1992.

Commentary & Analysis

Proverbial Philosophy: A Book of Thoughts and Arguments. Martin Farquhar Tupper. E. H. Butler, Philadelphia, 1892.

Ways of Wisdom. Edited by Steve Smith. University Press, 1983.

Wisdom. Edited by Robert J. Sternberg. Cambridge University Press, 1990.

NOTES

Chapter 1
1. Often used in talks and articles by a respected friend, Neal A. Maxwell.
2. Stephen R. Covey, *The 7 Habits of Highly Effective People* (New York: Simon & Schuster), 1989. See the Bicentennial Success Literature Review as described on pp. 18–19. This study was concluded nearly twenty years ago and, at that time, revealed a strong personality ethic in the success literature for the previous fifty years. Although there are some good signs as of late, the dominant theme in the success literature for the years since the study remains unchanged.
3. James Allen, *As a Man Thinketh*, vol. 2 (Bountiful, Utah: MindArt, 1988) p. 83.
4. Attributed to Albert Einstein.
5. Plato, *Apology, Crito, Phaedo, Symposium, Republic*, translated by B. Jowett and edited with an introduction by Louise Hopes Loomis (Roslyn, NY: Walter J. Black, 1942), p. 56.

Chapter 2
1. Adapted from S. Peele, *Diseasing of America: Addiction Treatment Out of Control* (Lexington, MA: Lexington Books, 1989), p. 147.
2. Charles Hummel, *Tyranny of the Urgent* (Downers Grove, IL: InterVarsity Christian Fellowship of the United States of America, 1967), pp. 9–10.
3. Attributed to Oliver Wendell Holmes.

Chapter 3
1. See Abraham Maslow, *Toward a Psychology of Being*, 2nd ed. (New York: Van Nostrand, 1968), and A. H. Maslow, *The Farther Reaches of Human Nature* (New York: Penguin, 1971).
2. This quote, attributed to George Bernard Shaw, was given to us by an associate and has inspired us for years.
3. Ralph Waldo Emerson, "The Divinity School Address," in *The Collected Works of Ralph Waldo Emerson*, vol. 1, "Nature, Addresses, and Lectures" (Cambridge, MA: Belknap Press, 1971), pp. 78–79.
4. Sidney Newton Bremer, *Spirit of Apollo* (Lexington NC: Successful Achievement, 1971), p. 167.

5. Many works are available on and by both Freud and Jung. Some of particular interest are: C. G. Jung, *The Undiscovered Self* (Princeton: Princeton University Press, 1990); C. G. Jung, "A Psychological View of Conscience," *Civilization in Transition.* Vol. 10 of *The Collected Works of C. G. Jung* (New York: Bollingen Foundation, 1964); and Erich Fromm, *Psychoanalysis and Religion* (Binghamton, NY: Vail-Ballou Press, 1950).
6. C. S. Lewis, *The Quotable Lewis*, edited by Wayne Martindale and Jerry Root (Wheaton, IL: Tymedale House of Publishers, 1989), p. 232.
7. Alfred N. Whitehead, "The Rhythmic Claims of Freedom and Discipline," in *The Aims of Education and Other Essays* (New York: New American Library), p. 46.

Chapter 5

1. Viktor E. Frankl, *Man's Search for Meaning* (New York: Pocket Books, 1959), pp. 164–66.
2. Benjamin Singer, "The Future-Focused Role-Image," in Alvin Toffler, *Learning for Tomorrow: The Role of the Future in Education* (New York: Random House, 1974), pp. 19–32.
3. Andrew Campbell and Laura L. Nash, *A Sense of Mission* (New York: Addison-Wesley, 1990), see especially chapter 3.
4. Fred Polak, *The Image of the Future* (San Francisco: Jossey-Bass, 1972).
5. Attributed to the eminent sociologist Émile Durkheim.
6. Eknath Easwaran, *Gandhi, the Man*, 2nd Edition. Nilgin Press, 1978, p. 145.
7. Viktor E. Frankl, *Man's Search for Meaning* (New York: Pocket Books, 1959), p. 172.
8. Attributed to William Ellery Channing, a nineteenth-century writer, social reformer, and minister.
9. This quote, attributed to Sir Laurens van der Post, writer, soldier, and filmmaker, was given to us by a South African associate.

Chapter 6

1. Howard Gardner, *The Unschooled Mind: How Children Think and How Schools Should Teach* (New York: Basic Books, 1991), pp. 3–6.
2. Eknath Easwaran, *Gandhi, the Man*, 2nd Edition. Nilgin Press, 1978, p. 145.
3. Quoted in Bill Moyers, *Healing and the Mind.* (New York: Doubleday, 1993), p. 310.
4. Quoted in Margaret J. Wheatley, *Leadership and the New Science* (San Francisco: Berrett-Koehler, 1992), p. 9.
5. See Sally Helgesen, *The Female Advantage: Women's Ways of Leadership* (New York: Doubleday, 1990); and John Naisbitt and Patricia Aburdene, *Megatrends 2000* (New York: William Morrow, 1990).

6. *Xenophon, Memorabilia and Oeconomicus,* trans. E. C. Marchant, The Loeb Classical Library ed. (Cambridge: Harvard University Press, n.d.), pp. 186–87.
7. Carol Orsborn, *Inner Excellence: Spiritual Principles of Life-Driven Business* (San Rafael, CA: New World Library, 1992), pp. 27–28.
8. Barbara Killinger, *Workaholics: The Respectable Addicts* (New York: Simon & Schuster, 1991), p. 115.

Chapter 9

1. Viktor E. Frankl, *Man's Search for Meaning* (New York: Pocket Books, 1959), p. 104.
2. Often quoted and originally attributed to Ralph Waldo Emerson.
3. John Sloan Dickey, U.S. educator, quoted in a private university's plans and goals report.
4. Vince Lombardi, *Colorado Business Magazine,* vol. 20, p. 8 (1), February 1993.
5. Stephen R. Covey, *The 7 Habits of Highly Effective People* (New York: Simon & Schuster, 1989), pp. 18–19.
6. David G. Meyers, *The Pursuit of Happiness* (New York: William Morrow, 1992) p. 197.
7. Ralph Waldo, Emerson, "Worship," in *The Complete Writings of Ralph Waldo Emerson* (New York: William H. Wise, p. 588.
8. Proverbs 4:23, *The Holy Bible* (King James version).

Chapter 10

1. Seneca, quoted in Burton E. Stevenson, *The Home Book of Quotations, Classical and Modern,* 10th edition (New York: Dodd, Mead, 1967), p. 1131 (from *Epistulae ad Lucilium,* Epis. LXXVI, section III).
2. C. S. Lewis, *Surprised by Joy* (New York: Harcourt Brace Jovanovich 1955), p. 177.
3. Peter Senge, *The Fifth Discipline* (New York: Doubleday, 1990), p. 14.

Chapter 11

1. *The Essential Gandhi,* edited by Louis Fischer (New York: Vintage, 1962), p. 193.
2. Hans Selye, *Stress without Distress* (New York: Harper & Row, 1974), p. 58.
3. W. Edwards Deming, *Out of the Crisis* (Cambridge: Massachusetts Institute of Technology, 1982) pp. 66–67.
4. Konosuke Matsushita, executive advisor to Matsushita Electric Industrial Co., Ltd.

Chapter 12
1. Stephen R. Covey, *The 7 Habits of Highly Effective People* (New York: Simon & Schuster, 1989).
2. *The Essential Gandhi*, edited by Louis Fischer (New York: Vintage, 1962, p. 255.
3. Martin Buber, *I and Thou* (New York: Charles Scribner's Sons, 1937), p. 3.
4. William Oncken. *Managing Management Time* (Englewood Cliffs, NJ: Prentice Hall, 1984), p. 106.
5. The watershed work on this topic is Robert K. Greenleaf's *Servant Leadership: A Journey into the Nature of Legitimate Power and Greatness* (New York: Paulist Press, 1977).

Chapter 13
1. Remarks by President George Bush in presentation of the 1990 Malcolm Baldridge National Quality Awards.
2. Kollmorgen Corporation 1979 annual report.

Chapter 15
1. Alice R. Trulock. *In the Hands of Providence: Joshua L. Chamberlain and the American Civil War*. Chapel Hill: University of North Carolina Press, 1992, p. 62.
2. M. Scott Peck. *The Road Less Traveled* (New York: Simon & Schuster, 1978), p. 15.
3. For an interesting book on this idea, see James Hillman and Michael Ventura, *We've Had a Hundred Years of Psychotherapy and the World's Getting Worse* (New York: HarperCollins, 1992).
4. C. S. Lewis, *Mere Christianity* (New York: Macmillan, 1952), pp. 109–10.
5. C. S. Lewis.
6. Ezra Taft Benson, "Beware of Pride," *The Ensign* (May 1989), Salt Lake City: The Church of Jesus Christ of Latter-Day Saints, p. 5.
7. Attributed to Gandhi.
8. Ralph Waldo Emerson, "Self Reliance," in *Essays: First and Second Series*, in *The Complete Works*, volume I (Boston: Houghton Mifflin, 1921), p. 90.

Epilogue
1. Bryant S. Hinckley, *Not by Bread Alone* (Salt Lake City: Bookcraft, 1955), p. 25.

PROBLEM/OPPORTUNITY INDEX

This index is designed to be a resource in accessing material in *First Things First* that deals with specific problems and opportunities around issues of time and quality of life. We've divided the index into areas affecting the personal and interpersonal dimensions. In some cases, we've referenced entire chapters or sections in addition to specific suggestions or ideas. The italicized references represent stories.

Determining what's important in the family, group, or organization

Increasing the effectiveness of the family, group, or organization

ABOUT THE COVEY LEADERSHIP CENTER

This five-hundred-member international firm is committed to empowering people and organizations to significantly increase their performance capability by applying Principle-Centered Leadership to worthwhile purposes.

The Covey Leadership Center's client portfolio includes two hundred of the Fortune 500 companies as well as thousands of small and mid-size companies, educational institutions, government, and other organizations worldwide. Their work in Principle-Centered Leadership is considered by their clients to be an instrumental foundation to the effectiveness of quality, leadership, service, team building, organizational alignment, and many other strategic corporate initiatives.

Their unique contextual approach to building high-trust cultures by addressing all four levels—personal, interpersonal, managerial, and organizational—is well renowned.

The firm empowers people and organizations to teach themselves and to become independent of the Center. To the adage that goes "Give a man a fish, you feed him for a day; teach him how to fish and you feed him for a lifetime" is added: "Develop teachers of fisherman and you lift all society." This empowerment process is carried out through programs conducted at the Covey Leadership Center in the Rocky Mountains of Utah, custom corporate on-site programs and consulting, and public Seven Habits and First Things First Time Management seminars offered in over seventy-five cities in North America and over forty countries worldwide.

CLC products and programs provide a wide range of resources for individuals, families, and business, government, nonprofit, and educational organizations, including:

Programs

Principle-Centered Leadership
  Week
Principle-Centered Leadership and
  Quality
The Seven Habits Internally
  Facilitated Leadership Course
Principle-Centered Leadership
  Internally Facilitated Course
First Things First Time
  Management Course
Seven Habits Sales Course
Seven Habits Seminars
Seven Habits Renewal Course
Principle-Centered Power Course
Seven Habits Family Course
Train the Trainer Courses for
  In-House Certification

Products

Seven Habits Executive
  Organizer
Seven Habits Audiotapes
Living the Seven Habits Audiotapes
Principle-Centered Leadership
  Tapes
Seven Habits Effectiveness Profile
360-Degree Stakeholder
  Information System
  (organizational diagnosis)
Principle-Centered Living Video

Custom Consulting

Custom Principle-Centered
Leadership Programs
Custom On-Site Programs,
Consulting, and Speeches
Custom Education Programs

Publications

Executive Excellence (newsletter)
The Seven Habits Magazine
The Seven Habits of Highly Effective
  People
Principle-Centered Leadership

Covey Leadership Center
3507 N. University Avenue
Suite 100
Provo, UT 84604
1-800-680-6839
International: 001-1-801-377-1888
Fax: (801) 342-6236

ABOUT THE AUTHORS

Stephen R. Covey, husband, father and grandfather, is an internationally respected leadership authority and teacher, and chairman and founder of the Covey Leadership Center. He received his MBA from Harvard and a doctorate from Brigham Young University, where he was a professor of business management and organizational behavior for twenty years. His book *The 7 Habits of Highly Effective People* has sold more than 4 million copies and has been translated into twenty-six languages. His latest book, *Principle-Centered Leadership,* is a business bestseller.

A. Roger Merrill, a well-known leader in time management and leadership development, is vice president and founding member of the Covey Leadership Center. He holds a degree in business management and has done extensive graduate work in organizational behavior and adult learning. He and his wife, Rebecca, are parents, grandparents, and coauthors of *Connections—Quadrant II Time Management.* Roger is also a contributing author to *Principle-Centered Leadership.*

Rebecca R. Merrill, mother, grandmother, homemaker, and accomplished author, has served in numerous leadership positions in community, education, and women's organizations. Coauthor of *Connections—Quandrant II Time Management,* she also assisted Stephen R. Covey on *The 7 Habits of Highly Effective People.*